HUSTLE

BELIEVE

RECEIVE

AN 8-STEP PLAN TO CHANGING YOUR LIFE
AND LIVING YOUR DREAM

≡PLUS 51 STORIES TO INSPIRE≡

HUSTLE

BELIEVE

RECEIVE

SARAH CENTRELLA
FOREWORD BY ED MYLETT

Skyhorse Publishing

Skyhorse Publishing books may be purchased in bulk at special discounts
for sales promotion, corporate gifts, fund-raising, or educational purposes.
Special editions can also be created to specifications. For details, contact the
Special Sales Department, Skyhorse Publishing, 307 West 36th Street,
11th Floor, New York, NY 10018 or info@skyhorsepublishing.com.

Skyhorse® and Skyhorse Publishing® are registered trademarks of Skyhorse
Publishing, Inc.®, a Delaware corporation.

Visit our website at www.skyhorsepublishing.com.

10 9 8 7 6 5 4 3

Library of Congress Cataloging-in-Publication Data is available on file.

Cover design by Brian Peterson

ISBN: 978-1-5107-4353-3
Ebook ISBN 978-1-5107-4355-7

Printed in the United States of America

For my crew: Kanen, Mira, and Izzy.
You are my reason.

Special love goes out to Charlotte Centrella, my Nonie. You have been my inspiration, motivation, and guru. You showed me that positivity and accountability are at the core of what makes a good human. Your unconditional love, support, honesty, and faith have saved me on more occasions than I care to admit. You are my rock. My OG. My crew.
I love you, Nonie.

And to my Auntie Maria: You were my very first editor starting when I was thirteen years old. You encouraged me to write stories even though I could hardly read or write, and I certainly couldn't spell! From day one you've been the greatest supporter of my attempts at writing. I am forever in your debt.

CONTENTS

HASHTAG DEFINITIONS

#BigPictureDream: Your overall desired end result; the experience and life you want to create.

#ItsTheJourney: Your specific dream might change over time.

#MoneyAintAThing: Money (or lack of it) is irrelevant.

#ChangeTheVoicesInYourHead: Turning negative self-talk into positive results.

#MottoForLife: The use of positive mottos and mantras to change your thoughts.

#LifePlan: A written plan with measurable goals for achieving success in all areas of your life.

#CreateAMovieInYourHead: The ability to turn your dream/future into a vivid "reality" in your mind.

#FutureBoard: The physical visual representation of your #LifePlan and #BigPictureDream.

#TheHustle: The work it takes to actively move in the direction of your dream.

#CourageOverFear: Using courage to make decisions that are not based in fear.

#ChillOut: Be patient!

#RelentlessPursuit: The refusal to give up, NO MATTER WHAT.

#FakeIT: Act as if it's already happened.

#Winning!: Anything positive that happens as a result of your hustle.

#ChangeYourCrew: Crew: The people in your life. Friends, family, coworkers, frenemies . . .

#EarthquakeMoments: How to get through difficult times. And why sometimes the worst moment can be a blessing in disguise.

#Manifesting: When preparation meets opportunity.

#ManifestThat: That moment when you are living out a previously defined dream/goal.

#HBRLife: Achieving financial success and living your dream for a lifetime.

FOREWORD

BY ED MYLETT

I started reading this book in December 2017 and honestly, it took my breath away. It is so powerful. Immediately, I began chasing Sarah to be a guest on my podcast *The Ed Mylett Show*, because I knew people needed to hear her story and the powerful information she shares in this book.

We connected instantly, from our very first conversation. I remember getting off the phone and thinking, *I just found a sister!* Sarah is incredible. She's one of my favorite people that I've ever met in the life strategies space, because she is REAL. Her genuine spirit and raw delivery shine through on every page. But it's the way she's turned her story into actionable tools that readers can apply that makes this so great.

Sarah is an inspiring example of how to turn your *test* into your *testimony*. She is proof that this works. Her stuff is REAL, and it's just *so good!* This is *not* the same old stuff that's regurgitated over and over in the self-help space. This is HER stuff! It's what she's learned through living it, which is such a powerful thing. What I love about Sarah is that she still believes she has a long way to go, and I can relate to that constant desire to become the person you were meant to be.

Sarah does such a great job of laying out HOW she changed her life with her #HBRMethod, that it's simple to understand her tools and put them to practice in your own life. I resonated so much with her strategies because they gave me both *comfort* and *strength*, the two ways I measure any good strategy. I wanted to bring Sarah on my show because I felt so passionately that millions of people need to know about her, need to hear this message.

Our podcast interview, by the way, was such an incredible and dynamic conversation that people have told us both how they paused the show to go buy this book! It was *that good*.

Go have a listen and see for yourself! You can find it on iTunes, Stitcher, Spotify, and on my website at www.edmylett. com/podcasts And take Sarah's advice--do the homework. Put in the work, and you will see the results.

ABOUT ED. Ed is a self-made multi-millionaire, the chairman of one of the largest financial organizations in the world, the best-selling author of *#MaxOut Your Life*, and a highly sought-after speaker. In 2018, he was named as the fastest-growing business personality in the history of social media. In his first year on Instagram, he went from zero followers to nearly a million! His podcast, *The Ed Mylett Show*, is No. 1 in multiple categories around the world; each new episode gets over 1 million downloads the day it drops. Ed's interview with Sarah is a must-listen!

Instagram & Twitter: @edmylett

Podcast: *The Ed Mylett Show* (subscribe!)

Website: www.edmylett.com

A NOTE FROM THE AUTHOR

Sometimes a conversation can change your life. I remember hanging up the phone the first time I spoke to Ed Mylett and thinking, *I will always remember this day*. I didn't exactly know *how* or *why*, but instinctively I knew my life would never be the same. And I was right!

If you are holding the *paperback version* of this book, then in your hot little hands is the result of that pivotal conversation.

The Universe delivers who and what we need, at the perfect moment when we are ready to receive it. It was no accident. It never is.

My heart is bursting with gratitude and thanks. Thank you, Ed Mylett, for all that you do. And a very special thank-you, to your #MaxOut army for responding so quickly and embracing me with such open hearts.

I am truly grateful.

Sarah

HUSTLE

BELIEVE

RECEIVE

HUSTLE

BELIEVE

RECEIVE

1. Let's G-O-O-O!!

!! Let's G-O-O-O !!

MY STORY

A text message changed my life. On the evening of September 7, 2008, I opened my husband's cell phone while he was in the shower to read: *I can't wait 'til you're finally free and all mine. No more sharing.* Those few words tore my world apart in an instant.

I'd been with this man half my life, since we were sixteen years old. We had an eight-year marriage and shared three beautiful children, including twin girls just over a year old. We'd been through it all: buying our first home, then losing it in foreclosure; being overjoyed when I got pregnant with our second child, then devastated when I lost it six months into my pregnancy. I thought we'd seen everything, but this I never saw coming.

I never saw it because everyone knew he loved me just a little more. They say in every relationship one person does that, loves the other more. The kids and I had always been his entire world. No part of me ever questioned that he'd jump in front of a train to save us if he had to.

I was all he ever wanted. Until I wasn't.

I set his phone on the bathroom counter and without a second thought threw open the shower curtain, turned off the water, and said "Get the fuck out." I watched him pull on his shorts in the hallway, still sopping wet, one leg and then the other. I crossed the room and opened the front door, pointed and yelled again "GET THE FUCK OUT!"

He kissed our son goodbye, tossed his wedding ring in my general direction, and walked out the front door, slamming it behind him.

He never came back.

Things had not been perfect between us prior to that day, I can't lie. We'd been struggling financially to the point of desperation for what felt like forever. We'd lost our home the year before and were forced into bankruptcy after our twins were born. Our life was in a noticeable negative tailspin. Losing everything we'd worked so hard to acquire had destroyed our pride and left us both feeling helpless, and miserable. I'd done everything I could think of to cut our budget and make it so we could pay the bills and still eat, but every month we fell further behind.

On the day he left, I didn't have five dollars to my name. Our electric, water, and gas bills were all past due with shutoff notices pending, and the rent was late. I hadn't worked in over two years, and the economy was in the middle of a deep recession. The car title was in his name, as was our bank account. Overnight, I went from desperate to stranded and destitute with no way to provide for my three small children.

That night I laid on the cold hardwood floor in our living room, my hair matted to the side of my head with tears that had finally run dry from my own dehydration. The only thought that floated in my semiconscious brain was, "How the hell can I do this?" I'd tried so hard to think of a plan, *anything*, but nothing came, except that question over and over again. It seemed completely impossible. Yet somehow, in that moment, survival mode also kicked in, and with it came even more questions. *Of course we'd have to move right away, but where?* I didn't have family who could take us in. *And we'd need to sell everything we owned, but how? And I'd need a job, but doing what? And how could I afford to work when daycare would take up most of my salary?*

All night these questions swirled in my head without answers.

The sense of utter helplessness was all-consuming. I was no stranger to hard times. I'd grown up in extremely difficult circumstances and had struggled all my life. I already knew what it felt like to go hungry; to not have a roof over my head or a bed to sleep in at night. But this was different. Being resilient and scrappy is fine when it's just you. But when you have children to feed, there's a new kind of panic that washes over you in overwhelming waves. In the past, I had always relied on #TheHustle to get me through anything. It was comforting knowing that no matter what came at me, I would always "find a way." But this time, I knew hustle alone would not save me, and I had no bright ideas.

In moments like these we are faced with two options: fall apart and ultimately disappear, or we can fucking fight! I knew I could never just give up, but I didn't believe I had what it would take to fight. Not this time.

About that time my girlfriend Charise walked in the door with her arms full of Costco boxes. She'd thought of everything: diapers and formula for the girls, dinner for the next week, and even enough cash to keep the electricity and water from being turned off.

That is the moment that has defined my #RelentlessPursuit. That is the moment I hustle and grind for.

Something inside me just shifted. A light went on deep in my core followed by a burning desire to never put myself or my children in that kind of position again. I made a promise to myself right then that I would not rely on anyone to provide for my family. I wouldn't borrow money from family members; I wouldn't beg for help. I would somehow pay my girlfriend back and figure out how to handle my business on my own.

Before this happened I'd always just thought I was unlucky and entitled to what little help I'd ever received. All my life I'd told myself this story, and *believed it. Nothing good ever happens to me. I work twice as hard as everyone else for half as much.* That was my core belief. And as a result, that was my *life.* No one ever told me that my life was the result of *my* thoughts, *my* beliefs, and *my* actions. I thought the only thing I could control was how hard I worked (#TheHustle), but that on its own left me feeling like I was drowning in quicksand. No matter how hard I worked, the results never showed. It took the catastrophe of that night, when my world collapsed in an instant, to spark within me a desire to drastically change my life.

That week I sold everything we owned and filed for divorce. I took the money I made from our belongings to pay the first and last month's rent on a really tiny, super-shitty, two-bedroom apartment. I had just enough left over for one more month of rent and a few groceries. That was all the money I had in the world. I didn't even have a bank account.

My older sister convinced me to get on food stamps, "Just until you get on your feet." I cried when the case worker took my story at the welfare office, but I knew I had no choice. I applied for every job I could find, but interviews were few and far between. When the second month came and my rent money was gone, I sold my wedding rings on Craigslist for a fraction of their value, enough for one more month's rent. When the woman came to pick up my rings, she looked around our little apartment, at my twins running around in their diapers, and said, "I don't want to know. Please don't tell me the story." She didn't want my misfortune giving her new wedding rings negative juju.

Things were certainly bleak, to put it mildly. It was terrifying, yet at the same time there was a new spark of hope deep inside me that wouldn't go away. Now I was in control of my future, and that was a whole new way of thinking about what was possible for my life. I remembered an *Oprah* show I'd watched where she'd talked about changing your thoughts because they have the power to predict your future. I mentally traced my life five years back and then ten years back and realized that everything I worried about, feared, and stressed over had become my reality. That was a huge revelation for me. I saw it plain as day: I'd created all those "misfortunes." I'd created that life. That was all the proof I needed. Even if it had only worked in a negative way up to that point, I knew I had nothing to lose and that possibility brought hope in a way I'd never known.

This book is *how* I went from a newly single mom with nothing, who was relying on state aid to survive, to an executive of a software company in just eighteen months. It's the story of *how* I manifested two #FutureBoards in four years and completely changed my life. It's *how* I went from living in a "poor me" world to being a "take charge of my future" badass. It's the tale of *how* I learned to dream HUGE and what it felt like to live out those dreams quicker and bigger than I'd ever imagined often without spending a dime of my own money. It's *how* I learned to work smarter and not harder. It's *how* I "*Changed My Crew.*" And it's the story of *how*, for the first time in my life, I learned to truly be grateful, live a "pinch-me moment" kind of life, and *how* I found my joy.

SARAH CENTRELLA (Me!) I am the single mom of Kanen, Mira, and Izzy; I live in Portland, Oregon; and I'm on a mission to prove that anything is possible for anyone! Author, coach, speaker, blogger, travel-obsessed marathon finisher, wine and food lover, dreamer, and doer.

Follow my journey on **Twitter, Facebook,** and **Instagram** (@sarahcentrella #HustleBelieveReceive) **Website:** www.sarahcentrella.com **Blog:** www.thoughtsstorieslife.com *My soundtrack: "All the Above" —Maino*

BUT FIRST . . .

#HBR Soundtrack: "Change Your Life"
—Iggy Azalea

You are about to embark on a journey that will last the rest of your life. This book is all about how you get from the life you're living now, to the life you dream of living. And just like anything that actually works, this journey requires a total mind shift, complete commitment, hard work, and most importantly, the willingness to *believe* you can make it happen.

It's one thing for me to tell you this, but who am I to you? To you, I'm just some chick whose marriage fell apart and manifested some pretty cool stuff off her #FutureBoard (yes, I got the Mercedes and the Louis Vuitton bag . . . but we will get to that later). You probably think I'm just another "life coach" with a story and a claim that what I did can also work for you.

Trust me, I don't blame you. I'm the biggest skeptic out there of anything that seems too good to be true. But this is *not that book*. So, to help put your mind at ease, I felt it would be helpful to share with you the stories of other people who are successfully living their dream using these exact same steps. People like NFL star running back Jonathan Stewart, a man who was raised by a

9

single mom with very little and who has gone on to make over $35 million as one of the league's highest-paid running backs. Or Anthony Tolliver, who dreamed of being an NBA player since he was old enough to talk and learned the mental skill set for success that I teach in this book and used it to fight for and achieve his dream. Or my aunt Anna Centrella Thayer, who's been a lifelong mentor to me and was the first person to show me the power of a #FutureBoard. Or Ryan Blair, who started out as a gang member and is now one of the highest-paid CEOs under forty.

#HustleBelieveReceive is filled with these stories. Amazing, inspiring, true tales of how real people are living the impossible. Each story is based on an interview I personally conducted for this book. These stories, in each person's own words, tell how they used these same tools to achieve success. Each has a unique twist, but the same steps are applied over and over again. I intentionally picked people to feature who are living out varied dreams: artist, author, fashion designer, NBA players, coaches, CEO, fitness instructors, Super Bowl champion, etc. Their backgrounds are as wide-ranging as yours and mine.

WHAT IS #HUSTLEBELIEVERECEIVE ANYWAY?

#HBR is a mindset. It's a way of life based on the belief that anything is possible if you are willing to bust your ass to achieve it and believe it will happen.

It is not a quick fix or a magic wand.

"Hustle" comes first because to get what you want in life you can't just "ask" for it like the original saying; "Ask, Believe, Receive" stated. Instead you've got to be willing, ready, and able to WORK for it, a.k.a. *hustle*.

You also can't achieve success or live your dream without **"Believing"** in both your dream and yourself. It's the foundation of anything you will accomplish in your life.

And finally, **"Receive"** means that you expect your *hustle* and *belief* to pay off. You EXPECT to *receive* and sustain success/ your dream for a lifetime.

In short, it is action, faith, and expectation.

WHAT IS THE #HBRMETHOD?

Simply put, the #HBRMethod refers to the eight steps for achieving success set forth in this book. Think of it like an eight-piece puzzle. You know, the kind that toddlers can put together? Each step is a piece of that puzzle, and all the steps are needed in order to complete the picture.

These steps are components that successful people use in harmony with each other to achieve their dream, and it is that combination that provides the magic ingredient of the #HBRMethod. No one step is powerful enough when used on its own, but together there is nothing you can't accomplish or achieve.

Each step has its own individual section followed by the related tools for success. Each one is noted by a hashtag meant to encourage you to join the conversation with others on this journey from around the world.

Let me be clear: I did not invent these concepts. Shocking, I know. People, like the ones featured in this book, have been using these basic tools throughout the ages without referring to them as the #HBRMethod (*obviously!*). I don't claim to be a guru or inventor of all things success! On their own, these steps are not revolutionary. But what I do believe to be revolutionary is the way in which they are presented: simple, clear, and combined as a powerful guide to success.

Most importantly this book explains *how* you can do it too, with examples of real people who live by these principles. These tools are ones you can apply at ANY STAGE of your life, regardless of your situation or circumstances. This book is for "regular people" like you and me; it's "real talk" and "on the level" (no BS). I don't believe in fluff, or crap, or words you've got to look up to understand.

HOW IT ALL STARTED

I discovered the #HBRMethod on my own journey going from *nothin' to somethin'* as I began recreating my life at the age of thirty-four. Over the past six years, I've learned that these steps are simply part of a successful person's DNA, whether they applied them knowingly or not. This is what I set out to prove in creating the #HBRMethod: I wanted to see if the steps I followed were also working for athletes, executives, writers, lawyers, actors, artists, or anyone else with a dream. I wanted to know if, regardless of the dream or circumstances, these fundamentals to success existed in individuals who were self-made. Overwhelmingly, the answer was *yes!* These people were not born with a special success gene that you don't have. Some began at the bottom or started later in life. Many were self-taught just like me, and all faced enormous challenges and overcame seemingly insurmountable obstacles to achieve their dream.

I was exposed to the very basic concept of controlling my thoughts from the Oprah show back in 2006, but the rest of these steps are ones I figured out as I went along. I didn't have time to read self-help books or study success strategies. I was busy learning how to survive as a new single mom, balancing a growing career.

In 2009 I met a football player named Kenjon Barner who played for the University of Oregon. That friendship proved to be pivotal in my quest to find success. What can a college football player teach a single mom in her mid-30s about living her dream, you ask? A lot! It was the first time I'd seen someone put into action the concepts that I'd heard on Oprah's show that day. I picked his brain about how he'd been able to manifest living his dream and how he was able to believe in it so completely. I asked questions—lots of them. And then I listened.

And that is how I learned that anything you set your mind to achieve, if you believe in it with your whole heart, work your ass off day and night for it, you will eventually live it! Kenjon was my living example, and I paid attention. Over the years, my network of players and coaches has grown exponentially. Some I've coached through transitions in their lives, and others are simply great friends, but all have reinforced the #HBRMethod by living it on a daily basis.

In May of 2014 I decided to try something I'd never done before: interview some of my athlete friends for my blog. The concept was "Inside the Mind of an Athlete," and for it I chose to interview five University of Oregon football players in five different stages of following their dream. I wanted to see if the #HBRMethod was indeed present in each of their journeys.

I started with a 2014 senior on the Oregon football team (Derrick Malone Jr.), then a recent graduate who was a free agent (Lavasier Tuenei), a newly drafted NFL player (Kenjon Barner), and finally a successful NFL veteran (Jonathan Stewart). The pursuit of their dream to play in the NFL was the common thread.

Their responses astounded me.

Here were five guys who were not into "self-help," or studying "success," yet they were living examples of everything I'd learned and applied to achieve my own success. All the components were there: #DreamIT, #DoIT, #SeeIT, #LiveIT . . . you name it. They were using the #HBRMethod to achieve their dream, and it was working! You will read each of their inspiring stories in the pages to come.

Then in June of 2014 I took my kids to see the Disney movie *Million Dollar Arm*. During the entire movie my son Kanen (who was eleven at the time) kept saying, "Mama, that's #Hustle-BelieveReceive!" Even at his age he was picking up on the steps the characters were using on their journey to live their dream. I came home that night and tweeted about the movie and how deeply it had impacted us, and it wasn't long before Ash Vasudevan (the real-life inspiration behind "Ash" in the movie) tweeted back.

That was the moment I realized I needed to find out if every successful person I knew was in their own way living the #HBR Method.

HOW #HBR BECAME A BOOK

For the last four years I have been writing books—three, to be exact. I'd written a book version of my blog *Thoughts. Stories. Life.*, and then rewritten it. And I'd spent all of 2013 writing my childhood memoir. I was tired—tired of the rejection and the whole process. But deep down I always knew there was one book I still needed to write . . . the story of *how* I'd changed my life and was living my dream.

Then I had an idea that changed everything.

I would interview fifty-two successful people from all walks of life to see if the #HBR Method was also present in their stories, and I'd incorporate that into the book of how I'd changed my life.

My first thought was: *Let me start with the people in my circle.* I began mentally going through my list of friends, family, mentors, and clients to see if they fit the description of *"successful people living their dream,"* and to my amazement almost everyone I knew fit that description perfectly. Then I turned to Facebook. I wrote a post letting my friends know that I was looking for the most successful people they knew to interview for this book. The result is that almost everyone featured in #HBR is a friend, client, or someone who was referred to me through that Facebook post.

Think about that for a minute.

There are over fifty people featured in #HBR, each of whom is incredibly successful in their chosen field, while I'm a struggling single mom from Oregon! All of the people featured are following their passion, and they are all in *my "crew"* (or are one degree of separation from it). These are the people I've deliberately surrounded myself with over the past five years as I've been creating my new life. They are the ones who've shown me this method of success in various ways, the ones I've learned from like a sponge, the ones who have elevated me at every step along the way.

This book is the result of my journey to uncover the simple, common steps to success that bind each of us together. I simply asked each person featured to "tell me your story," and I listened as they talked. It's important to note that I intentionally chose to have them tell their story before I asked any questions related to their success. I didn't go online trying to see if I could figure out their philosophies, I just sampled people from every category I could think of that were living their dream, and let them talk. To my amazement, these steps organically appeared in their stories over and over again the same way they had shown up with the Oregon football players.

My goal is that you will finish this book with NO MORE EXCUSES! That it will give you the tools and proof you need to begin living the life you've always dreamed of for yourself.

Life is short. This is our one shot. Shouldn't it totally kick ass?

Your future is in your hands. The guide to creating it is literally at your fingertips at this very moment. All that's required of you right now is . . . *DESIRE*.

Desire is the only element that I cannot give you. I cannot make you *want* to change your life or live your dream. That's on you. But if you have the hunger, I can show you how to cultivate it.

WHAT TO EXPECT

There are 8 teaching chapters in #HBR covering the 8 steps to the #HBRMethod. Each chapter will be followed by six featured stories as examples of the steps in this book. Those steps will be indicated by their *#name*. Feel free to consult the glossary of terms at the back of the book if a step hasn't yet been defined.

#HBRSOUNDTRACK

I'm a HUGE believer in the power of **music** to change your mood and lift your spirits. Music has always had a very emotional effect on me. A great song can take me from bummed-out to top of the world in three minutes flat. Its power can't be underestimated.

When you are starting this journey you need all the support you can get, and one of the easiest ways to get it is from listening to empowering music whenever you can. It will speed up this process for you, reinforcing everything you are learning. So under each of the eight steps you'll notice the #HBRSoundtrack song for that chapter. Listen to it and see if you can understand why I chose it for that step, and start to make it your anthem. Start also looking for songs that affect you in a positive way and make a playlist. I have a list of my top thirty motivational songs on my blog if you need ideas.

WHAT YOU'LL NEED

A writing journal and a pen. Write in your journal after you read, or at bedtime. Write what you're thinking, planning, and how you're going to make it happen. You'll also need the journal to log your homework, a.k.a. "Your Hustle."

The journal is not only your plan for the future; it's your proof that YOU created your future. I love going back and reading my goals and journals from a few years ago because they totally predicted this moment: the one when you're holding a book I wrote! My journal (and blog) are proof that I planned it out long ago and then followed the #HBRMethod to make it happen.

This book can only change your life if you put what you are learning into daily practice, and the best way to do that is to keep a daily journal. Write down how your day was, if you practiced what you learned, and be sure to always write your "wins," (any positive things that happen in your day) because you will have them, I promise.

YOUR HUSTLE

Each section of this book contains steps to success with corresponding homework. I call this "your hustle" because it quite literally is the work you will need to put in if you expect to get results. I expect you to do the homework. You cannot be successful if you are unwilling to put in the work required. It's that simple.

The good news is this: The #HBRMethod will bring you almost instant peace and relieve the anxiety of living a life that otherwise may feel out of control. #HBR gives you the tools to control what is within your ability, and teaches you how to release the anxiety of what's outside your control. It also provides you with the tools that will shape and create your future, controlling what was previously "unknown." That is pretty powerful. I bet you didn't even know you had that in you, did you? But you do. We all do. It just takes training and daily practice. Over time, you will learn how to control and change your future outcomes.

My hope is that this process is fun for you—that it enables you to unlock boundaries that have held your life captive, and that you learn how to dream big. I hope that you see your life for all it *can and will* be, instead of what it currently is *not*. I hope #HBR inspires and motivates you to ACTION and to find your own #RelentlessPursuit. And I hope it empowers you to change your life the way so many people have changed theirs by following this method.

JOIN THE MOVEMENT

Create your own #HBR journey and follow others around the world on social media who are also using the #HBRMethod to change their life and live their dream. Studies have proven that whenever you're trying to create a new habit, whether it be something specific like losing weight or as holistic as changing your life, it helps to be surrounded by likeminded people. Post your #HBRSelfie and show us Your Hustle!

Join the conversation about #HustleBelieveReceive, the book, and the people featured in it:
Instagram: @HustleBelieveReceive
Website: www.hustlebelievereceive.com

#HBRSTORIES

ANTHONY TOLLIVER

KIMBERLEY HATCHETT

KENJON BARNER

ANTHONY TOLLIVER'S STORY

Anthony was at the airport waiting between flights when I caught him for our interview. I'd worked with him a few years before as a coach and mentor. I remembered what a powerful story he had, so I was ecstatic that he'd be willing to share it with all of you.

"My first disappointment in basketball came when I was in kindergarten," Anthony told me. "I told my mom I really wanted to play on a team, so she took me down to the gym to sign up for basketball, but we were told it was too late. Registration had ended three days before, and there was no room left for me on the team."

That was the first time Anthony learned about resilience and what it means to want something more than the urge to quit. "Since I couldn't play, I spent as much time as I could watching the game of basketball. Especially NBA games. I watched Michael Jordan play every chance I got, and that passion just got stronger as time when on."

Anthony officially started playing basketball on a team in first grade. He loved it, and he was pretty good at it too. In the third grade, he joined an elite team that made it all the way to the state championship in Kansas City, and they won. They went on to place third in the national competition.

"It was pretty cool for a third-grade kid, being a part of something like that." Anthony told me. "And from a very young age I was exposed to talent outside my school, and outside my state, so I realized quickly that I wasn't the world's greatest player. I was good, but I recognized that the competition was fierce. I knew I wasn't even the best player on my team. It was a great lesson to learn early about being humble."

Anthony was the tallest player on his team, which gave him a distinct advantage—until he got to middle school. "It was the first time that kids were not only better than me, they were also taller. I understood that I needed to develop special skills to stand out as a player. There were things beyond my control. I couldn't control my height, I couldn't control how good other players were, but I could control the effort I put into developing my skill level. So in middle school I was determined to become a skilled shooter. That was something I could develop with patience and practice (#TheHustle)."

In middle school, Anthony considered quitting basketball. He worked hard but wasn't getting playing time. "But my mom was a huge encouragement for me. She talked me through those tough times and encouraged me to keep fighting for my dream." Anthony's mom was a teacher for thirty years, a single mom raising three children, and the center of his world. Having a mother who was a teacher meant that academics always came first, and lucky for Anthony they also came naturally.

His good academic history came in handy when colleges began to recruit him his junior year of high school. He chose Creighton, a smaller college than many of the ones that had scouted him during his breakout senior year.

"I have wanted to play basketball in the NBA since I've had life (#BigPictureDream). I have no memory of not having that be my dream. I was five years old telling everyone I was going to play in the NBA," Anthony told me. "While growing up there were a lot of sacrifices I made to achieve my dream. When my friends were roller-skating I was practicing my shooting, I was that guy. I had a laser focus ever since I can remember. That has always been my goal, and I've made choices in my life accordingly (#RelentlessPursuit)."

"The level of hard work comes from my mom," Anthony continued. "She put in those long hours and hard work to raise us on her own. My goal was to provide for her so that she didn't have to work as hard. I wanted her to have time and resources to focus on herself instead of us. I always wanted to be able to retire her. I had all these plans to let her enjoy her life. That was my motivation. It was never to be rich and have a huge crib; it was to take care of my mom. That was the thing that kept me going. All through college I'd call my mom after every game and we'd talk about it and she'd always encourage me."

After college, Anthony didn't get drafted into the NBA. But he did get invited to training camp in Cleveland, where LeBron James played at the time. "I remember as a kid I always had this fantasy of opening our refrigerator and having it stocked full of everything imaginable to drink (#CreateAMovieInYourHead). I remember going to camp and opening the refrigerator in the training room and there it was, stocked to the brim with anything I'd ever want to drink (#ManifestThat!). There was a cook, who'd make your meals to order. It was crazy. But it was also the best motivation. It was a taste of what that life was like and it solidified my dream even more."

Cleveland didn't end up signing Anthony to a contract after preseason ended. Instead, Anthony spent the next two years playing basketball overseas and in the NBA's developmental league, waiting to be called up to the NBA.

When I asked Anthony why he didn't quit through all that disappointment and struggle, he laughed. "My goal since I was in kindergarten was clear; a goal I'd worked for my entire life

(#LifePlan). I was determined to live my dream. My dream was not to go to an NBA camp, and play against NBA players at camp. Or to earn a paycheck playing ball overseas. Or to play in the D-league. It was to have a career as an NBA player (#BigPictureDream). My goal was to say 'I made it,' and I played, and I was a good shooter. Most people expected me to go make some money overseas, and call it a day. No one expected me to have a career in the NBA. Whenever I got cut, I just told myself I didn't want to be that guy who quit just because he 'barely made it' (#MottoForLife).

"I wanted to be a 10-year veteran, I wanted to last. No one thought I'd make it to the NBA, not even my coaches, but I always knew (#BelieveIt). I kept telling myself if it's up to me, then I am going to make it. If it's just that I need to work harder, and get better, then I will do it. I knew that if it was within my control I would make it (#ChillOut)."

That chance came in his second year playing overseas when the San Antonio Spurs called Anthony and signed him to a preseason contract (#ManifestThat!).

"Visualizing has always played a big role in my life (#CreateAMovieInYourHead). As a kid it was like my fantasy world, dreaming to be an NBA player, watching those players on TV. As I grew up and learned how the NBA works, I started to analyze the other role players on the team, not just the star players. There were roles on the team that were not just for the big stars; I knew my role on a team was going to be one of those supporting positions. I started to really focus on what they did to become successful and that was the biggest motivation for me.

"It was more realistic, to look at position players and say 'I want to be like that,' than dream of becoming a Michael Jordan. I started to visualize myself in those roles, and started implementing those tools in my game. Robert Horry was one of the guys I looked at as my example, thinking to myself, '*I could do that. I could do his job*.' It's ironic that when the Spurs signed me it was because they released Robert Horry. I'd literally taken his job (#ManifestThat!). I visualized that happening, and it actually became a reality!"

Anthony described the moment when he felt like he was finally living his dream. He laughed and said, "I have three! The first one was at the Cleveland training camp. I was with guys who were way better players than me. They were bigger, more talented; I was definitely the underdog. But I thought, 'I could make the team.' The rule for making the team after training camp is: If you don't get a phone call by 5 P.M., you've made the team. I left practice on the last day of camp and went back to my hotel to watch the clock. I was so nervous waiting for that call, it was making me crazy. I needed to pick up my eyeglasses from the store before it closed, so I decided to do it while I waited. I actually lost track of time and when I looked at my phone in the store it was already 5:05, and I had no missed calls from Cleveland. I got in the car and started bumping, '*Welcome to the good life*' (#ManifestThat!)."

"The other moment I remember was after being bounced around overseas, then to the D-league, and then to several short-term NBA contracts, I was starting to really question my dedication and my dream. So when I was called up by Golden State, I wasn't expecting to play very much, but my big moment came early on when we played the Lakers, and the coach started me. So there I was standing on the court at tip-off, giving Kobe Bryant a handshake before the jump ball. That was when I really felt like, '*Okay, this is crazy, I'm living that dream I had in kindergarten*.'

"The last one was when I signed the contract with the Spurs. I was in Vegas with my mom and got that first paycheck signed by the NBA. That was such an amazing feeling, to see a check written in your name by the NBA and share that with my mom."

In his first game with the Spurs, on October 22, 2008, Anthony played his career-best game (up to that point). "It was the game that felt like 'I made it.' I called my mom as soon as I got out of the locker room, like I did after every game. She was so excited; we talked about the game and what this meant for our future. It was a great moment."

The next day Anthony got a call after practice. His mother had suffered a sudden heart attack, sitting in her chair where she'd watched his game. The TV was still on when his sister stopped by the next afternoon to say hello, and discovered their mother had passed away the night before.

"It was so shocking." Anthony's voice went quiet, and I realized this is something he rarely talked about. "I was really down and confused after that. My faith was the one thing that kept me from losing it. I've never been one to rely on anything such as drugs, or alcohol, or anything like that to get me through hard times. I've always relied on God and on my faith, and that's the only thing that carried me through.

"I was able to see my mom alone before the service, and I had a moment with her where this incredible peace washed over me and I knew I was going to be okay. She'd given me everything I needed, raised me with the tools to succeed, and taught me how to be a good man. She had done the job that I needed her so much to do, and I felt so blessed. God gave me such overwhelming peace that day when I was with her. I cried at the funeral, but I haven't cried since. She's been with me all the way. I look just like her, and my son looks just like me. She is here with us all the time. The time when it was the hardest was on my wedding day. I wanted her to share that with me. I still think about her every day and she is always here."

After his mother passed away, Anthony struggled to redefine his motivation for following his passion (#EarthquakeMoments). He leaned on his faith and his family, as again he bounced around from team to team, on short-term contracts. He would play for ten days here, and twenty days there.

Since 2008, Anthony has played for nine NBA teams. He's signed a two-year contract with the Minnesota Timberwolves, and has played in the NBA playoffs twice—once as an Atlanta Hawk and in 2014 as a Charlotte Bobcat. Anthony credits his shooting skills and "team player" attitude as the reason his career as a position player has been so successful. Those skills he developed young and focused on are the same ones that enabled him to live his dream. He's achieved his lifelong goal of becoming an NBA veteran, and is going on his eighth year in the league.

ANTHONY'S ADVICE TO YOU

"Nothing replaces hard work (#TheHustle). Don't let anyone tell you that you can't do something. When it comes to your dreams, people around you can discourage you only if you let them. If you have that dream, go for it 100 percent (#RelentlessPursuit)."

ANTHONY TOLLIVER is a power forward in the NBA. He currently plays for the Minnesota Timberwolves; he is also the cofounder of Active Faith Sports. Follow his journey on **Twitter:** @ATolliver44 **Instagram:** ATolliver44 **Website:** www.ActiveFaithSports.com

KIMBERLEY HATCHETT'S STORY

I first met Kimberley via a Facebook post in which I'd asked my friends about the most successful person they know. One of my Facebook friends whom I didn't personally know responded that he knew just the woman I was looking to interview. I must say that I'm so grateful he was kind enough to make this introduction, because Kimberley has become not only an amazing mentor to me, but a great friend as well. You will notice connections to Kimberley in several stories to come.

On the day Kim called for our interview we had never previously spoken. I knew she rarely gave interviews so I was understandably nervous, but anxious to hear her story. She was the first female athlete that I'd ever interviewed or discussed the concepts behind the #HBRMethod. My background up to that point had been working with male athletes in the NFL, NBA, and collegiate level, so I was eager to hear her perspective.

I asked Kimberley to tell me her story . . .

"I started running competitively when I was thirteen years old. It was my dream to be an Olympian, and at fifteen I had the opportunity to join an elite running club, and train with Olympic Gold Medalist Carl Lewis and his sister Carol (#DreamIT).

"I have an identical twin sister who also competed in track and field, and parents who fully supported our dreams. My mother was a schoolteacher, and after school she'd drive us three hours to train with the Lewis's.

"For me my hustle and my passion started with my parents, believing in us and telling us we could achieve greatness.

My father was this beautiful, larger-than-life spirit, who was also an athlete and taught us at a young age to go after what we wanted. He also taught us how to quiet our mind in a stressful situation. That ability to keep calm and focus under intense stress that I learned as an athlete, is something I rely on in business all the time (#ThinkIT)."

When Kimberley was a junior in high school she tore her ACL. "Back then that injury destroyed an athlete. We didn't have the medical advances there are today, back then it was a career-ending injury." Kimberley told me, adding, "But I fought it. I rehabbed it, and worked extremely hard to come back, ultimately getting a scholarship to the University of Virginia (#RelentlessPursuit)."

Her dream was to compete in the 1984 Olympics, and she spent her entire college career working toward that goal. When her friends were joining sororities and going to frat parties, she was training, or sleeping, or mentally preparing for a track meet (#TheHustle). When they were on the beaches of Miami for spring break, she was on the track for hours at a time perfecting her craft. But in 1984 she suffered a truly career-ending injury at her Olympic trial, one not even she could overcome (#EarthquakeMoment*)*.

Yet she wasn't willing to give up so easily. She moved to New York City and took a low-level job at Chase bank while still trying to train and rehab her injury. But it soon became apparent that it was time to face the reality that her dream of being an Olympian, which she'd worked for since the age of thirteen, was not going to happen (#ItsTheJourney). It was time to redefine her dream and figure out what the next chapter of her life would become (#LifePlan).

"I decided it was time to take the skills that made me successful as an athlete and transition into business full time. Those skills are what got me through Harvard Business School. Having mental toughness (#ThinkIT) and the ability to believe in yourself and your goals (#BelieveIT), the mindset of never giving up, of working harder than everyone else and staying focused (#RelentlessPursuit)—I relied on all of that at Harvard. When I graduated I knew I wanted to be in investment banking, but I wanted the independence of being my own boss. I looked at all the options and settled on personal investments.

"I knew the risks were high, much higher than taking a job in banking with a nice starting salary like my fellow graduates were doing. Here I was taking a commission-only job, having just graduated with a huge college loan to repay. I was willing to step out on faith and take the opportunity and risk (#CourageOverFear). But I made a goal, to repay my $50,000 student loan my very first year (#SayIT). At the end of the year I'd not only paid my loan in full I'd made that amount three times over, doubling what I would have made had I chosen the 'safe route' (#ManifestThat!).

"You have to be willing to fail. And if you do, you get up and try again. The people who are very successful are those who take the risk without fear of failure.

"I used to daydream all the time. Sitting at my desk calling through the Yellow Pages all day, thinking about what my life was going to be (#CreateAMovieInYourHead). I imagined my apartment, where it would be, what my life would be like, all of that is what kept me going in the beginning. And then it all happened! Only way bigger and better than I ever could of imagined" (#HBRLife).

Every year since the inception of the list, Kim has ranked among the "Top 100 Women Advisors" in the world, a list compiled by Barrons. She has remained the only African American woman on the list. She's also made the top 1,000 coed list five out of seven years. She has set a new bar, accomplishing what no other African American women before her ever had, proving anything really is possible for ANYONE. In 2014 the Network Journal named Kimberley one of "The 25 Most Influential Women in Business." Today she is the Executive Director of Morgan Stanley, managing over $2 billion in personal client assets. She has truly created a life beyond her expectations.

"I have always recognized that it could be gone in an instant. I manage private investments and I've seen really bad days, days when clients lose millions of dollars because the market takes a turn. So I never take it for granted (#GetGrateful). I always just wanted to stay grounded and teach my daughter that this life isn't 'normal.' That we needed to be grateful and remember that I didn't grow up this way, and try and teach that to my daughter."

I think so many of us have a dream, but we have a very difficult time believing it could be possible for *us*. But even still, we have role models, people who are already living those dreams who give us the possibility that it *could happen*, at least in theory. It takes a true visionary to have a dream, look around, and realize that you don't see one single example of anyone living that dream, and still go for it. That's what most people like to call "impossible." But it's only "impossible" until *you make it possible*. And that is what Kimberley has done; she's proven that barriers and boundaries only stop us if we allow them to stop us. If we want something bad enough, believe in it with all our being, find joy and passion in it, forge ahead no matter what the obstacles, we will realize it.

KIMBERLEY'S ADVICE TO YOU

"Find the thing that brings out your passion, which you fully believe in. I was, and am, passionate about preserving people's wealth. That ignites passion in me; it's what I love, and what I'll probably never retire from doing. So find something that brings that out in you.

"But remember, there is always a balance in life; make sure you enjoy it. Take time for yourself, and to meditate, and spend time with your family. It's not a fulfilled life if it's only about work; you need to find a balance."

KIMBERLEY HATCHETT is the Executive Director of Morgan Stanley, Private Wealth Management Group. She is also a gifted speaker, sharing her story to inspire young people to go after their dreams. Kimberley has interviewed the likes of Tyra Banks and Jane Fonda for Morgan Stanley's authors reading series. Follow her journey on **Instagram** @khatch1234

KENJON BARNER'S STORY

I first met Kenjon in 2009. It was coming up on my son Kanen's eighth birthday and I was struggling to find something special to do for it. I didn't really have any money, still living paycheck to paycheck. Even though I'd accepted a great job, it came with a small salary and I knew I couldn't afford to throw him a party (#MoneyAintAThing!).

Kanen and I are huge Oregon Duck football fans; back then we'd watch every game together in our cramped apartment living room. We'd play catch with a football during commercial breaks, trying not to send a long pass through the window. Football was *our thing*; it was how I tried to supplement for the loss of his father's presence in his life.

One night I had an idea. What if Kanen could play catch with an actual male instead of his mom? And what if I could convince an Oregon Duck player to be that guy as a surprise for Kanen's birthday? Why not? I believed in dreaming big. It was worth a shot. So I went on Facebook and "cold-called" Oregon's star running back Kenjon Barner.

I was blown away when Kenjon ("KB" as he's known to friends and family) responded that he'd be happy to help me surprise my son, and play football with him. It was January, just a week after Oregon played in the BCS Championship game, when Kenjon walked out onto the field to meet my son. Needless to say it was one of those once in a lifetime, pinch-me kind of moments, that for my son, was larger than life (#ManifestThat!).

Since that day we have become great friends and much of what I learned in my early days of starting over, on how my mindset affected my outcomes, came from Kenjon. I'm sure you can see why . . .

Kenjon grew up in a home full of love and competitive brotherly rivalries. His parents had their hands full, with six boys and a girl. So from a young age he learned that confidence was everything! As a kid it was actually basketball where he excelled, and it's what gave him that confidence from the start. "I played basketball from the time I was three years old, it's all I ever wanted to do," KB told me when I asked him when *football* became his dream. "I wasn't really even thinking about football; I'd never played it, except with my friends in the yard growing up. But basketball was what I loved and was good at, and it's what my family expected me to play."

In seventh grade Kenjon's dad came to his son's room to wake him up for his early morning practice. But this time he didn't want to get out of bed. "I was so tired and I told him I wasn't going to practice. I told him I wanted to quit. My dad looked at me and said 'Then what are you going to do?' It was such a huge part of my life, it's like how do you quit the one thing you spend most of your time doing?

"I looked at him and said, 'I am going to play in the NFL' (#SayIT)."

Kenjon had never played football before. He had never studied the plays or worn a uniform, but when he said it out loud to his dad (#SayIT), and later to his friends they knew he was serious. They wondered if he had lost his mind, but they knew he was serious! "When I set my mind to something, I let nothing stand in my way. I was a confident kid. Growing up as the youngest with five brothers, you kinda have to be! I've always believed in myself (#BelieveIT).

"But all through my freshman and sophomore year of high school I was just thinking, *man, I gotta find a way to get a job when I graduate high school.* No one in my family had ever gone to college, it's just not what I was exposed to, it wasn't an expectation I had."

In Kenjon's junior year of high school he was offered a college scholarship to play football. "I thought, *wow that's crazy!* But in the back of my head I was still thinking, *I really need to get a job.* My mom was so excited by the thought of me going to college that there was no way she was about to let me miss that opportunity. And by the end of my junior year I got to a place where I believed it was possible for me.

"I absolutely believe that if you set a goal and a dream you can achieve it. I verbalize a goal and believe it, and know I'll achieve whatever I set out to do. My junior year of high school when it came time for the state football awards, I missed the award for first team all-state. I felt robbed. After the awards I was upset, and I told my dad I would 'make 'em pay!' I said, 'I'm gonna score 40 touchdowns and rush for 3,000 yards next year' (#SayIT). The next year I scored 47 touchdowns and rushed for 3,124 yards (#ManifestThat!).

"You've got to believe it with that kind of confidence (#BelieveIT). If you don't believe in it then how can anyone else? People thought I was crazy, but my family knew that if I said it, I would do it. You've gotta have that faith, and that confidence."

Kenjon went on to be one of the most acclaimed running backs in the history of Oregon football. He was the first Duck since 1965 to score touchdowns from punt returns, rushing, receiving, and kickoff returns. He played in the Rose Bowl in 2011, the BCS National Championship game in 2012, and the Fiesta Bowl in 2013.

On April 27, 2013 Kenjon was drafted into the NFL in the 6th round by the Carolina Panthers.

I asked him what that felt like. "It was the most stressful, annoying, frustrating, happiest three days of my life! My agent had warned me not to watch the draft live, and to just wait for a call, but of course my family and I watched it nonstop. But then when I got the call from Carolina on the third day, wow, that was amazing! It was such a celebration for my whole family. It was the happiest day of all our lives."

I asked Kenjon what it felt like to live out that dream, running out the tunnel onto an NFL field for the first time (#Manifest-That!). "My first preseason game I wasn't nervous." KB told me. "I thought something was wrong with me because I just felt so calm. This is what I'd dreamed about and worked for all my life, a moment like this. Looking up in those stands and seeing thousands of fans, I was just thinking, *wow, this is so crazy!* And as soon as I got out there they called my play as the first play of the game, and then suddenly I was a nervous wreck. I hadn't expected to be taking the field for the first time in the first play of the game. They gave me the ball and I fumbled it, and we lost possession of the ball.

"When I make a mistake like that, I can't let it go. I choose not to let it go, because it motivates me and keeps me present. I take that negative energy and channel it for motivation (#ChangeTheVoicesInYourHead). And the next time they called my play I was ready; I ran the ball for a touchdown.

"In order to do something you need to be able to *see* yourself doing it first. I visualize the game before I play (#CreateAMovieInYourHead). I see myself running for a touch-down. Then when it happens I'm not surprised because I've seen myself doing it and I'm prepared. I think of it as God gave me that vision, allowed me to see it, and then he enabled me to live it out. If you do what you're supposed to do, and put in the work, then what's meant for you will come to you. You have to trust the process and be patient (#ChillOut) and know that if you do all the preparation, then when your turn comes, you will be ready."

KENJON'S ADVICE TO YOU

"If you're not willing to work hard, don't expect it to happen."

KENJON BARNER was drafted by the Carolina Panthers in 2013 and traded to the Philadelphia Eagles in 2014. In 2018 Kenjon won the Super Bowl with the Eagles. Can you say #ManifestThat!? Follow his journey on **Twitter** @kbdeuce4 and **Instagram** @justmekb24

II. The 8-Step Plan

STEP 1: #DREAMIT

"Being realistic is the fastest road to mediocrity. WHY would you EVER be realistic?" —Will Smith

WHAT'S YOUR DREAM?

STEP #1: DREAM IT

WHAT DO YOU WANT?

When's the last time you truly gave this question some serious thought? It seems simple enough on the surface, but I find that most people I coach have no idea what they really want. So ask yourself: What do I honestly want my life to be like? You would be surprised at how many people can't answer this question, without the words "money" or "to be successful." Neither of those answers count. You're going to have to do better than that!

This saying is posted on my office wall:

If you don't know what you want, you'll never know when you've got it.

I encourage you to write that down someplace where you can see it as well, because it might be the truest statement I've ever heard. This chapter will teach you how to discover what it is you want out of your life. But you must be willing to buy in; you need to do the work with me. You need to make the commitment here and now: that this isn't just a book you're reading for the hell of it, it's a tool to quickly and easily change your life and teach you how to live your dream. And I can't help you change it unless we know where it is you want to go. We need that picture, that vision, that goal, to be as clear as an IMAX movie screen playing in your mind all day. You have to see it, love it, and be passionate about where you're about to go; that's what will get you there, and fast!

#BIGPICTUREDREAM

It's important to identify from the start what your #BigPicture-Dream is. I call it this because I want you to begin focusing on your end result—not reaching one goal, or a few milestones, but really starting to imagine, and then work for the whole big picture, or the LIFE you want. When you start out focusing on what this life will look and feel like, then you will be open to the journey it will take you on to achieve it. I can almost promise you that you won't reach it via your exact plan; it will most likely be a windy journey so focusing on the end helps you curb any disappointments or setbacks along the way, and helps you take advantage of opportunities that come.

This exercise will help you get started . . .

What did you want to be when you were a little kid? Say, nine years old? You know, those times when you closed your eyes and daydreamed in class, or on long car rides, or all day every day. What kind of potential did you believe the world held for you? What made you excited?

As kids we had this amazing tool called an imagination. And for a few years, before "reality" was beaten into our brains, we had free rein to imagine life any way we wanted it to be. Those "daydreams" are often the core of what we truly love in life;

they hold the key to our passion, even if the format changes over time.

EXAMPLE

In my childhood imagination, I was a famous singer. I bought backup tracks and practiced singing to them in front of my mirror, using my curling iron as a microphone. I perfected my autograph, signing blank pieces of paper for hours at a time. I had it all down like a movie in my head, all day, every day. That fantasy made me so happy. I used to love to slip into that fantasy world no matter what I was doing—cleaning, schoolwork, riding my horse, whatever. I'd play it out like a script, picking up where I'd left off the last time. I knew what I wanted to be when I grew up. I wanted to walk out on the stage, hear the crowd, hold the microphone, and say "Thank you for coming."

Then the world beat the dream out of me, and the reality of life took over and I found myself living the kind of life I never envisioned at all when I was young. I was a broke stay-at-home mom who was afraid to look into a mirror, let alone sing into one. I'd forgotten the joy that vision had brought to me, and forgotten the idea that great things might actually be possible for me. When I was a kid, I loved the way my last name rolled in pretty scribbles across the page when I practiced my autograph, and I vowed never to change it. So when I got married I protested for several years the idea that I needed to give up my last name and learn a whole new autograph. But eventually I gave up both: my name and my dream.

As I began rebuilding my life after my divorce, I slowly started giving myself permission to dream again. To remove the boundaries of "reality" from those dreams and just put them out into the Universe. So I identified them (#LifePlan) and began working toward them every day.

My #BigPictureDream was to share my story with the world through multiple forms of media, the biggest of which was speaking in front of a live audience. It wasn't until after my first speech, in which I stood in front of a thousand strangers, held a microphone, and said "Thank you for coming," that I realized I had just lived out my childhood fantasy. And later, when I signed copies of my coauthored book (*Adventures in Manifesting*) at the back of the room, I realized I was signing the exact same signature (my maiden name) I'd practiced when I was twelve years old. I had manifested the very dream I'd held so close as a child, the one that brought me so much happiness and provided a means of escape from my dysfunctional upbringing. The dream and experience of living that dream were the exact same. Both dreams had been centered on inspiring and uplifting people. I'd always wanted to do that through singing and music, and now I was doing it through the spoken word. Only the medium had changed.

But I never would have come back to this dream, or identified it in the first place, had I not sat down to evaluate what it was that I truly wanted from my new life. It took almost three years from the time I first identified that dream on my first #Future-Board, to the time I lived it. And it started with just a spark, and remembering the joy I'd found in it when I was a child.

I want you to find what brings you the most joy, or did when you were younger. It might seem ridiculous and out of place in your grownup life, and that's OK. That's just the dream on the surface. Be patient and explore it further; I bet whatever was at the core that attracted you as a child is still what will fulfill you as an adult.

This is the most important part . . . Dream BIG!!!

It seems crazy, I know, but most people really struggle with how to dream big. It's human nature to shoot down your dreams, to discount them, or question their validity. If you're feeling stuck, you are not alone, trust me. I find that in the beginning, one of the things my clients have the most difficulty with is giving themselves permission to dream. It's been so ingrained in us from the time we were children that dreaming is a waste of time, and that what we should focus on is what is "realistic" for us, that we feel guilty even when we have permission to dream. At first it almost feels too selfish to dream big. You might not feel like you deserve your dreams to come true, or that you're worthy of success or wealth. It's so easy for us to get stuck in the box we came in, believing that the only thing possible for us is within those four walls. But I want you to begin to realize that there is NO BOX at all. Just an open space for you to create your own kingdom.

When I put my #FutureBoard together for my office at work, I remember thinking how crazy every picture looked to me at the time. They all represented a life so far removed from my reality that it was laughable. I was struggling to pay rent and buy groceries at the time, yet I was putting up pictures that represented the woman I'd created in my #LifePlan. It was ridiculous. But it made me so happy, unexplainably happy, to make that board and find the pictures that matched my plan.

#ITSTHEJOURNEY

It will likely be a long and winding road that takes you from where you are today to living your #BigPictureDream, and over time your specific goal/dream might change. Knowing this from the start will help you stay aware and take advantage of opportunities that present themselves along the way.

There are many examples in this book of people who worked extremely hard for a specific goal only to find out that achieving it didn't bring them the happiness they expected, so they adjusted their dream to something similar that fulfilled their passion. But the journey of accomplishing that goal always puts them ahead of the game as they pursue the next dream, so it's never time wasted. The journey makes you wiser, brings amazing people into your life who otherwise would not be there, and enriches your life, even when it's difficult.

EXAMPLE

When I started rebuilding my life in 2008 my dream was to be a corporate boss chick. I built my whole #LifePlan around who this woman would become. But somewhere along my journey to becoming a boss chick, my passion began to find me. My #BigPictureDream had always been to become financially free, have flexibility in my job so I could be with my kids, to travel, and to mentor others. But back then I never would have expected it to turn into my present-day dream. Now my specific dream is to leave the corporate world and become a bestselling author, coach, and speaker. However, the criteria for my #BigPictureDream is exactly the same. Only my specific goals/dreams changed over time.

So, be open. You never know what the Universe has in store for you. And if your passion/dream is currently undefined, simply focus on the #BigPictureDream of the life you want, and the specific passion will rise to the top when you're ready to receive it.

#MONEYAINTATHING!

You don't need money to start living the life of your dreams!

This is my favorite concept of the #HBRMethod. Sounds crazy, right? I promise you it's the God's honest truth. No matter what your current financial situation is (even if you're broke!), money is NOT a requirement or even a necessity when it comes to you living the fabulous life of your dreams.

Money is irrelevant when it comes to manifesting your dreams. Will Smith said that when you decide you're going to do something or become something, "the Universe gets out of your way." It responds to your decision, and your commitment to achieving the end result. It is not limited by something as lame as money.

I know you don't believe me, so here are just a few examples that prove this theory to be true.

EXAMPLE #1

In the fall of 2009 I accepted a job with a legal software company based in my hometown of Portland, Oregon. I had relentlessly followed up with the CEO after my first interview because I was convinced the job had amazing potential and I was determined to get it. Each time I went in for an interview, I practiced my steps: #ThinkIT, #SeeIT, #BelieveIT, and #SayIT. I had total faith I'd get an offer. But weeks turned into a month, and still there was no call.

Finally the day I'd waited for arrived, and I was sitting in the boardroom with the CEO and a written offer. It was the first time we'd ever talked about salary after having endured multiple interviews, and I was sitting in the chair looking over the offer, *devastated*. It was half of what I'd expected it would be, and less than I was paid at the job I currently held. It had only been a year since my husband left and I was still relying on food stamps to survive. I knew there would be no way I could afford a pay cut, even if the potential and job title was amazing.

I explained this to the CEO and reluctantly declined the job, feeling defeated and broken on my drive home. As I pulled into my driveway, my phone rang. It was the CEO offering to match my current salary if I'd take the position. I was ecstatic! Even though I knew the position wouldn't offer more money and that my family and I would still be financially strapped, I knew I'd be happy.

On my first day of work I carried in my rather large corkboard covered in pictures of the life I was working to achieve, and set it up at my cubicle. It was the same #FutureBoard I'd made back in 2006 when I was still married. On it were pictures of places I dreamed of visiting: New York, Las Vegas, Los Angeles, and Hawaii. There was a picture of a Mercedes, a Louis Vuitton bag, and a "26.2" marathon sticker.

I had been on the job about three months when the CEO called me into his office and said he'd like to offer me a new role: Director/VP of a new division he was planning to launch. It came with a minimal raise but a lot more visibility and travel.

On the day before my first business trip I packed up my laptop and double-checked that I had everything I'd need, when

I suddenly noticed the picture on my #FutureBoard. It was a photo of the Hollywood sign above a picture of Times Square in New York. I looked down at the printed piece of paper in my hand: my e-ticket to Los Angeles and then on to New York.

I'll never forget standing in the middle of Times Square at midnight and letting the intense joy wash over my entire body. I closed my eyes and inhaled the smells of the city and took in the sounds of the taxi horns blasting. All of it was a manifestation of my dream. I was standing in the middle of the picture that had hung on my wall for three years.

I had seven dollars in my bank account on that trip—not even enough for a slice of pizza. But I didn't go hungry. Nope, instead I was eating at amazing restaurants and staying at a beautiful hotel in Midtown. I was living my dream and it wasn't costing me a single penny. I had manifested the first of many all-expenses-paid trips that to me were not just about having to travel for my job. They were also proof that I could live the life I so desperately wanted and was working to create, even though technically I was still pretty broke.

It was a few months later that I found myself in Las Vegas for a week-long convention. Once again, personally, I didn't have a penny to my name, yet I was aware enough to recognize that I'd manifested the exact experience I'd dreamed about, all the way down to "randomly" staying in the exact same hotel I'd had in my picture.

EXAMPLE #2

In 2015 I had accrued enough miles to book a first-class trip to Los Angeles with my son. Though I've come a long way since 2009, I'm still a single mom supporting a family of four, so I always have to budget. I don't make the kind of money the people who normally take first-class vacations make. Nevertheless, I was able to take him for three days. I had purchased first-class airfare, a stay at an amazing hotel, tickets to Universal Studios, and his dream rental car. Our trip included a day at the beach and dinner in Beverly Hills. That ENTIRE trip cost me $300! The best part was when Kanen and I stood in front of the Hollywood sign for a quick picture. Even though I'd manifested versions of this LA trip before, I manifested the BIG ONE five years later.

Our job is to dream it. It will come bigger than expected, at a time you least expect it.

EXAMPLE #3

In one of my favorite examples of #MoneyAintAThing!, I learned that ANYTHING is possible. In 2010 I asked my son Kanen to tell me his dream, and without skipping a beat he said, "I want to go to a Baltimore Ravens game and meet Michael Oher!" We had just seen the movie *The Blind Side* about Michael Oher's life and Kanen was obsessed with it. I looked at him and just shook my head. What was I supposed to tell my kid? That his dream was virtually impossible? That only some dreams come true? Nah.

So we cut out a picture of the Ravens' home stadium and added it to my #FutureBoard. I had no idea how I could make this dream a reality. It seemed like the most impossible of them all.

In the spring of 2011 I was unexpectedly laid off from my dream job, and it wasn't long before I was once again worried about how I'd make ends meet. The last thing I was thinking about was flying across the country to a Ravens game. Money was once again extremely tight, so buying airfare, paying for a hotel, and buying the tickets would be impossible. Not to mention: How on earth would I be able to get Michael Oher to meet my son?

It was around that time that my connections in football were quickly growing, and one day I got a message on Facebook from retired Ravens quarterback Anthony Wright. He'd heard that I was coaching players through their transitions in and out of their professional careers, and wanted to talk. When I mentioned my son's dream in passing, he immediately offered to get us tickets to the game if I ever decided to go. That suggestion set pure magic in motion.

That day I decided to see how many airline miles I'd accumulated over the previous year of business travel. I had exactly enough for two round-trip tickets to Baltimore. I booked them on the spot, afraid that if I thought about it too long I'd let doubt creep in and change my mind. I was going to step out on faith and make my son's dream a reality.

But there was still the question of how we'd meet Michael Oher. I reached out to one of my connections, a former Oregon player who now played for the Ravens, to see what strings he could pull. He couldn't promise anything, he told me, but he'd try.

On October 11, 2011, my son Kanen and I walked to M&T Bank Stadium from our hotel in Baltimore. He was more excited than I'd ever seen him, talking a mile a minute. When we arrived at the Will Call box office to pick up our tickets, inside the envelope were two seats in the coveted lower level, and two sideline field passes.

There are no words to do this part of the story justice: the moment when I walked with my son past the players' locker room. We then proceeded out the team tunnel onto the football field, under a banner that read **Relentless Pursuit**.

We watched the team take the field and go through their warm-ups, the atmosphere electric. And then I noticed Michael Oher on the other side of the field; he was walking directly toward us. He walked right up to my son and said, "So I hear you've been looking for me!"

That entire trip, including an experience that money could not even buy, cost me $150, including the hotel.

See videos from this trip on my YouTube channel @Sarah-Centrella and read the real-time blog post with pictures on www. thoughtsstorieslife.com

For more amazing examples of #MoneyAintAThing from my #FutureBoard, check out the tag on my blog "Manifest That!" Photos of the dream and reality are on my Pinterest @SarahCentrella under the board called "My Reality Board."

Those are just a few examples of how money has NOT been a factor for me in living the life I desired.

If I can do it, so can you. And don't tell me you're not capable of that, or that you can't do it. You wouldn't be reading this book if that was the case.

CLIENT EXAMPLES

The examples I gave above might seem a little "too good to be true." Luckily they are all posted in real time on my blog and YouTube, but you may still be thinking I'm full of shit. But I can assure you it's very real (though I did make up the cool name)!

EXAMPLE #1.

Sarah Joyce Bryant (@thenightwriter) was a client in my #HBRBootcamp. When she started class she was really struggling. Financially things had been very tight, she was in an unhealthy relationship, and worst of all she had been dealing with some serious health issues for years. By week two the boyfriend was gone, and Sarah Joyce was starting to focus on rebuilding her life and getting to a positive place.

But her health continued to sideline her progress and mental focus. She couldn't seem to find a doctor willing to actually listen and provide help. She'd gotten an experimental prescription in the past, which improved her condition, but it was $540 per month and insurance wouldn't cover it. At that time her financial situation had been better, but now there was no way she could afford that medication.

I told her that the #HBRMethod works for all aspects of our lives, not just the really big stuff, and so she went to work applying it. A few weeks into boot camp and Sarah Joyce not only found a doctor willing to hear her, but also someone who was willing to give her the medication that would make her better, and the best part? This time it was 100 percent covered by insurance.

Before #HBR she thought that the lack of money was a barrier she could not overcome to get to the medication she needed, but in the end it was FREE.

EXAMPLE #2

Nicky Peet (@nickypeet44) is one of my coaching clients who lives in France. When we first started working together Nicky too was struggling with her finances, and the stress that it brings. We worked on learning to let go of that stress and replace it with #TheHustle and #BelieveIT, and slowly things started to shift for Nicky. She got a raise at work, began growing her Reiki business, and for the first time in her life got unexpected checks in the mail (#Winning!).

One of Nicky's dreams was to focus on her passion for photography, but for that she needed a good camera, and she knew she didn't have the money to go out and buy one. But she kept that wish close, and went looking for one anyway, just to get the feel of it (#FakeIT). When she saw the exact camera she'd been dreaming about marked down to an unbelievably low discounted price, she knew it was a sign. And for the first time in a long time she had the money to take that opportunity on the spot. She recognized that she had manifested this camera at a price she could afford, and she stepped out on faith, knowing that money would continue to come in (#CourageOverFear).

The point of all these stories is to help you to wrap your head around the concept that you must #DreamIT without the restraint of "money" in the equation. The lack of money will never be what stands between you and your dream.

YOUR HUSTLE

Grab your journal and pen.

Now your fun begins! I want you to create a #BucketList. This is my all-time favorite exercise in the #HBRMethod, for the following reasons.

1. It teaches you how to dream big, which should feel absolutely liberating, exciting, fun, enjoyable, inspiring, or whatever else you want to call it. It's designed to help you dream bigger than you've ever imagined was possible for your life.
2. It takes money out of the equation and focuses on experiences. By its very nature it breaks down the barriers to what is possible for you, because the whole idea of a #BucketList is that they are moments you want to experience (or live out) before you die (or *kick the bucket*, hence the name). So when you think of it that way, there

should be no limits on those desires, right? *Who's to tell you what you can or can't do before you die? Who's to tell you that someday you wouldn't have a limitless bank account?* Think of this as a "fantasy life" if that helps you to remove the barriers of reality.

This list has no right being "realistic." I don't care if you think these things are out of your reach or not. I want you to put down EVERY experience, every moment you want to live out before you die. No ifs, ands, or buts. Just write them all down.

To help get the creative juices flowing, pick a quiet spot to do this homework. Choose a quiet time during the evening when the kids are in bed (that's what I do), or out in nature where you can clear your head—whatever physical location and time of day is most relaxing for you. Get comfortable, maybe grab a glass of wine, put on some nice music, get a pen and paper, and . . . let your imagination run wild.

Here are a few questions that will help get your creative juices flowing. You'll need to have at least twenty items on your list before you can move on to the next chapter.

- What have I always wanted to do/try?
- Where do I want to travel? Why? What do I want to do when I'm there?
- What's the scariest thing I've ever wanted to do/try?
- Where else would I want to live?
- What do I want to accomplish in my lifetime? (Run a marathon? Write a book? Start a business? Etc.)
- What would I do if I won the lottery? (actual things you would DO)
- What would I eat? Where would I eat it?
- Who would I meet?

So what's on your list?

Now when I ask you, *What do you want?* I bet you can answer the question. You've taken some of those restrictive barricades away that have held you captive and are starting to sense that there really might be a pretty kick-ass world out there, and that maybe, just maybe you're entitled to experience it. Now we're getting somewhere!

*If you need inspiration, check out my personal #BucketList on my blog www.thoughtsstorieslife.com and search "bucket list."

#HBRSTORIES

ASH VASUDEVAN

NIKKI MAcCALLUM

STEPHANIE THAVIXAY

RYAN BLAIR

CHARISE WELLER

ASH VASUDEVAN'S STORY

#BR STORIES

Ash's interview was the very first one I ever conducted specifically for this book. I'd just finished my blog series with the Oregon football players, but that was different. I knew football. I especially knew Oregon football, and I also personally knew all but one of those guys. But I'd never done an actual interview with a total stranger on a topic I didn't really know much about—in this case, baseball. I felt so inadequate and nervous. What if I made a total fool of myself? What if he thought my questions were stupid, or hated how I wrote his story? To say I was using #FakeIT is an understatement; that and my #MottoForLife mantras were what gave me the balls to carry out the interview that started it all.

Thank God Ash couldn't have been kinder or more gracious; he put me at ease right away when he called for our interview.

This is the story of a dream that seemed totally crazy, an impossible mission . . . to find talented baseball players in India, a country where cricket is the national pastime and baseball was a complete unknown. This is also the story of what it takes to succeed, how to step out on faith when you believe in your dream, and how to silence the critics and achieve the "impossible."

Meet Ash Vasudevan, the real-life inspiration behind the 2014 Disney film *Million Dollar Arm*.

"In 2007, when we were first starting out with the idea for the reality show 'Million Dollar Arm' in India, 99 percent of the people we spoke to about it thought we were insane. The people in the United States thought it was a totally crazy idea; they didn't like the format or location. They thought if we were going to do an open 'talent' search we should go to Asia or South America, places where people knew about baseball. But we wanted to go to a place where the market was untapped. Everyone we talked to in India thought it was a ridiculous idea as well. 'Do a show for cricket,' they said. 'Why would you do it for baseball? No one knows what baseball is in India!' But we KNEW the talent existed in India; we just weren't sure if we could find it. It was like finding a needle in a haystack," Ash said.

Ash is known for his love of the unknown, his passion for creating and funding unique projects with great stories. "The opportunity to explore and do things that no one else has done is what drives me. And normally when everyone thinks an idea is insane, that's when I know it's something special. I'm known for taking risks, and I knew the talent was there to be discovered."

Ash and his business partner Will (Chang in the movie) run an investment company around unlikely (high risk, high reward) projects. "We fund those," Ash told me, explaining why he decided to support JB Bernstein's initial idea. "He was one of the most successful sports marketing gurus in the world. We all very strongly resonated with the idea, the impact that basketball has made in China; we knew it could have a similar impact with baseball in India. And from a sheer numbers standpoint we never doubted the idea, or that the talent existed. We always knew we had to be the one to go make it happen. We had an unshakable conviction that it would work, we were convinced of it (#BelieveIT)."

On their very first scouting trip to India, Ash and JB asked San Francisco Giants pitcher Brian Wilson to come to India to help them get a good read on potential talent. "We went to one of the hallowed grounds of Indian cricket, where all the best players train and set up a small pitching mound. Brian, who was recovering from surgery at the time, went out on the mound and threw a few soft pitches. Pretty soon all the kids had stopped what they were doing and were crowding around him. About 200 kids, watching this 6-foot-2-inch big man throw a baseball. Most of the kids were shy, and didn't understand what Brian was doing or why we were there, but then a nineteen-year-old lanky kid walked up to Brian and said; 'So all you have to do is throw a ball?' He watched Brian do his wind-up, and throw a few pitches. Then he took the ball, and without trying to get into form or copy Brian's technique he threw a 90-mph fastball. And then we knew we were on to something (#ManifestThat!)."

During our May 2014 interview, Ash indicated that in Season One nearly 30,000 kids tried out for a chance to play baseball and be on the show. In Season Two about 150,000 kids came out, and in Season Three (Fall 2014), they were expecting that close to a million kids would try out. "We wanted to crack that market, and I think we have done that. Major League Baseball is hoping to set up a training facility there and train young athletes, which is an amazing partnership we have with them now," Ash told me (#HBRLife).

"Recently JB [Bernstein] and I were in India to attend Rinku's brother's wedding (one of the two winners from Season One and the movie), and I was shooting footage of this wedding processional and the number of kids who came up to Rinku (the winner of Season 1 of Million Dollar Arm contest) to take pictures with him. It was incredible to see that. He's their role model, and that is such a powerful moment to be a part of, to see what he means to those kids and how much he loves to give back to them. We are just so proud of both of them. They are family to us; we are all very close.

"Now kids in India have an example of what could be possible for them, they see Rinku do it and they believe they can, too.

Now we see kids trying out who have spent time watching him play on YouTube and are studying the game of baseball to be prepared for tryouts."

ASH'S ADVICE TO YOU

"Don't think of yourself as an average person. If you have the luxury of choice and time, take advantage of it. Life does not give you many opportunities to redo those decisions. Lastly, move outside your comfort zone.

ASH VASUDEVAN is the Founder of Apex Entertainment and is a tech venture capitalist. Follow his journey on **Twitter:** @ashedge

NIKKI MacCALLUM'S STORY

I met Nikki one afternoon for drinks in New York City. I was in town on business and a former client of mine insisted Nikki and I meet, promising we'd get along great! I'm always interested in connecting with great people so I was happy to oblige, and I'm so glad I did!

"When I was little, all I ever wanted was to be on Broadway (#BigPictureDream)," she began. "It's a goal I've had from day one, and I wanted to do whatever I could to make that happen.

"My mom was a music teacher, and I remember falling asleep listening to soundtracks of Broadway musicals at a very young age. I was a shy kid growing up, and to help overcome that I did plays all through my school-age years and throughout high school. My dream was to go to NYU and study musical theater, but I wound up getting my Bachelors of Music instead of Fine Art; that way I'd have something to 'fall back on' as my mother put it, in case performing didn't pan out.

"My parents were very supportive of my dream, but I'd always worried that I wouldn't be able to support myself in New York and knew I needed to find a 'day job.' So I answered an ad that said 'Actors make great telemarketers.' That began my dual life."

Nikki took the sales job in the legal industry, working nine to five so she could pay rent and stay in the city. But she was still committed to her dream of being on Broadway, getting up at five A.M. every day to go on auditions before work. She used any spare money to perfect her craft, by taking voice lessons, acting lessons, and anything she could think of that would make her the best actress she could be. "I did it day in and day out," she said.

"At the same time I was doing a lot of Internet dating!" Nikki told me, laughing. "It was just too hard as a single woman to meet guys any other way when I was working full time and pursuing my dream. I started writing a one-woman cabaret called *Matchmaker Matchmaker I'm Willing to Settle!* It depicted in a comedic way, what it was like to be a single woman Internet dating in New York."

Nikki began calling around looking for a producer for her show, and she started getting feedback that she should turn it into a full off-Broadway musical with an original script and score. "Through that process I met my two collaborators who cowrote the show with me. I've always tried to identify my strengths and weaknesses and surround myself with people who are strongest in the areas where I am weakest (#ChangeYourCrew)."

Nikki's musical *Matchmaker Matchmaker I'm Willing to Settle!* Premiered at OBERON in Boston, on the American Repertory Theater's second stage in July 2011.

"It's very easy to get stuck in your original dream and be narrow-minded about it. I had to be open to new ideas and follow through on them, even though it was different from what I'd originally planned (#ItsTheJourney).

"My dream now has definitely shifted to being a writer instead of being on Broadway. Now it's my goal to get my stories out there and affect people's lives through my writing. I've written my memoir, and I'm constantly trying to do at least one thing every day to move my book and dream forward. Whether it's contacting people for advice, researching, sending out query letters, or reaching out to my network, my goal is to work at it on a daily basis (#TheHustle)."

NIKKI'S ADVICE TO YOU

"You have to remove the phrase 'I'll be happy when' from your vocabulary.

"Be good to yourself, because there are days when you don't see any progress. You start telling yourself all this negative stuff. Get the attention off yourself, and get out of your own head. I'll go outside and high-five a random stranger! Sometimes you just need to shock your system to get perspective.

"Remember that the most successful people were once where you are. They struggled just like you.

"And lastly, realize that people will surprise you. The ones you thought would have your back may not, and the ones you thought wouldn't give a shit can change your life."

A few months after our interview Nikki called to tell me that she'd signed a publishing contract for her memoir 26.2. #ManifestThat!

NIKKI MAcCALLUM is the author of *26.2*, a memoir. Her off-Broadway musical has had five productions, and is in the process of being rewritten for an even bigger production. She has preformed as a soloist at Lincoln Center, 54 Below, and Birdland. Follow her journey on **Twitter:** @NikkiMacCallum and **Instagram:** @nikkimacncheese

STEPHANIE THAVIXAY'S STORY

One day I got a package in the mail from my best friend. Inside was a simple white T-shirt with the word "#MomLife" in black letters across the chest. I'd seen her post a picture wearing a similar shirt and thought it was so cute, so my friend had ordered one for all her mommy friends. "You should check this girl out who makes these shirts, she's bustin' her ass and doing really well," she told me.

So I looked up Stephanie's Instagram and liked what I found. I'm blessed to be able to share her story with you.

"About four years ago I had my major #EarthquakeMoment, as you say," Stephanie began. "I was a 24-year-old mother trying to make it with my young children. I never went to college, and had no particular job training or special skills. I felt lost, and the more my mom tried to convince me to go back to school the more upset and depressed I got.

"Then one day the mother of my lifelong best friend took it upon herself to publicly attack me on Facebook in a way that broke my heart, and made me seem like I was a 'loser.' She said I would never amount to anything. I was devastated. It was such a personal attack that it put me into a deep depression, and soon I realized that I was losing my friends as a result of all that was said.

"So here I was last year—no job, no degree, and very few friends left in my life."

Then in the fall of 2013 Stephanie had an idea. She'd always loved to draw, and she sketched out a stick-figure mother and child with the hashtag "#MomLife" and asked her boyfriend if she should make herself a T-shirt with it. He thought it was a cute idea, and so did a girlfriend who suggested she try to sell the shirts.

By this time, Stephanie had finally gotten a seasonal job offer at a retail store to help earn extra money for her family for Christmas and knew she couldn't afford to order extra shirts to sell. But two days into her new job she was laid off.

"I just remember riding the train home and crying. I was crushed. I felt like such shit. Like everything people had said about me over the last few years was true. That I was really not going to ever be successful."

The next day Stephanie ordered 25 T-shirts with all the money she had to her name, $200. When the shirts came a few days later she took a blanket and her son to the park, and laid all the shirts out in neatly folded rows on the blanket. She chose a busy park in downtown Seattle where pedestrians and wealthy stay-at-home moms would walk by pushing strollers, in hopes the shirts would catch their eye. For hours they stood by the blanket, but no one even looked their direction.

She didn't sell a single T-shirt.

"I was so mad at myself, I thought that I was crazy. That I'd just wasted the little money we had to buy a bunch of shirts that no one even wanted to look at. I started questioning my decision. But something deep down, something unfamiliar to me said I shouldn't give up that easy. I didn't know what to do though, or where to start. So I just let the idea go for a few weeks, and left the shirts in my closet."

About three months later Stephanie decided to give it one more try (#RelentlessPursuit). She figured she had nothing to lose and needed to find a way to get her money back. She got on Instagram and began looking for moms with the most followers, and asked if they'd consider wearing one of her shirts and posting it on Instagram. One of the first people she asked (#SayIT) was Loren Ridinger from *Keeping Up with the Kardashians*. She sent shirts off to anyone for whom she could find addresses and asked that they take a picture in the shirt and tag her.

A few weeks went by and nothing. No shoutouts. No sales. And then one day her Instagram started blowing up. Within minutes she'd gotten hundreds of new followers and likes. When she opened her account she saw that Loren had posted a picture of her T-shirt with a shoutout. "That changed everything," Stephanie said (#ManifestThat!).

"At that time I just wanted to make sure I got my money back. And of course I hoped that people would like my shirts as well, but I wasn't sure what it could become. My boyfriend and I had always wanted to start our own business, and this is the one that we acted on when the idea came to us, even though we didn't really know what we were doing (#CourageOverFear). I didn't know what to expect when I started. But over time I've learned about running a business, having a website, negotiating contracts, finding quality companies to make my shirts . . . all of that has been a huge learning process for me (#TheHustle)."

Before long, several NBA wives were wearing Stephanie's shirts.

"It's so crazy to see my shirts on celebrities. It's such a blessing that people love them and are willing to support my brand and my dream. It's funny how the people who left my life a few years ago because they thought I was a 'loser' have come back and now suddenly think what I'm doing is 'pretty cool.' But in the beginning they definitely didn't support me, so I've not allowed them to suck me back into their drama (#ChangeYourCrew).

"For me, the best part is the feeling of accomplishment that I've gotten from starting my company. Knowing that I was able to do this without a degree, on a limited budget, and as a young mom with no experience, makes me really proud." In

2018, Stephanie left her "real job" to pursue her passion. She cofounded Gifted Customs LLC, where she not only creates and sells her #MomLife brand, but designs and prints custom clothing for clients as well. She even manifested her big dream of having her own brick and mortar store!

STEPHANIE'S ADVICE TO YOU

"You don't have to know everything when you start; you just have to do it (#DoIT). You will learn as you go, and grow, and you never know where an idea can take you."

STEPHANIE THAVIXAY is the CEO and cofounder (with her boyfriend) of Parent Approved Apparel, the company behind the #MomLife brand. Follow her journey on: **Twitter:** @momlifemomlife **Instagram:** @momlifemomlife **Website:** www.paapparel.com

RYAN BLAIR'S STORY

I must confess that when Ryan called for our interview, I was a bit nervous. I don't get easily starstruck or intimidated by many people, but Ryan's story is pretty impressive and I really didn't want to make a fool of myself or come across as a total hot mess (which I am!). One of my followers on Instagram had suggested I reach out to Ryan, and I'd immediately sent him a tweet asking if he'd be willing to share his story. It only took a few minutes for him to tweet back that he'd be happy to, and today was the big day.

So I asked Ryan to tell me his story . . .

"Growing up I was in an abusive family, surrounded by drug use and alcoholism. My childhood years were extremely tough; my father was a very abusive man, beating anyone in the family if he was in a bad mood. I learned that lesson at the age of three. In school I was always in special education programs; I suffered from ADD and grew up with that constant fear and a lot of negative self-beliefs. My family moved around a lot throughout my childhood, so I overcompensated for the dysfunction at home by playing sports, and being good at it. But over time I built up a lot of anger towards society and especially 'rich people,' as I watched my middle-class family begin to lose everything.

"When I was thirteen years old my dad disappeared for good, and as a result my older brothers and sisters turned to drugs, alcohol, and gangs to cope. It was just my mom and me from that point on, and she was working ten to twelve hours a day, seven days a week just so we could survive. It didn't take long before

I started hanging with the wrong crowd and getting arrested. I saw the struggle my mom faced being poor and I knew I didn't want that. I didn't want the middle-class life either because I'd seen that get stripped away from our family when my father left. So that left one option, by default—I decided I wanted to be rich *(#BigPictureDream)*.

"I realized I was a natural leader and quickly rose to a position of leadership within the gangs where I grew up in Los Angeles. I saw that gangs were really just underground illegal businesses, where the leadership could make good money. I saw how people could hustle to make cash quickly. To me gangs were a way to get money, and that motivated me. As a result I spent the majority of my teen years on probation from age fourteen to eighteen, and was forced to go to school just to stay out of juvenile detention. By this time my grades were so bad that I could no longer play sports, which was something that I loved and had always provided me with a positive outlet with positive male role models. I had no mentors or males to look up to in my life, no one who believed I was capable of more than the life I was living.

"The turning point came in my life when I was about eighteen and my mom started dating a very successful real estate investor. He took me under his wing, and began teaching me about his business and how to become a man. That was the first time I was really exposed to true entrepreneurship—*the legal kind!* My mentor taught me about feeding my mind with books; he gave me my first copy of *Think and Grow Rich,* and other self-help books. He taught me how to expand my vocabulary; at the dinner table he would teach me why what I said was just as important as how I said it (#SayIT). He taught me how to dress and carry myself like a man (#FakeIT), and taught me the business of real estate investing. He never had a son of his own and I think he had a desire to teach what he knew and wanted to give back; as a self-made man he took the time to teach me everything he knew (#MoneyAintAThing!). In those days he was flipping about a hundred houses a year, and was one of the most successful residential investors in Southern California.

"He was a great man.

"I paid attention, because I saw guys making a few grand a week in the gangs, but he was making $100 grand a week through real estate; I wanted that. Because I didn't have a high school diploma it seemed like the best way to make money was to follow in his footsteps, and I began investing with his help in smaller real estate projects.

"There was a part of me that thought 'maybe I could have that kind of life, the life of the rich and famous.' I started to believe that if I applied myself I could get it (#BelieveIT). My mentor really helped me reprogram my belief system, and because he was in my corner I knew I had an asset and that helped me change my identity. I began to try to fit in with his new crowd (#FakeIT), eventually moving in with him, and I felt like the Fresh Prince of Bel Air. All of a sudden I was living a whole different life (#ManifestThat!). It changed my entire reality. I was surrounded by wealth for the very first time, and exposed to things I'd never seen before, walked on marble floors . . . that kind of thing.

"He taught me it took ambition and creativity to make money. I'd say something like, 'it takes money to make money' and he'd say, 'No that's what people say who want to make excuses. It takes ambition to make money' (#TheHustle). He was the first man to tell me he was proud of me; it was the first time I had any positive reinforcement."

When Ryan was nineteen he started his first business and has since created seven businesses from the ground up. He is known as a serial entrepreneur, building and selling companies for millions. He is the cofounder and CEO of ViSalus, a company with over \$1 billion in revenue in 2013. In 2012 Ernst & Young named Ryan Entrepreneur of the Year. His autobiography *Nothing to Lose, Everything to Gain* reached number one on the *New York Times* bestseller list. Ryan truly is living proof that it doesn't matter where you start, or what condition you find your life in—it's possible to turn it all around.

"I've always been a dreamer; growing up in a tough environment you have to dream to cope. I would lie in bed at night and be as visual as possible (#CreateAMovieInYourHead), dreaming about international travel, the house I'd live in, the cars I'd drive, receiving awards. I always dreamed I'd do something in film, and be on the *New York Times* bestseller list, and I've lived out those dreams. As time went on, my dreams grew and one was to be Entrepreneur of the Year, and last year I was. And once I was exposed to a different life, I could envision it even more.

"My mentor taught me how to write my own story (#WriteIT). I designed it (#LifePlan). The first step and the easiest thing to change, is the 'outside you.' You can do that first, and then you can start changing yourself on the inside. Change what you wear, dress the part. Watch your expressions on your face and your body language. Fix your 'first impression.' Those seemingly small changes will create big changes inside you over time. I always tell people that you need to spend as much time working on the inside as the outside; you have to feed your brain with positive information. When you change the outside it helps you change your beliefs about yourself, and begins to reprogram you to become successful."

RYAN'S ADVICE TO YOU

"Change your environment. Do not spend any time around anyone who's not supportive of your plan or doesn't support you. Give them a few warnings and then cut them loose (#ChangeYourCrew). You have to be willing to cut people loose if they are not on board. You will not get to where you want to be if the people around you are not on the same path.

"Learn and grow. Always be studying and growing. Feed your mind, read.

"Balance your health and your mind and body with your success. Keep your health a priority.

"Never give up (#RelentlessPursuit). It's a marathon. It took seventeen years and ten thousand hours of work per year to get me where I am now. It's trial and error sometimes, but you have to live it."

RYAN BLAIR is the CEO of ViSalus. His book *Nothing to Lose, Everything to Gain* hit #1 on the *New York Times* bestseller list. He was named as a top-earning CEO under 40 by Ernst & Young, and his documentary *Nothing to Lose* has gotten widespread critical acclaim. Follow Ryan's journey on **Instagram:** @ryanvisalus **Twitter:** @RyanBlair **Website:** www.ryanblair.com

CHARISE WELLER'S STORY

Charise and I met when I was a twenty-two year old server, living with my Noni (grandmother) in Monterey, California. We worked at a popular restaurant called Lallapalooza, and were both engaged to be married in 2000.

Charise is the reason for my #RelentlessPursuit. She's my girlfriend who showed up at my house the day my husband left with everything the kids and I most desperately needed. Five years later I asked Charise to join me for lunch. I handed her an envelope with tears in my eyes. Though Charise had never wanted or expected that I repay her the money she brought me that day, it had remained a personal goal of mine. I love her for trying to not accept the money, but I love her even more for providing me with the motivation to succeed, even if that was never her thought or intention. It just shows that you never know what your gestures of kindness and support mean to someone.

When I learned that she was starting a line of natural home and body products, I begged her to share her story.

"When we met all those years ago I was not only working at the restaurant, I was also running my own brick and mortar high-end gift store in Carmel, California. I wasn't taking a paycheck from the store, and was drowning in credit card debt to buy groceries, gas, and pay my bills. When I realized that formula would never work long-term, I took action (#TheHustle). That's when I took the job as a server at Lallapalooza. I'd work at the store from eight A.M. until five P.M., and then go to the restaurant and work until two A.M., every day. I put my tips back into my business, and worked around the clock."

When she got married in 2000 Charise sold her store and moved to Southern California, where she took a position in PR with the Los Angeles Dodgers. When their first daughter was born, her husband accepted a position in Portland, Oregon, so the family would need to relocate. This meant Charise would need to leave her job behind. That's when she decided to stay home and raise their daughters rather than look for another position in Oregon.

"As a mom with four little girls trying to raise my family in the healthiest way possible, I felt totally inundated by infectious disease. It seemed as though cancer was everywhere; it's affected so many people I know. I just thought, *am I doing everything I can to protect my family?*

"I had this moment when I realized that I didn't really know what I was giving my kids in the products they used. I started paying attention to the labels but didn't understand what everything was on the ingredient list, so I spent weeks and weeks studying labels. I looked up every ingredient and learned as much as possible so I could find out if these ingredients were harmful or not. The more I learned the more I understood what these chemicals were capable of, including causing cancer.

"At first I felt very overwhelmed by all this new information and looked around for an easy fix, and for products that would be safe for my family. But what I was looking for did not exist.

"I became a closet botanist, experimenting and mixing natural ingredients to make replacement products for my family. I thought, if I can't buy it then come hell or high water, I would make it rather than continue to give my children something I knew was harmful. I became a total nerd, spending all my nights reading and researching to find out how to do this (#TheHustle)."

Charise started slowly, creating each recipe with care and purpose, testing formulas, mixing potions. She'd order a few natural components one week and the rest another. "It took a long time for this process to come to fruition," she told me. "I didn't have disposable money so I got one ingredient at a time, and slowly I began making what I needed.

"I started by replacing our kitchen cleaners, and sleep aids, and then our medication. My family had been on medications for allergies, ADHD, and anxiety, and I was able to replace those drugs with my natural hand-curated alternatives."

It wasn't long before Charise's business began to grow organically. "People were literally knocking on my door, asking me what I was working on and asking to buy my stuff. I live in a suburban area where neighbors know each other and word spread quickly; it kinda went viral.

"When I began this process I had no intention of selling anything! I just had the goal of making my family as safe and healthy as possible, but the products were good and people wanted them.

"I started in my garage with nothing but a folding table to work on. When it was freezing, I worked. When it was hot, I worked. And when I wasn't creating I was learning everything I could about how to make healthy products (#TheHustle). That research took a long time, about a year. And it took total determination (#RelentlessPursuit).

"Once I recognized the need for my products, I decided to turn it into a business; it was the next logical step. Life is crazy; as a mom I didn't have 'free time.' My husband travels and I have four little kids. It seemed ludicrous to add this to my plate, but I chose to give myself the time. I didn't rush it. If I was going to do this I wanted it to be perfect. Every little aspect of the business was critical in making my products what they are today.

"At that point it stopped being just about my family, and became something I could do to help other families live a healthier life. In a way my passion fell in my lap, and became something much bigger than me.

"During this process I've had moments when I felt very overwhelmed, financially strained, and felt like I was in this alone (#EarthquakeMoment). When you're following your passion you are your own cheerleader. No one cares if you win or lose but you. Those are low times, but you gotta want it bad enough to cheer yourself on.

"Even when it's difficult and frustrating I've never thought, *I can't do this anymore.* This is what I am supposed to be doing; this is my calling.

"I had to release myself of the guilt of being a mom who's also working, because I know that what I'm doing is bettering my family. Balance is one of those things that is an illusion when you're building something from the ground up. If you're striving just for balance, especially as a mom, there is no such thing! Maybe that will come later, but when you're in the hustle there is no time for balance.

"I've worked in my car; I make notes and lists constantly. I work on flights, I work when my kids are at tae kwan do. I don't waste moments. I take advantage of any down time to get work done (#TheHustle)."

CHARISE'S ADVICE TO YOU

"So let's talk about the excuses. Some people like to use circumstances as an excuse for not following their passion. With that attitude there will ALWAYS be something that will stop you. The only time we make excuses is if we are trying to live a lie. Be honest; live your truth.

"You need to find ways to do your passion, regardless of the obstacles in your life; if you make excuses then you will fail (#RelentlessPursuit).

"One of my biggest pet peeves is when people say 'I can't.' It's something I don't allow to be said in my home (#SayIT).

"Don't take a break from your hustle. Small breaks lead to bigger ones, so don't stop; every day just do one little thing (#TheHustle)."

CHARISE WELLER is the founder of Weller Tribe. She is a wife and mother of four girls and lives in Sherwood, Oregon. Follow her journey on **Twitter:** @wellertribe **Instagram:** @weller_tribe

#GETGRATEFUL

STEP 2: #THINKIT

"What you think, you become." —Buddha

#GETGRATEFUL

Definition: "If you want to find happiness, find gratitude."
—Steve Marabolin

Hate your life? Welcome to humanity! Many of us at one point or another have hated our life and tried to drown ourselves in a pool of self-pity. If you have never felt that way, I'm super jealous. But at some point most of us have found ourselves bitchin' endlessly to anyone who will listen about how much our life sucks, and if you haven't I bet you know someone who has, so you get the idea. You know ... *Your job sucks, you have no money, you're sick of being broke, your relationships are all hot messes.*

I get it. I was there.

In 2006 while pregnant with my twins, I found myself in a destructive hellhole. I remember stressing endlessly about finances as I packed up our foreclosed home and prepared to move into a rundown rental. I felt defeated and broken, having spent years trying to establish a respectable life for my then-husband and son. It seemed like the world was dead-ending as everything I had was stripped away.

The more I obsessed about how bad shit was, the worse it got. Almost daily. It felt like standing under an avalanche and not having the energy to get out of the way. Hopelessness is a dangerous thing. Bitchin' about our issues is equally as dangerous; it's what creates the feeling of hopelessness. The more I focused on and verbalized my problems, the worse they became.

Your thoughts predict your future. Period.

If there is one thing you take away from the #HBRMethod, let it be this: what you think about and obsess over will become your reality. You are a reflection of everything you receive. So if you want blessings in your life, #GetGrateful. Act blessed. If you want love, give it. If you want success, *act* successful. If you want to live your dream, obsess about the moment when you are living it, and how happy it makes you. So this is the good news: Anything you dislike about your life today, you can absolutely change. And it all starts with #GetGrateful.

STOP BITCHIN'

The best way to get grateful for your current situation is to stop bitchin' about what you don't have. You can't be thankful if you're constantly complaining. It's crazy how much power our words hold. And even crazier still the control our thoughts have on our words, emotions, and future.

If you don't believe me, take a few minutes to think about all the things you don't like about your life at this present moment. Write them down. Then ask yourself: Have those issues gotten worse or better over time? My guess is they have not gotten better. So when they started going sideways, can you recall stressing about them? Obsessing until you felt physically ill at times? Did you talk about those problems with your friends and family or anyone who would listen? Did you tweet about them? Write a negative status update about them on Facebook? Find a quote that really stuck it to the person you were mad at and posted it on Instagram? We've all done it. I'm as guilty as the next person, but what was the outcome? Did your problems magically fix themselves by doing any of those things? Did they make you feel better, or eventually worse?

Think about your list of problems for a minute. Do they occupy the majority of your mind space? If so, then you are in a downward, self-fulfilling-prophecy spiral. What you've thought about, and talked about, has become your daily reality.

Think on that a minute.

By complaining about your problems, verbalizing them, and allowing your feelings associated with those thoughts and words to change your mood, or even make you physically ill, you have actually made those problems *bigger*. Instead of solving them, you've made them much worse. Because *you* are responsible for your problems. I know, *ouch*.

But bear with me here.

EXAMPLE

When I first learned of this concept back in 2006, it took a long time for it to really sink in. The fact that I was the one creating my problems and making them worse was not something I was ready to accept. I'd lived my life up to that point with the philosophy that I was just terribly unlucky and that no matter how hard I tried, nothing good would ever come my way. I believed that, *completely*. And (total shocker), that's exactly how my life was playing out. Totally *unlucky*, and super shitty.

Before we lost our home, I lost a baby. After we lost our home, we were forced to file bankruptcy. It was like the hits were always lined up and coming at us full-speed. It's all I'd ever known. I was so used to struggling, to being poor, that it was my normal. It's the design I'd unwittingly laid out for my life somewhere along the way, and I was fulfilling my destiny to a T.

I felt there was nothing in my life to be thankful for. I'd made my problems so big that they dwarfed and concealed my blessings. I would love to sit here and say that when the light went on, I began doing the work to turn my life around. But sadly, I didn't have the strength yet, the accountability, or the tools to do so. Instead I made a #FutureBoard and tucked it under my bed so my husband wouldn't see it and make fun of me. I tried to ignore the little voice of hope in the back of my head; it seemed too unrealistic in my world at that time, to have *hope*.

And then September 7, 2008, happened. And my life fell the fuck apart. When my husband left, I was at the bottom of rock bottom—the place where it really can't get any worse. If I thought my life sucked before, it was a stroll in Central Park compared to what I was facing starting on that day. But for some reason, not fully understood by even me, instead of sinking further into the "my life sucks, nothing good ever happens to me" black hole I'd lived in the past few years, something in me chose to fight. I can only credit my children for giving me the desire to stand and get my shit together. Well, that, and the lack of any other option. It's funny how when you make up your mind to succeed and realize there are no alternatives, you can actually do just that.

What was the thing that slowly began to change my life? *Gratitude*.

I had nothing when he left—no job, no income. I couldn't stay in the home we were renting even one month without his income. I had no formula or diapers, no bank account or car in my name . . . *nothing*. But oddly enough, that was the day I learned the meaning of the word "gratitude." I learned that when my whole life was collapsing around me, I still had something to be thankful for—my babies and I were still together. I knew that as long as the four of us were together, we would make it. Somehow we'd survive. I'd *make it happen*.

It's ironic how sometimes it takes having everything stripped away from us before we realize how good we really have it. I was alive. I was breathing and healthy, and so were my children. That really was all that mattered; everything else was superficial and could be fixed, somehow. And so every day, in those early black weeks, I sent up a gratitude prayer for every tiny little thing I could think of.

It suddenly became clear how I'd manifested all the bad in my life up to that point, how everything that I'd feared and obsessed about became my reality.

The first thing I realized was that I had total control over my bitchin'. I was determined to reverse my thought process and results, so if it meant stopping myself every time I started to speak negatively about my life, then that's what I did. I paid attention to my thoughts, and I watched my words carefully. My new motto became: *If you don't want it to come true, don't say it* (#SayIT).

I posted this mantra on my bathroom mirror:

If you're not grateful for what you have, you'll never get more to be grateful for.

Learning how to be grateful has been a major key to my success. It's turned my mindset around completely, and that has changed my outcomes. Being grateful is still what gets me through tough times, and it's something I consciously practice on a daily basis. It's how I teach my children to react in their world, and how I choose to live, day in and day out. I choose to relish even the smallest "wins" or blessings, and ignore the setbacks as simply part of the journey (#Winning!).

THE EASY GUIDE TO BEING GRATEFUL NOW!
YOUR HUSTLE, PART 1

Grab your journal and pen and complete the following:

1. Make a list of every single thing you can possibly think of that you are thankful for in this moment, on this day. List even the things you take for granted, like having a place to call home, heat and electricity, food to eat, and so on. List a minimum of twenty.

2. Choose the five items on your list that you are most grateful for. Really think about each one.

3. Close your eyes, and imagine your life without each of those things on your list. One at a time. Picture your life without your family and friends or without a bed to sleep in at night and food to eat. Walk through this exercise slowly; try to visualize in detail what your life would be like without everything you take for granted.

   Have you ever really taken the time to imagine your life without a place to live? Where would you go if you lost your home tomorrow? Or your job? Or your health? Or the basic necessities of life? Most of us never do that. We take it for granted. We think the world is ending because we can't afford to pay our cable bill. Let me reassure you, the sun will still rise even if your cable is shut off for nonpayment (I speak from experience here).

4. Go back to your "grateful thoughts" about each item on your list, and name at least three reasons why you're grateful for each item.

5. How did that exercise make you feel? Do you legitimately feel grateful for your blessings now? Write about what you're feeling in your journal.

6. Post your list where you can see it every day—maybe on your bathroom mirror so you can read it over while getting ready in the morning.

The purpose of gratitude is to make us aware and present in our lives, to teach us not to take anything for granted. It's so easy to get caught up in our daily life and forget all the good things that are part of our environment. Gratitude lets you reconnect with all of that—it keeps you present in the moment and focused on your goal.

As you move through the steps of the #HBRMethod you'll find there will be times on your journey when you seem to be stuck in a rut, or when things aren't turning out as planned—that will be your indication that you've let your gratitude practice slide. Don't let it slide.

#CHANGETHEVOICES
INYOURHEAD

Have you ever stopped to listen to the voices in your head? Do they like you? Do they encourage your dreams and build your self-esteem?

What about the thoughts that don't do this? You know the ones I mean, those that tell you you're fat and unattractive; the ones that remind you all day how much your life sucks; the ones that tell you no one will love you; the ones that say you're not good enough or that say you suck as a parent; or that there will never be enough money; or that you'll never be successful. Whatever your demons are—and we all have them—now is the time to rewrite the script in your head.

This is the most difficult part of your journey. Changing these voices is harder than believing, because if you can master this, then believing will become second nature. So know that going in. This will be the fight of your life, *every day*. This requires straight mental hustle. The first week will be a total struggle; it will leave you mentally exhausted, but hopeful and excited. Then after that it gets easier every day. But those thoughts never fully disappear; it's our job to recognize them when they show up and send 'em packin'!

EXAMPLE

Think of your brain as a 1990s cassette tape—you know, the kind that would play over and over when you hit "repeat"? But remember how you could make your own mix tapes by pressing "record" and just like that a new song would cover up the old one? These tools will help you record over those old distractive thoughts to create a new tape.

There's a tape that's been playing on loop in your head as well. Pick a part of your life you would like to change, any part. What is the tape saying about that part of your life? Is it positive or negative? When you think about it does it make you feel better or worse? If worse, does it have the power to actually change your mood? Does it make you feel depressed or make you irritable? Does it make you act on those feelings (like snapping at your kids or spouse)? Does it put you in a "funk"? Is it all you think about?

EXAMPLE

I have struggled with my weight my entire life. I was never what would technically be considered "fat or obese" but I was overweight, and have always been on the curvy side. But obese is how I've always FELT regardless of my pant size or the number on a scale. That was the message I fed my brain since I was about nine years old. It didn't matter that when I got married I was a lean, six-pack-fit size eight. Nothing I could do was good enough to change that message I constantly gave my brain. All day I'd catch myself saying, "I'm fat, I look terrible in these jeans, I'm not pretty." It was my constant obsession. It destroyed my mood and depressed me. Those thoughts completely controlled me.

When I finally figured out that what I obsess over actually gets worse, I was scared shitless! I realized that it was much harder to get the motivation to work out and eat healthy when I was constantly telling myself how repulsive I was. How could I tell my body all day long how much I hated it and then expect it to magically change on its own? It made no sense.

The one thing I knew I could change was how I *thought* about it.

It took a while, but one day I woke up, looked in the mirror, and really liked what I saw. For the first time in my life, I could see myself the way other people saw me. I *felt* beautiful. I *was* beautiful. Somehow in the months of applying #ChangeTheVoicesInYourHead and #MottoForLife, the weight had just come off. I had always worked out regularly, but this time was different. Somewhere in between "this feels ridiculous," and forty pounds lost, the struggle had stopped. I'd quit fighting my positive thoughts and the negative ones had become scarce, and then the day came when all of it was actually true. I was fit and I was beautiful (though that still sounds a little crazy to say!).

It wasn't magic. It was hard work, both mental and physical. But as with any habit, it gets easier and more intuitive over time if you are consistent. That's #HustleBelieveReceive right there.

My first step had been to kill the negative voices in my head. It took commitment and awareness on my part though, and thus it will on your end too. You need to listen to those voices, so you can stop them in their tracks, and one of the best ways to do that is to use your "I am's."

YOUR HUSTLE, PART 2

It's time to rewrite your story, and redefine who you are.

I am not a particularly religious person, so if you are not either I hope this homework assignment does not offend you.

- I want you to go to YouTube and watch Joel Olsteen's speech about the power of the words "I am."

• Now write out 25 positive "I am" statements about yourself. For example, "I am smart," "I am confident," "I am beautiful."

About a year ago I was in a rut that I was afraid I would not be able to pull myself out of. I was so close to giving up on my dream. I stopped writing. I was beginning to question everything; I'd seen such little progress that I allowed doubt to nearly sabotage all my hard work and #BigPictureDream.

One night I watched an Oprah show with Joel where he talked about the importance of what follows "I am," and something inside me clicked. I then watched the above-mentioned YouTube video about ten times. Putting into practice my positive "I am's" reinforced a breakthrough that catapulted my manifesting in 2014 and ultimately led to this book. What Joel talks about here is exactly what the #ThinkIT step is all about.

I hope this exercise creates a breakthrough for you and that you say them to yourself all day every day and use them to combat any negative thoughts that creep up.

#MOTTOFORLIFE

Mottos and mantras are one of the best ways to retrain our brain and turn negative thoughts into positive outcomes. Think of your negative thoughts as a computer virus. If someone sent you a corrupted email that you knew would destroy your computer's hard drive, would you open it? I hope not! The same rule applies here. Those negative thoughts are poison. If you allow them to go unchecked they have the power to destroy all the work you are doing to change your life.

GIVE THEM NO MINDSPACE. Change the subject on your thoughts, have your mantra ready, and kill them in action.

THE POWER OF "PAUSE"

When negative thoughts come up, recognize and acknowledge them, and then just ask them to PAUSE. If you tell a brain who's been trying to solve a problem for years that you're just not going to think about it anymore, it will probably start to panic and create even more anxiety. And that is not our goal. Baby steps are just fine. So when that thought comes in just say, "I see you, but let's think about that in an hour." In that hour, be determined not to think about that subject AT ALL. This technique relieves immediate and constant stress because you've promised you'll get back to it later. Then when it comes up again do the same. See if you can push it back one or two more times. This is teaching your brain how to think as told rather than think how it wants.

Then keep your promise. Pick a time of day that works for you to sit down and actually think about whatever is the stressful issue. Allow yourself ten or fifteen minutes to think about it and maybe write it out. This is your time to "deal" with whatever's been bugging you.

If it tries to steal your sleep and keep you up all night, say, "I will sit down over my morning coffee and figure this out tomorrow." You are forcing yourself to limit those thoughts to a specific time where you can give them the attention they need, devise a plan to work on your issue, and then you're closing the door on those thoughts for the rest of the day.

It's kind of like weaning yourself from those old habits instead of going cold turkey. And that's just fine; it works the same way, because we are becoming actively aware of our thoughts and choosing not to think about them every time they pop up. Then when you are stronger you can reverse those negatives, and eventually use #MottoForLife to reinforce your new belief system.

All of this is a process, and a journey. It takes time. Be kind to yourself. Recognize how far you've come in just picking up this book and wanting to change. So don't be hard on yourself. These thinking patterns don't change overnight or without work, but it can be done. And the payoff is LIFE-CHANGING!

MENTAL TENNIS

A metaphor I share with my clients to help them better understand this concept is to think of those negative thoughts as a tennis ball. When you're on the court playing tennis and the ball comes your way, you try to hit it back over the net, right? You don't just stand there and let ball after ball land in your backcourt. No, you run your ass all over the court trying to return those balls as fast as they come.

"Mental tennis" works the same way. When negative thoughts come in say, "Nope! Not right now," and you simply hit it back by reversing that thought. The reverse of that negative thought then becomes your mantra, which can help keep those thoughts fewer and farther between.

For example, if the thought is "I'm fat and ugly," you simply recognize it and then tell yourself "I am fit and beautiful." Every time you say, "I am fit and I am beautiful" you're telling yourself a whole new story, one you will eventually believe, turning it into your new truth.

Now I understand that this is going to feel . . . how shall I put this? Like total bullshit! When you first start practicing these steps it feels pretty fake, ridiculous, and unnatural on every level. I get it; it felt exactly the same way for me and everyone I've ever coached. It's new to us; our brain doesn't know what to make of this conflicting information at first. This is a different message from what it's used to receiving so in the beginning your brain will try to reject your new thoughts. It might even try to add more negativity like, "This won't work" or "It's stupid."

But just trust me on this—the more you fight through and practice these steps the easier it will become. That's the beauty of this—IT WORKS!

GO-TO MOTTO

My very first motto was "I can do it; I am strong." I was in spinning class on my lunch break in 2009 and I wanted to get off that bike and walk out of class more than I'd ever wanted anything in my life. The more I thought about it, the more my legs started slowing down and my body prepared for the moment I'd give the command to bolt.

I've walked out of class before, on days when I just didn't have the energy or wasn't feelin' it, so my mind and body already knew it was an option. But for some reason that day instead of getting off the bike I decided to look up at my own eyes in the mirror. This was something I'd never had the courage to do in class before. When I did so, the only thing that came into my head was "I can do it; I am strong." I said that motto over and over the entire rest of class, refusing to think of anything else. I was shocked to find that not only did I finish the class, but also I felt AMAZING!

That little motto has gotten me through everything I've faced ever since. It doesn't matter what I'm going through, or how low I'm feeling, if I say that motto twenty times (especially looking in a mirror!), it will totally reverse my mood and get me back on track.

Mottos are an amazingly simple way to retrain our thinking. Find one that is easy to remember, gives you power, and can apply to any situation, and say it over and over whenever you need a boost. They are especially helpful when you are starting to fall into a negative thought pattern. Having mottos ready, and practicing them, can turn those thoughts and your mood around in just a few minutes.

EXAMPLE

The biggest source of stress my entire life had always been the lack of money. It was all I ever thought about, all I ever talked about. I could see no end to my money problems, just a deeper and darker hole. And total shocker—I kept manifesting more bills and less money.

My obsession with lack of money was so bad it made me physically sick to my stomach. It robbed me of sleep and tormented my mind every single day. It was a problem I was constantly looking for ways to solve. I'd sit at my desk at work and write out all my bills, over and over again, as if seeing them on paper would make them disappear. Toward the end of my marriage it was the dominant conversation piece, to the point that if we talked about anything else I felt we were being irresponsible and not trying to "solve" our money problems.

It was a monster that lived inside me.

Once I realized and accepted that as fact, I wasn't about to keep the same negative pattern going in my new life. At all costs I was determined to change my future results.

I first made a commitment to stop talking about money. Period. Since I had nothing nice or positive to say about it, I was no longer allowed to verbalize anything related to "lack of money," even though I had less of it than ever before. All my years of stressing about money had never actually solved a thing, so instead I chose to focus all my attention on being grateful for what I had. When I wanted to complain that I didn't have the money to keep the cable on, I would instead verbalize how grateful I was that the rent was paid and the lights were still on.

A few years ago when I was trying to transition from a place of "struggle" to a place of "thriving" financially, I came up with a new motto. This time I used it to "say" what I couldn't yet generally verbalize. I wasn't confident or comfortable enough to own a financially free future, so to get me to that point I used the motto: "I am healthy. I am happy. I am beautiful. I have more than enough to provide for myself and my family." Notice how I put the financial part last; it wasn't even something I could make a motto solely around. I had to start small until it became something I could truly speak and own.

It's taken me years of dedicated effort to correct the negativity I had around money. It took baby steps. A little here, a little more there, but every step has gotten me closer to owning my financial future instead of it dooming me. Once I was able to begin releasing its grip on my life, things began to quickly change.

YOUR HUSTLE, PART 3
Grab your journal.

What are the top five things in your life that causes you to have negative thoughts? Is it your health? Your finances? Your relationships? Your job? Whatever it is, write down five mottos that address each of those five stressors. Make them just a sentence or two, something you can easily remember. Read them several times, then put them on a list beside your bed and read them every morning and before bed.

Now, every time one of those pesky thoughts come up you have your tennis racket ready to hit them back! Say that positive motto ten times in your mind over and over until you've changed the subject in your brain. Repeat this every time those thoughts come up.

TIP: Be careful not to make these too "pie in the sky." They need to connect with and motivate you, but not be so unrealistic that they become powerless. Example: if you start out broke and your motto is, "I am wealthy beyond imagination," this will not be effective. After all, your subconscious doesn't even understand what "beyond imagination" means! That motto would set you up for disappointment because anything less than "wealthy beyond imagination" would mean you're not successful, which is of course ridiculous. Instead start with a motto like, "There is always enough; everything is taken care of," or something along those lines. And when you've mastered that, upgrade it.

#HBRSTORIES

DERRICK MALONE JR.

LONNELL WILLIAMS

JAMI CURL

DAN FELIX

JENNY G. PERRY

DERRICK MALONE JR.'S STORY

Derrick is the very first interview I ever did. *Ever.* It was the first time I'd attempted to write about someone else's life, or to write a story that wasn't my own. I felt so incapable, but he trusted me and I'm forever grateful. It was this interview that sparked the idea for my five-part "Inside the Mind of an Athlete" blog series, which eventually became the foundation for this book.

I met Derrick through our mutual friends on Facebook and his teammates, whom I had coached. For three years I mentored him before we ever actually met in person, over lunch in 2014 after I'd done his interview.

He grew up in the Southern California town of Culton, a community known for turning out skilled football athletes from its high school. Derrick remembers how, as a kid, football was always part of his life, even though he didn't formally start playing until the eighth grade.

But football was always there. His father Malone Sr. was an excellent running back in high school and had dreams of his son playing quarterback. But Derrick was more interested in baseball and basketball, even though he spent every evening playing football at the park with his friends. Or at recess. Or before and after class. Still he wasn't sure it was what he wanted to do. It wasn't until his breakout game playing safety during his junior year of high school that he thought maybe he was actually good at football.

After that game college recruiters began circling like sharks. It was then that he finally began to see what his family and friends had known for some time: that he had a gift that could change his life.

"My confidence and belief in myself comes from my family," he told me. "Growing up, our home was full of love. My mom, dad, and grandmother believed in me to the fullest. They instilled that confidence in me. They told me to never settle, to always expect more because I 'deserved it' (#BelieveIT)." That core foundation helped Derrick get to the place he is at today, one where he truly believes in his ability, the future, and his ultimate dream.

Derrick's first "impossible dream" was to play football for the University of Oregon (#DreamIT). It had always been his top choice for colleges, and when they were the first to show interest in him, and ultimately the one from which he accepted a scholarship, it was the realization of his dream (#ManifestThat!). Oregon was life on a grand scale! ESPN highlights and national networks even featured games on Saturday afternoons.

"My dream now is to play in the NFL," he said. "It makes everything you've done along the way, all the sacrifice, all the things you miss out on, worth it (#TheHustle). It's the payoff (#HBRLife). There are a lot of limitations that come with the responsibility of being an athlete. My life is not like the life of a 'normal' college student; there are sacrifices and struggles that come with the glory moments. It's the proof that all those little things really meant something, and the reward for putting in the work to graduate with two majors. And it's the ultimate chance to make your family proud of you. It's an opportunity for me to be a role model to the younger generation, to make an impact on others and help change their lives (#BigPictureDream.) This is what we work for (#RelentlessPursuit)—that validation, that reward.

"I imagine it every day. It's a lifelong thing. I close my eyes and visualize, I constantly daydream about it, all day every day

(#CreateAMovieInYourHead). It's a way of life, and it's been like that since I was a kid. I've always been able to make a movie in my head and focus on it (#SeeIT).

"My coaches during my sophomore year were the ones who really instilled that dream in me. They told us every day that making it to the league should be our goal, that we should work for it, and that it was possible. I knew the odds were small, but I wanted to be part of those small odds. And over time I began to really believe it that it would happen (#ChangeTheVoicesInYourHead).

"Regardless of how hard and disappointing it is at times I've never even considered giving up. I never quit; it's not in my nature (#RelentlessPursuit).

"When I need motivation all I have to do is call my mom. I hear the pride she has in me, and it puts a smile on my face. I just want to make her even more proud. That is why I do this. And I do it for my aunt, who passed when I was in high school. Whenever you think of giving up, you just gotta remember why you're doing it in the first place and get back to work."

I asked Derrick about the moment when he felt like he was living his dream and he said, "Running out of the tunnel to play in the Rose Bowl. I watched the game as a kid at my grandma's house, and remember thinking those players looked so big, and it seemed so impossible, and then I lived it (#Manifest-That!). Being with my family and sharing that experience with them, and holding the trophy after we won, it was the happiest moment of my life, a dream come true (#GetGrateful).

"My mantra is Oregon's motto: *Win the Day* (#MottoFor-Life). It's tatted on my arm, and it's what every day is about for me. Just go out and no matter what I'm doing, whether it's practice, a game, training, eating right, or choosing not to go out, all of that is my hustle (#TheHustle). It's all part of just winning today."

DERRICK'S ADVICE TO YOU
"Win the Day."

DERRICK MALONE JR. is an undrafted free agent in the NFL. Immediately following the 2015 draft the Atlanta Falcons signed him. He is also a blogger, writer, and poet. Follow his journey on **Twitter/Instagram**: @PoeticSoul_ **Website:** www.impoeticsoul.com

LONNELL WILLIAMS'S STORY

Everything always happens for a reason that is bigger than we can see on the surface. Such was the case regarding my first meeting with Lonnell Williams. We were both selected by producer Marc Anthony Nicolas to tape a quick viewer segment for the CBS show *The Talk*. Our segments aired back to back, and when I saw Lonnell's I took notice. He had that exuberant, loving-life aura, and I quickly looked him up on social media and began following his journey on Instagram. We interacted a few times as the months went by, and I couldn't help but notice that he was living life to the fullest and following his dream, as was I.

So I reached out and asked him if he'd be willing to share his story.

"Growing up as a black gay kid, who was not comfortable in my skin, I was always trying to be what everyone else wanted me to be. I knew exactly what I didn't want to be, even though I wasn't yet sure what I did.

"My family ran the gamut; one side of my family was well-off, and the other side had many drug addicts and alcoholics, as well as poverty. But having that mix and being exposed to culture at a young age is what helped me get to where I am today. I grew up in the Bay Area in California, and my parents divorced when I was a young kid. I went to school in Oakland with my dad's side of the family, and then would spend time with my mother in San Francisco. That mix showed me there could be something different from the life I knew in Oakland.

"I have always been driven by a need to enjoy life and have fun (#BigPictureDream), and even in high school I wanted to find a summer job that was *fun*. So I went to work at an amusement park even though it was forty miles away. I wanted to put fun first in my life and do things that bring me joy."

In high school he was obsessed with going to college at Pepperdine University in Malibu, California (#DreamIT). He told everyone, including his teachers, of his dream. They all thought that he was crazy. "You'll never get in," they told him.

"The first time I did a 'vision board' (#FutureBoard), was in high school, even though I didn't know what one was at the time. But I got brochures about the school and I'd sit on my bed staring at those pictures (#SeeIT) and imagining myself going to Pepperdine (#CreateAMovieInYourHead). I spent all my time learning everything I could about it (#TheHustle)."

Lonnell wanted to be a TV broadcaster and Pepperdine was his first choice. Yet after submitting his applications, he received acceptance letters from his two backup schools, but still nothing from Pepperdine. Finally the acceptance letter came and he was beyond thrilled (#ManifestThat!). "The next day I went to school and told all my friends. I thought they would be happy for me but instead they would say stuff like, 'How are you going to pay for it?' I realized then that no matter what you accomplish in life, someone is always going to try and steal your joy."

Two years into his broadcasting degree at Pepperdine, Lonnell realized he really didn't enjoy being a broadcaster, or producing the news at all. "It was just draining my spirit. It was so depressing!" he said (#ItsTheJourney).

One afternoon he went with a friend to the set of a sitcom, where he had an "aha" moment: "I realized that a sitcom was much more along the lines of what I wanted to produce. My dream was to work on the show *A Different World*."

When he graduated, he looked up the top five shows on TV and wrote a letter to each of their executive producers (#TheHustle). But the one he wrote to *A Different World* was extremely passionate, far more so than the others. "I was getting ready to take an internship with another show because I'd not heard back, then finally I got the letter from the show's producer. She wanted to meet me, even though she wasn't hiring, because she could sense my passion from the letter." (#Winning!) The meeting was amazing, and in its own way a dream come true, so Lonnell let it go. He figured what was meant to be would happen (#ChillOut).

"A few days later, I got a call saying they'd like to offer me an internship," Lonnell said (#ManifestThat!). He was eventually offered a full-time position on *A Different World*, where he worked for three seasons (#HBRLife!).

Lonnell spent several years working on TV shows and concert series, and one day he looked around and noticed that he was surrounded by all these "haves." "I wasn't one of them," he said. "I had to recognize that, and let it go because I didn't like the person I was becoming."

"So I took a year off to figure out what I really wanted," he said (#ItsTheJourney).

One afternoon a friend talked Lonnell into going with her to an open hiring call for an airline flight attendant. It wasn't even something he'd ever considered doing, but he was offered the job. "The blessing that came out of it was that I was able to start traveling. My first trip was to Milan, Italy, and I remember pinching myself thinking *how did this happen!?* (#GetGrateful)"

"In 1997 I was working for the airline as a concierge. My job was to be the one responsible for all the big-time VIPs, getting them in and out of the airport."

On a daily basis Lonnell dealt with huge celebrities, but the two he wanted to meet the most had not come through on his shifts. Then he heard that Janet Jackson was coming to town as a guest on *The Oprah Winfrey Show*, and that he would be escorting her! "I asked Janet for tickets to the show and she got them for me!" he said. "I went to the show's taping and afterward I got a chance to meet Oprah."

There he stood in the receiving line waiting for Oprah to shake his hand, and wracking his brain for something clever to say that would make a lasting impression. He watched her make her way down the line and heard each person saying "I love you! You look so beautiful!"

"I knew I couldn't say that!" he laughed. "Oprah gets to me and I say, 'Oprah, I just want to say thank you for bringing love back into the realm of human consciousness.' And the next thing I know her hands were on my cheeks, and she was talking to *ME*! We were actually dialoging (#ManifestThat!).

"I knew then that our paths would cross again (#BelieveIT)."

It was about this time that the Internet was really starting to take off, and YouTube was taking over. "I started paying attention and saw that in the LBGT community people were not connected. There needed to be a way to bring people together. My gift is the ability to approach people without judgment, and so I launched a YouTube channel to fill that void in the community." Before he knew it Lonnell was being invited to big events to cover them for his show. "It was a gift and a huge blessing to be in that position."

A few years later Lonnell had taken a position as a flight attendant for corporate and private travel. Three years into this position he was sent to a mandatory training, and when he walked into the class he saw the only other black man he'd ever seen flying as a private flight attendant. That man turned out to be Oprah's personal flight attendant. "Of course we became friends!" Lonnell said with a laugh.

"One day I get a call from him and he tells me that Oprah is looking for another flight attendant, and he asked me if I'd be interested in submitting my resume. I had been happy with my current position, but who passes up a chance to work with Oprah!?"

Before the interview process began Lonnell made a decision to lock down all of his social media. "I wanted to sell an image of what I wanted them to know about me; I was afraid to show them who I really was."

After making it past several rounds of interviews, Lonnell got word that his final test would be to take an actual flight with Oprah and see how the two of them get along. But a week passed, and still no word as to when this flight would take place. "I was in Chicago walking past a Starbucks and I saw the front page of the paper with the headline 'Drama Aboard Oprah's Private Jet.' Needless to say he never heard back from Oprah's team about the interview, and had to accept that all of this had happened for a reason (#ItsTheJourney).

A few years later Lonnell got the surprise of his life.

"I tweeted Oprah and she tweeted back!" Lonnell said with exuberance in his voice (#Winning!).

From that initial interaction Oprah invited him to a Lifeclass taping in Chicago and from there, the friendship has grown into a lasting and genuine connection. "The lesson I learned from that whole experience was that I needed to always be my true self. Because when I was afraid to be authentic (locking down social media), the doors closed. But once I embraced who I am and was true to that, the floodgates opened. And ironically it was social media that is responsible for our friendship (#CourageOverFear)."

LONNELL'S ADVICE TO YOU

"You must have a dream, and you must dream big (#BigPictureDream). Put the vision out there and you'll be surprised at how it comes to you. Listen to the whispers; be open to realize that your dream comes from a narrative that you didn't expect (#ItsTheJourney).

"What I've learned is that if you stop and listen to the jabber of the words that pass your jaw, I guarantee you that your life is a direct reflection of your words (#SayIT). Your life is what you say. Instead of being stuck in the story of why your life is the way it is, change the way you talk about it (#ChangeThe-VoicesInYourHead)!

"Say affirmations every day (#MottoForLife): *I am loving. I am loveable. I am loved.* Write it on the mirror (#WriteIT). It's absolutely critical. Make it a habit.

"Be grateful and appreciative of every little thing (#Get-Grateful). Prosperity is not really a financial state; it's being able to appreciate where you are right now (#MoneyAintAThing!).

"You are in control of your own destiny.

"A miracle is simply a shift in your perception. If you change how you think about something it changes the world around you (#ThinkIT).

"Align yourself with joy, health, peace, and prosperity and that will be what shows up in your life. Plant the seed, then water it with gratitude and love. Remember that you just can't rush it (#ChillOut), trust that it will grow if you do your part (#TheHustle).

"Be fully present in your life.

"Remember you are worthy. Unworthiness is a cancer to the soul. If you subconsciously feel that you are not worthy of those blessings they will vanish. If you believe in lack and limitation don't be surprised when it shows up!"

LONNELL WILLIAMS is the host and creator of the YouTube series 3LWTV, where he covered Oprah's The Life You Want Tour in 2014. He is also a social media correspondent for Access Hollywood, The Insider, OWNTV, and ET Now. Follow his journey on **Instagram:** @3lwtv **Twitter:** @3lwtv **Website:** www.3lwtv.com

JAMI CURL'S STORY

I met Jami at an event in Portland called Project Breakfast.
I'd been invited by my girlfriend Charise Weller, and when I
learned that the event would be held in a real live candy factory,
I couldn't wait to go! I just knew Jami must have a great story;
after all, there are not many people I know (okay, none but Jami)
who own a candy factory!

"I've always been interested in hard work," Jami started. "I got
my first job when I was twelve. I wasn't necessarily driven by the
desire to make money; I was just excited to work. I wanted to do
things well and work was a great way to get positive feedback,
a way to know that you're doing a good job. I've always been
self-motivated; it's something that comes from inside me. All
through high school and college I'd worked in the food industry, scooping ice cream or waiting tables, and it was something
I really enjoyed."

After Jami graduated college in Ohio, a friend read an article
about Portland, Oregon, that said that it was a city raised on
coffee, beer, and books. "We thought that sounded like Utopia!"
Jami laughed. So they packed up their car and the two girls
moved to Portland, where Jami took a job in marketing.

"I started my master's in Public Administration because
it seemed like the right thing to do to advance my career. It
wasn't long before I was questioning that decision because I
really missed working in the food industry. So I started baking
on the side, making cakes for people at night and on weekends.

I was working full-time in a good job, but one that I really didn't like, going to school, and trying to find the time to keep baking cakes.

"That's when I decided to quit school, quit my job, and open a bakery (#CourageOverFear).

"I think it's important to have faith in your decisions, even if people don't agree with them. I just knew it would work (#BelieveIT). I had proven people wanted my product by successfully selling them on the side (#TheHustle). It wasn't a rash decision. I put thought into understanding the market and knowing it was the right time, and then I just did it (#DoIT).

When I asked Jami where the courage came from to quit her job and follow her dream, she explained, "You have to believe that it will happen (#BelieveIT). You can't set yourself up for failure by doubting yourself."

Jami acted quickly, and just three months after she'd quit her job, the doors to her bakery officially opened. "I needed to do what made me happy and stop doing what I was *supposed* to do." Her bakery was called Saint Cupcake, and in those early days she was the only person baking, working twenty hours a day, seven days a week (#TheHustle).

"The work was backbreaking, especially those first six months before I could hire someone. I've always been the type who wanted to do it myself if I could, but it was never-ending. I did that for almost nine years (#TheHustle). By that point we had nearly forty employees. It was a lot of work but a lot of fun.

"Eventually it got to the point where it didn't make me happy anymore. In those eight years I took two vacations; the rest of the time I was at the bakery, *all the time* (#TheHustle).

"I started playing with caramel recipes and selling them at the counter. That's where I began to slowly come alive again, and started finding joy and excitement in something." Jami told me.

"I made a decision to sell the bakery and close it, and that's how QUIN Candy Factory came about (#CourageOverFear)."

At QUIN, Jami made products that could be shipped, not ones that go bad the next day. She had a small staff of fourteen people, and each candy was handmade. Over time as the business grew, Jami would be able to hire people to take on various roles and become more hands-off, helping her reach that coveted work/life balance.

"I think that a lot of people confuse the feeling of failure with the judgment of others. If you are worried about what others think, then that will limit your happiness. It's totally normal to be open to changing course as you are going; dreams change and grow over time. If you find that something doesn't make you happy, make a change (#ItsTheJourney)."

Jami had never worked in a candy factory before and had to learn quickly as she went along. There was the creative side business—the marketing and PR. She made all the recipes, set up partnerships, and learned about production, inventories, and costing. "I'm working just as hard as I did with the bakery, but it's less physical (#TheHustle)."

"I am definitely living my dream." Jami told me. "When I had the bakery we were known only as a cupcake baker, and it drove me crazy. Now I'm recognized as a business owner and respected in a different way. That allows me to educate and mentor others, which is something I love to do. I'm hoping to write a recipe book and continue sharing my knowledge with others. I'd love to have more QUIN retail locations open up in the future across the country. I want to do work that makes my child proud of me."

JAMI'S ADVICE TO YOU

"No one else is going to care as much about your vision as you do. You have to act like that every day. Your job is to believe in it every day (#BelieveIT)."

JAMI CURL owned QUIN Candy Factory in Portland, Oregon, prior to its closing in 2018. She is the bestselling author of *Candy is Magic*.

DAN FELIX'S STORY

JaTara Wright, one of my Facebook friends, contacted me after she saw my initial post about looking for people to interview. She suggested I reach out to Dan, who was one of her mentors. When I did, he was kind enough to agree to share his story even though he's a pretty private guy and he didn't know me from Adam!

"I was born in the United States but spent my childhood grow-ing up in the Caribbean, where I watched my grandmother work incredibly hard. She made dresses and sold them in a little shop that was in front of her house. I saw what it was like for her to run a business, and that was my first understanding of true entrepre-neurship, which was a great example for me. I get my work ethic from my mom and my grandma; they were a great example of what you can accomplish with hard work. My grandma was an amazing woman who took in children to provide a better life and education for them in Haiti."

When Dan was thirteen years old he moved back to the United States with his mom, who worked incredibly hard to begin building a life for them in the States; even still it was a bit of a culture shock. "In the Caribbean there were not the ameni-ties I was exposed to in the States; life was much more simplistic there. When I lived in the Caribbean I wasn't even aware that life wasn't luxurious the way it can be in the States because I didn't know the difference."

It was the '80s and Dan was living with his grandmother's brother, who was a judge, which exposed him to a whole dif-ferent kind of lifestyle from the one he'd known growing up. "I started playing basketball when I moved to the United States," Dan said. He was tall so it made sense; he saw the attention the athletes were getting and he wanted a taste of that. "I had never played organized ball before in my life, but I used that as motivation to get better, because I was terrible when I started! My sophomore year I got better because my work ethic was so strong. I was determined to learn the game (#TheHustle). By my junior year I was really good. It shocked people. Then my senior year I was the shit!" Dan laughed (#ManifestThat!).

Then suddenly, Dan suffered a serious knee injury and just like that, basketball as a career was over for him (#Earthquake-Moment). "I hit a brick wall after that, trying to find something that interested me. I was lost without ball. I really thought that it would be my ticket."

Dan tried acting and music, but he needed a job to make money for acting school. He decided to take a summer job at a market in New York City; its flexibility allowed him to be a movie extra on films while still making money for school.

One day he showed up late for work after being on the movie set all day and got yelled at. "I was really mad because the manager yelled at me in front of everybody, so I walked out and that was it. I've never had a typical 'job' since."

Dan took a commission-only sales position after that and "I've been building my own business ever since" he told me. "I started selling toys, in a business-to-business commission-only role, and it was exciting for me to hit major sales goals. In a year I built a team and an office in New York, and from there I began building teams all over the country." His business currently has offices in seventeen states (#ManifestThat!).

"Eventually I was able to build my own music studio and fulfill my dream to create and produce music. I started investing more into building my brand including Billionaires Row and Unison Solar Company (#HBRLife)."

Dan's dream was to retire his parents and build his grandmother and mother a new home in Haiti (#DreamIT). "My mother had begun a renovation on my grandmother's house and I was able to help completely renovate it and open a grocery store for her in Haiti, both of which were able to withstand the Haiti earthquake. But after that it was my motivation to move my mom and grandma to the US so they could live with me in Miami. And I was able to retire my mom, which was a realization of my big dream."

I asked Dan to describe the secret to building a business empire and he said, "My mind is always sharp (#ThinkIT). I am constantly looking for ways to keep it focused, because there is inevitably a next level that you are trying to reach (#HBRLife).

"If you don't visualize your goals and dream, they will never come true (#CreateAMovieInYourHead). I would picture things so big that people would make fun of me. I would tell people the things I wanted to do (#SayIT) and nobody believed me. When I rebuilt my grandma's house I visualized seeing the reaction on her face (#BigPictureDream), and that gave me a great deal of motivation.

"As soon as the new Bentley come out I got it, and people were in shock. But I'd always pictured it (#SeeIT), and then I did it (#ManifestThat!). Saying it created the motivation to keep going, even when I didn't want to. When I speak it (#SayIT) and I envision it, I can feel it. I already know it's coming (#BelieveIT). I put blinders on to anything else (#TheHustle). I don't wanna hear what anyone has to say about it (#ChangeYourCrew). Sometimes it can rub others the wrong way, because they might think that you are being cocky, but I have always been humble.

I'm just so dedicated to achieving my goal that people think I'm emotionless, but it's just pure focus (#RelentlessPursuit).

"You can teach yourself all of this through practice (#HBRMethod). Develop good habits. If you are always waiting to *have* it first, then you will never actually *be* it. Believe that you already *have it* because then you can *become* it (#FakeIT). Train yourself to turn these things into habits, and that will turn into success. This makes you fearless and will keep you going (#CourageOverFear)."

DAN'S ADVICE TO YOU

"Be patient (#ChillOut). Be okay with not doing it right the first time; it takes time to get it right.

"There is no power in going to work for other people, because you can always get laid off. But if you choose to make your own money, then no one can take that away."

DAN FELIX is the COO and cofounder of Billionaires Row, a lifestyle brand and champagne line. He is also a hip-hop music producer for his studio Cold City Productions and the owner of Face Advertising. Dan was a self-made multimillionaire by age thirty-five. He has two beautiful daughters—Tatiana, who attends St. John's University (pre-med) and Abigail, who just started Montessori school. Follow his journey on **Twitter:** @dfelix25 and **Instagram:** @facebillionaire

JENNY G. PERRY'S STORY

I "met" Jenny on Facebook a few years ago; like-minded people have a way of attracting. I was so impressed with her success as a writer and coach and loved her bravery in helping to redefine a sexy, confident woman. I'm so glad she was happy to share her personal story.

"When I was in fifth grade I was teased for being overweight, even though I really wasn't. The kids called me 'porker.' I just wanted to be liked and was really sensitive about it. I realized at a young age that I was defined by my body."

When she moved schools in sixth grade at the age of eleven, no one in the new school called her fat anymore. "But I didn't know how to deal with that either. In high school I gained some weight because of all the negative feelings I had towards myself, and then I felt pressure to lose it. So I became bulimic.

"I had so much shame as a bulimic because I didn't have the willpower to become an anorexic. I began to do a lot of research on eating disorders. I became so depressed and started cutting myself to deal with the depression and internal pain, and was put on Prozac. I tried to commit suicide twice, and had to get my stomach pumped. I just got to a place where I didn't want to be on the planet anymore. I was so uncomfortable in my own skin.

"When I finally got through that dark place I decided that I didn't want to be on meds anymore. I wanted to feel the highs and lows; I no longer wanted to be numb."

In Jenny's junior year of high school she went away for an inpatient program to treat her eating disorder, where she stayed for six months. Her struggle with bulimia dominated a year of her life, and through treatment and therapy, she realized that her life really wasn't that bad. "I then made a conscious decision that it was time for me to shut that door. It was just a decision I made, that I was not going to do it any more."

"Then I went to college and started partying my butt off! It was all too much for me; I got alcohol poisoning and had to leave school and go home." So Jenny moved back in with her parents and decided to go to culinary school. "My life had no direction at that point. I met my husband my second semester in culinary school just a year after I graduated high school, and my daughter was born a month after I turned twenty.

At twenty-five Jenny found herself with two kids, and again battling her weight. "I really lost myself during that time. I'd lose a bunch of weight and still not feel the satisfaction I was searching for. I asked God to give me perspective without tragedy. I wanted to be a pillar of light, even though I didn't know what or how I would become that."

When Jenny turned thirty, and had her third child, she again fought depression, panic attacks, and darkness. "That was when I decided I really needed to make a change. I began to read everything I could find on how to change my thoughts and my life. I was totally committed to it."

After her fourth child was born Jenny again wanted to lose weight, but this time she decided to use what she was learning about controlling her thoughts and apply it to her weight loss.

"I started by visualizing my new life and my new body. This time I gave myself *love* (#CreateAMovieInYourHead). I had to pay attention to my internal voice, and unravel what I really believed. I needed to rewrite my story.

"I realized that I had to focus on my energy and keep it positive (#ThinkIT). I told myself that I was beautiful (#ChangeTheVoicesInYourHead) and sexy, because I said so (#SayIT)!

"It's been four years since I totally reinvented my life. I pulled away from all the people who were not positive influences in my life (#ChangeYourCrew), and I made a choice to be whoever I wanted to be regardless of people's opinions. I felt it was time to let my *whooohooo* out!" Jenny laughed.

Jenny began sharing her true self on her blog, and started a Facebook page, where she gave herself permission to be authentic. "It was wild!" she told me. "To let my inhibitions go, and not care what people thought of me for the first time in my life, was liberating. But sometimes being yourself makes the people around you uncomfortable, and I noticed some of my friends stopped talking to me. It happens when you find your passion and are pursuing your authentic happiness. Your circle of friends gets smaller (#ChangeYourCrew)."

Jenny wrote the book *Sexpot with Stretch Marks*, in 2014. "When you've gone through hell and back, you just naturally want to help other people. That was my hope with my novel, that it would help someone else. You have to fully love yourself and become your own BFF. I took all my mistakes, took the lessons and richness from them, and used it as the power to create my change. I finally found my passion and my purpose, and it's to use my story to help and inspire others."

JENNY'S ADVICE TO YOU

"Doubt is normal. If you don't have doubts, then I don't believe you! Everyone has them; it's natural as you make changes in your life and pursue your passion. But doubt is fake. It's not real; you have to put it in perspective. You have to take the leap of faith and trust that it's going to work. Doubt is there to keep you small.

"Reinvention is possible at any stage in life. Entertain the thought that this *is* possible; let it marinate. Just think, what if this really could be possible for me? Let other people's stories inspire you, and just know that if it's possible for them then it is for you too!"

JENNY G. PERRY is the author of *Sexpot with Stretch Marks*. She is also a coach, blogger, and mother of five! Follow her journey on **Twitter:** @JennyGPerry **Instagram:** @JennyGPerry **Website:** jennygperry.com

STEP 3: #SAYIT

"I believe you can speak things into existence." —Jay Z

#HBRSoundtrack: "Fight Song" —Rachel Platten

When I started this journey in 2008 I was alone. I mean really, *really* alone. My family had withdrawn after my ex-husband left, and friends weren't sure what to make of me as a newly single mom. All anyone had ever known was Sarah "the wife." Watching me try and pick up my life was uncomfortable for most.

I get it now, but I didn't then.

I can count on one hand those who stayed close in the early years; to this day those people are part of my *ride or die* crew. But back then on most days I felt totally and utterly abandoned.

Looking back I believe it was a blessing in disguise. I think that if the people whom I'd always counted on stayed in my life I would have never made the changes I desperately needed to make. It's hard to change your life when people around you can't support that decision; it's too easy to get sidetracked. The benefit of being so isolated was that no one talked me out of my dreams.

And then I discovered Facebook.

Believe it or not Facebook became a powerful tool as I learned to #SayIT. I found that if I put a goal as my status update (back in the day when we still had "walls" and everyone was manically obsessed), that I was almost challenging myself to make it a reality. That's how I verbalized my desires and put them out in the Universe. And it worked! It held me accountable. My "friends" checked in on my progress and a whole new world opened up to me. Suddenly I was less alone and what I said would happen actually did.

In 2009 a coworker of mine named Doug Dingus asked if I'd ever considered writing a blog. We went on sales calls together and I'd tell him crazy stories about my life as a struggling, newly single mom. He was fascinated by my determination and hustle. He knew I was dealing with everything alone and kept telling me to write and post my stories on a blog. I laughed. "I am no writer!" I told him. After all, I'd taught myself to read at the age of thirteen. "I'll just embarrass myself," I told him. Plus I'd never read a blog in my life; I wasn't even sure what "blogging" was. If those reasons weren't enough, the thought of technically figuring out how to use a blog seemed beyond daunting.

But Doug insisted, and one day while the boss was at lunch he sat at my desk and helped me to start my blog. When he asked what I wanted to name it, the first thing that came out of my mouth was *"Thoughts.Stories.Life."* And the rest, as they say . . . is how I got here.

Thoughts.Stories.Life. became my voice to a world, even though I never expected people to listen. I honestly didn't write for anyone but me; it was my way of getting things off my chest because I had no one else to talk to. It was how I put my plan out in the Universe, how I expressed my goals and desires without the fear of judgment. Ultimately it became the way I applied #SayIt.

Then in February of 2010 I was in New York with the CEO of my company for a work convention. On one of those nights I sat in a lobby bar in Midtown having drinks with Bill, one of my clients, when somehow the topic of my story and blog came up. I'm not sure how, because at that time my blog was still anonymous and I hadn't told a soul about my story. But when we were done he said, "Sarah you HAVE to tell the world your story! It's so inspiring and I bet you could help a lot of people manifest a new life the way you did. Just face your fear and claim it! Put your name on it."

As fate would have it that next week a story I'd written and submitted about how I was working on changing my life went viral on the Internet—WITH MY NAME ON IT! I thought they would let me know before it was published and I could decide if I wanted it out there or not, but nope! There I was on Google for the whole world to see.

At first I panicked and begged them to take my name off the story, but it was already out there. I remembered what Bill told me, and I decided to face my fear and own my truth (#CourageOverFear).

Those events changed my life.

WORDS HAVE POWER

I always tell my kids: "If you don't want that to come true, DON'T SAY IT!" I have instilled in them even at their young ages, that you don't say negative things about yourself, your future, or other people, because it will come true.

Luckily the opposite is also true. If you #SayIT you are giving it power. You are turning a thought and an idea into something REAL. When we verbalize our dreams and desires it gives them wings. This might be a bit girly, but I think of them as fairy dust. When I speak my dreams they float away like fairy dust, going to make those words a reality.

When you own your #LifePlan and dream, you change how you speak about it. Instead of saying "IF I become X," you say "WHEN I become X." It's really that simple. You start verbalizing to anyone who will listen, or on social media, or however you can be held accountable, that you ARE working to achieve your dream. You talk about it in detail as if it's a GIVEN. You know it's coming. Not *if*, but *when*.

EXAMPLE #1

I will never forget the very first time I verbalized my dream to share my story with the world through multiple forms of media, including TV. More specifically I'd always envisioned that one day I'd be interviewed by Oprah or a show on OWN TV (her network). This was a dream (#DreamIT) I'd held close to my heart for about two years (well longer, but two years actively thinking about it), but I'd never had the courage to #SayIT out loud.

Then one day those words tumbled out of my mouth.

I was on an incredibly terrible date. I'd been living outside Seattle, Washington, in a rundown suburb and was trying my best not to hate my life. It was gray and raining every day. I'd not been on a date in months, so I accepted some guy's invitation to meet for drinks one dreary night in February. We'd exchanged a few messages on Match.com and before I knew it there I was in a dingy, deserted Applebee's on Valentine's Day, wishing I'd just stayed home. I immediately knew I'd never see this guy again, so when he asked me what I did for a living I took that opportunity to verbalize my #BigPictureDream.

I just said it.

I can still remember having an out-of-body experience as if I were watching myself tell this random guy my biggest dream, the one I'd never before spoken about. I could feel the words pass my lips, and hear them burn my ears. But there it was. It was done. I figured this was the perfect way to release those words into the Universe with as few repercussions (since no one I knew was shooting down those dreams) as possible.

That poor guy must have thought I was crazy, as I just boldly claimed my future. Either that or he thought I was full of shit. But either way, I sat on that bar stool and said, "I am going to tell my story on TV. And one day have my own show. And meet Oprah. And write a book. And help change the world." (Maybe I got a little carried away . . . but hey!).

He just stared at me and asked for the check (which I paid).

But I knew in that moment that I'd given wings to my dream. The Universe had been given an assignment to make my dream a reality.

Roughly eighteen months later I was in Chicago as a guest on the Steve Harvey Show. It was my national TV debut. The topic was dating (about which I happen to blog a lot), but I was also given the opportunity to tell a bit of my story. It was exactly what I said would happen that day in Applebee's (#ManifestThat!).

The show had flown me into town a few days before our taping, and on Sunday I ventured out of my hotel to brave the fourteen-degree winter weather. I hopped into a cab, and headed to Harpo, the headquarters of Oprah's empire OWN TV. I've had the dream to meet Oprah ever since I can remember; being at Harpo was something I'd envisioned for years. When the cab driver pulled over, I stepped into the snow and stood in front of the Harpo sign. I snapped a selfie and tweeted it to Oprah and the president of her TV network, Sheri Salata, with the tag #DreamComeTrue.

Just being in front of that sign was the realization of a dream I'd had for years (#Winning)! Here I was on an all-expenses-paid trip to Chicago (#MoneyAintAThing!), standing in front of the building where Oprah filmed her show, shows that helped to change my life. I asked the cab driver to wait for me as I walked up to the front entrance and looked through the windows. I paused and played the #CreateAMovieInYourHead of my moment. I wanted to remember it—*The girl standing outside these doors dreaming of one day walking in.*

That night I got a Twitter notification that Sheri Salata had just "favorited" my tweet and followed me! I started screaming! I just knew something more was coming, it HAD to be. And then my phone buzzed again; this time it was a direct message from Sheri: *"Hey Sarah . . . U r amazing! S."* I couldn't believe it!! That meant she knew my name and had read my story . . . that was more than I could have hoped for (#Winning!)!

The next afternoon I was having lunch at the Polo Lounge, a place where Oprah had once interviewed Justin Bieber. I just wanted to feel her presence on that seemingly miraculous Monday. And then my phone buzzed—it was an email from the office of the EVP of new programing at OWN TV asking for a meeting while I was in town. I *freaked the fuck out!!* But I wasn't surprised. I KNEW it was coming; my belief at that point was strong enough to move a building (#BelieveIT).

On Tuesday morning we taped the live portion of the Steve Harvey show, and afterward I hopped in a cab and headed back to Harpo headquarters. This time I had a one-hour scheduled meeting with three top producers of the network. This time I could walk inside those doors. I waited in the lobby where I'd seen so many photos of Oprah standing. I was living a dream bigger than I'd even dared to imagine less than 48 hours before (#ManifestThat!).

My dream was to meet with the producers and have Oprah or Sheri know my name, and it had come true. Who knows what the future will hold, but I know that I manifested that experience. It would never have come about had I not found the balls to #SayIT.

In September of 2018, I found myself sitting at a beautiful dining room table, in a gorgeous Los Angeles home. I was excitedly (and nervously) telling three amazing women my story and how I'd changed my life using #FutureBoards. One of those present was Sheri Salata! It was at HER invitation that I'd got on a plane and flow to LA to teach her how to make my #FutureBoard. We spent the afternoon collaborating on a project together and the entire time I just kept thinking, "Holy shit! I'm in Sheri Salata's house! And we are working TOGETHER on a project!" The full-circle irony of the moment was not lost on me. I was sitting across the table from the woman who created the Oprah show that had changed my life. Four-and-a-half years after that first initial tweet, we were working together! You never know when your dreams will manifest, which is why you have to constantly be hustlin' toward them no matter what. You never know who is watching and waiting for your time to be right to give you the opportunity of a lifetime.

EXAMPLE #2

On my very first #FutureBoard I had a picture of the marathon sticker "26.2." Now I have no idea why in hell I put that sticker on my board because I am NOT a runner, yet there it was. When a coworker asked me if I wanted to train with her for the Portland marathon in 2010, I thought, *What the hell! Let's check that off my list.*

So I joined a running group and began the grueling six-month training program. This wasn't something I advertised, though. Deep down I doubted if I'd actually go through with it, and thus I didn't want to deal with the humiliation when that became my reality.

Shocking as it is, I quit four months into training. I felt very gratified that I didn't need to face negative comments on Facebook for failing to go all the way.

Fast-forward to January 2014 when I was setting my goals for the New Year, and I saw that damn sticker still hanging on my #FutureBoard. Even worse, every time I lectured Kanen about how "*You can never quit, not even when it gets tough,*" he'd joyfully remind me that I quit the marathon training, and I'd shake my head and finger at him, but had no witty reply.

So that is how I finally DECIDED to train for and RUN the Portland Marathon. This time I'd concretely made my decision and there was nothing that would prevent me from showing up on race day and getting my fucking authentic bumper sticker to put on my damn car! I knew this time I would use the #HBRMethod to accomplish this insanely enormous goal; I could never do it alone.

So I went to social media and let the world know my goal. I then started a blog series called "Marathon Life" where I chronicled the entire six-month training process and how #HBR got me through it. I knew that if I put it out there it would happen.

It was on those ten- and fifteen-mile Saturday morning runs that the #HBRMethod began to officially come together in these eight steps. During those hours and hours alone with my thoughts, proving to myself that this method works on something so tangible as making one foot follow the other, mile after painful mile, was when it all clicked.

On October 4, 2014, I crossed the finish line of the Portland Marathon after running for more than seven hours. I could barely walk, most of the race volunteers had packed up and gone home, the fans were long gone . . . but there stood my three babies and my girlfriend Jackie waiting with signs that read, "*You can do it mama! #HustleBelieveReceive!*" (#ManifestThat!)

My son realized that day that his mama won the argument (even if it took a few years).

Watch the video "Impossible Is Nothing" on my YouTube channel and read the blog series about this journey on my blog www.thoughtsstorieslife. com listed under the tag "Marathon Life."

YOUR HUSTLE

Grab your journal.

Read over your last homework assignment—the five mottos you wrote and your "I am's." Then go to your bathroom, turn the light on, and look in the mirror. Yup. I want you to speak them out loud to yourself. I want you to hear those words and see the reaction you have to them. Look at yourself. Hold yourself accountable. Make them YOUR mottos, your truth. Your Future.

Say them daily until you BELIEVE them, and they are just who you ARE. And then make new ones to step up your game to the next level and do the same thing.

Post a few of them on your wall, or #FutureBoard, or the inside of your mirror, some place you will see them every day. Say them out loud when you are driving, over and over. Make them your status updates, tweet them, Instagram them. Surround yourself with them.

Just like every step in this book, it's all about putting into practice what you've learned. It will do you NO GOOD if you don't actually put in the work as it's laid out in this book. So let's get some results, baby!

#HBRSTORIES

LEAH LaBELLE

RASUAL BUTLER

JAYSON HAWKINS

KITHE BREWSTER

TODD WASHINGTON

BOB OWEN

LEAH LaBELLE'S STORY

I met Leah at my friend's holiday party in 2014, and it wasn't long before we were swapping stories of how each of us were hunting down our dreams with #RelentlessPursuit.

This is her story.

"I come from a musical family. My parents were extremely famous musicians in their home country of Bulgaria, each a member of a popular music group. When they met they decided to form a group together and used music to come to America during the communist regime in Bulgaria. So I've had music in my blood from the very beginning.

"Before I was born they formed a Christian group in the United States and traveled the country performing. As a little girl I was jumping up on stage and singing with them; music was my first love. At the age of three there are videos of me singing in their studio. It's just been such a natural thing for me.

"I was about seven when *Sister Act 2* came out, and I was so excited! It was the first time I realized I could turn music and singing into a job and I knew that's what I wanted to do (#BigPictureDream).

Leah was sixteen when *American Idol* began its third season. She heard they were doing open auditions for the show in New York and she'd always dreamed of going (#DreamIT). "I walked into my mom's room that day and saw she was booking travel on the computer. She surprised me with a trip to New York City for my birthday, which just so happened to be the same dates as the audition (#Winning!)!"

When they got to NYC on Friday evening for Sunday's open audition the line was already 250 people deep. They camped out until it was her turn to sing on Sunday, and she made it through to the next round, which meant she'd get a chance to sing for the judges Randy, Paula, and Simon the next day. Again she nailed her audition, advancing to Hollywood Week. (#ManifestThat!) It was the start of her junior year of high school when she left for *American Idol* in Hollywood. "Each week I made it to the next round of competition, and then into the top twelve. At that time *Idol* was in its prime and the entire nation was watching; it threw me into a world of red carpet events, press, and media. It was crazy. I learned so much about myself and the music business during that process, but I thank God that I didn't win. I was just too young at that time and not developed enough as an artist."

When Leah was voted off the show she went back to high school. "I learned that people aren't always happy for your success and your friends can turn on you; it was really hurtful (#ChangeYourCrew)."

The second hard lesson Leah learned was that the music business can be pretty brutal. One of the producers for American Idol Top 12 Album offered to take her under his wing and introduce her to management, a lawyer, and producers, essentially to help assemble an A-list team to kickstart her solo career. Leah was excited, but after her meetings there was no follow-up. She tried countless times to reach him, only to find out he'd been busy doing the same for the artist he'd just signed, Rihanna. "That messes with you a little bit, especially when you're young and naive. You start to question if you're good enough, or pretty enough. It's a blow (#EarthquakeMoment)."

"I was obsessed with Pharrell and N.E.R.D. growing up, and at seventeen they came to play a show in Seattle. I was dying to meet him, and one of the local radio station DJs knew me and let me go to the meet and greet after the show. I was sitting in this room by myself with my poster, so nervous and not sure what to say, but I have learned to always trust my intuition, so when he walked in I stood up and walked right up to him. I put out my hand and said, 'You're gonna produce my whole album one day!' (#SayIT, #DreamIT) He looked at me and was like, 'Really??? What do you sound like and how old are you?' We chatted for a few minutes and then he left." Despite the brief interaction, this encounter would one day reveal its outcome to both Pharrell and Leah.

Leah moved to Los Angeles when she was twenty-one to pursue her dream of becoming as a solo artist, and for five long years hustled her butt off. She learned that it wasn't enough to just perfect her craft as a singer; she had to make connections and work the business side as well. One of her first industry connections encouraged her to start a YouTube channel and begin building back her fan base from *Idol*. "I've gotten so much love from my fans on YouTube, and so many amazing opportunities have come from it," she told me.

One day she got a message from pop singer Keri Hilson saying that she wanted to meet Leah and possibly sign her as an artist. "I'm so grateful to Keri for that opportunity, I went on the road with her singing backup vocals, and I was able to meet so many people in the industry."

One afternoon Leah was in the recording studio with Keri and heard that Pharrell was in the building recording in a nearby studio. "Keri's manager suggested I sing for Pharrell's manager, and when I did Pharrell walked out of his studio and said, 'I heard you. Can you do that again?' I sang it again for both of them, and then reminded Pharrell of the time I said he'd produce my album one day, and he remembered that moment

(#ManifestThat!). We talked for a few minutes and then went our separate ways."

After Leah stopped working with Keri, she started singing backup vocals for Jordin Sparks, who was opening up for the Jonas Brothers world tour. "Even though I didn't wanna be a background singer, [I] had to really humble myself as an artist because it was a way to pay my dues and learn even more about the business. I was torn though because I really wanted to do my own thing, but it was a great experience; we also opened for Britney Spears.

"There have been a lot of highs and lows along the way. The lows are really tough. I got to a place where I was drained. I started thinking that I was becoming someone I didn't know, I wasn't happy doing it anymore. I'd lost the joy of music. It was an emotional roller coaster, and I was tired.

"I hit rock bottom one day and I remember crying myself to sleep. It was my lowest point when I really did want to quit (#EarthquakeMoment). The next morning I saw a tweet from Jermaine Dupri: 'Follow me so I can DM you.' He said, 'Have you checked your YouTube message?' I hadn't for months, and sure enough there was a message from weeks ago not only from him but one from Pharell as well (#ManifestThat!)! Pharell's assistant asked me to come to Miami the very next day!"

Leah went to Miami and spent a day in the studio with Pharell. And before she knew it she was on a plane to New York City to meet with Jermaine Dupri and L. A. Reid. "We got to L. A.'s office and he said, 'Okay, sing.' I sang a few songs for him and he was lovin' it. He said he really believed in me and wanted to sign me right then (#ManifestThat)! I literally went from crying myself to sleep, to a few weeks later singing in front of L. A. Reid!"

That set a crazy whirlwind in motion for Leah, who

thereafter signed her record deal and then recorded her first major album. That spring her first single dropped, and she was doing the full promo tour in New York with Pharell. This included features in major magazines. She also performed at Essence Festival and won a Soul Train Award (#HBRLife)!

"I've always believed that when you speak your dreams out loud they will happen (#SayIT). I used to say them to my mirror when I was growing up; I've always been that way. Saying it out loud helps me process my thoughts and makes me surer of what I want.

"Things don't happen overnight, but when they happen it feels like it's overnight. It took eight years from the start of *Idol* to my first major record deal (#ChillOut), but when it came it felt like it was overnight! It took eight years from the time I told Pharell that he was going to produce my album to the time when he actually did. That's why you gotta always stay ready (#TheHustle). Even if nothing is happening, you can't slack. You gotta believe that you will be called (#BelieveIT), put in the work while you wait, and then when you are, you'll be ready (#RelentlessPursuit).

"I have been on this journey to succeed with a full-on belief in myself and the gift God gave me. (#BelieveIT) My journey is not like anyone else's. My story will not be like anyone else's. My talent is unique to me."

LEAH'S ADVICE TO YOU

"If you are pursuing your dream you must be insanely passionate about it in order to stay sane. But also understand that it won't be easy and nobody from the outside will ever understand how hard you are working in the silence.

"Work hard for what you want because it won't come to you without a fight (#TheHustle). You have to be strong and courageous and know that you can do anything you put your mind to (#RelentlessPursuit). If somebody puts you down or criticizes you, just keep on believing in yourself and turn it into something positive (#ChangeTheVoicesInYourHead).

"Always remember that you are going to be fine. No matter what you're going through, you are going to survive so let time do its thing.

"Nothing can set you back unless you allow it to."

Tragically, Leah was killed in a car accident in January of 2018.

RASUAL BUTLER'S STORY

It was at the Christmas party when I met Leah LaBelle that I first learned of Rasual. As soon as I told her the concept for this book she said, "You have to interview him!" It took nearly eight months for our schedules to coincide, but I was thrilled when I finally got a chance to hear his story.

"I started playing basketball when I was about seven years old. It was around the time my father died. He had just returned from fighting in the Vietnam War when he was killed in the streets. No one knew who killed him and it's remained an unsolved murder (#EarthquakeMoment).

"My father was my best friend. He'd just bought me a Knight Rider Big Wheel bike and taught me how to ride it. I was really hurt by his death. I didn't know how to handle it, other than to be angry."

After Rasual's father died his mother took him to live with his grandfather. She wanted him to have a man in his life, someone to help him process the anger into something positive.

"I grew up in South Philly, and my mother was worried about me because I'd started getting into trouble at school. I remember one day my grandfather's friend took me to a basketball court, and talked to me about being upset. He said, 'It's okay to be angry and upset about what happened, but instead of acting out that anger, imagine what the guy looked like who killed your father. Pretend that the basketball rim is his head and the ball is a brick; if you want to hurt him, that's how you do it (#CreateAMovie-InYourHead). You get the ball to go in the hoop and that's how you do damage to him every time you make a shot.'

"After that I started obsessing about basketball. I got all my anger out on the court; it was therapy for me. Then I started loving it, and got good at it."

Rasual didn't play organized basketball until middle school, and in seventh grade started for the varsity team. At six foot two he was one of the tallest kids in school, and all that practice turned him into a good shooter. It wasn't long before he noticed the positive attention his playing got him in school, even from the principal. He became even more determined, practicing every day after school.

"I loved to play so much that I missed my curfew a few times because I was so into the game, and I knew my grandfather wasn't happy about it. So one night walking home I realized that I needed to have a talk with him. I turned off the TV and asked if I could talk to him. I was thirteen years old and I'd never done anything like that before, but I told him that I was going to use basketball to go to college and move us out of that neighborhood (#SayIT). I told him I was going to make a better life for us, and help him out. And I told him that if he ever wondered where I was after school, or if I ever missed curfew again, to just go to the court, because that's where I'd be, working (#TheHustle). I couldn't believe I had the courage to say it because I'm a bit of an introvert, and he couldn't either. But he became my biggest supporter after that.

"I believed that basketball was my destiny, I knew God whispered it in my ear, and I had faith that it would happen (#BelieveIT).

"I remember telling my teachers and friends that I would play in the NBA one day, and they said 'it's a one in a million chance.' And I always said that 'one' would be *me*. I just believed it. The more people told me I couldn't do it, the more determined I became."

For his freshman year of high school Rasual was accepted into a prestigious private school called Roman Catholic, which had consistently ranked in the top twenty-five nationally for basketball. He was one of just a handful to ever make the varsity team as a freshman, an accomplishment he didn't fully understand at the time.

"When the basketball rankings came out at the beginning of the year I was ranked 200/200 in the tri-state area. I remember being really upset that I was ranked at the bottom of the list; I got home and cried. But that just made me obsessed about getting better. I said to myself that when I was a senior I would to be the number-one player in the tri-state area (#ChangeTheVoicesInYourHead). My senior year I was the number-one player in that area and the number-five shooting guard in the nation (#ManifestThat!). After that I saw what I was capable of when I pushed myself. I just kept becoming a student of the game and always practicing. I studied what NBA players did, how they eat and worked out. I thought, 'If that's where I want to be, then I need to do what they did'" (#TheHustle).

His junior year of high school Rasual got the opportunity of a lifetime, to work out with a trainer who only worked with professional players, one of whom was Cuttino Mobley who played for the Houston Rockets at the time. Cuttino invited Rasual to go with him to Houston to work out with other pros. "That really lifted my confidence because there I was in the gym with some of the greats; I was kinda starstruck at first. But these guys were asking me if I was preparing for the draft, and I was holding my own. That just kicked me into another gear."

Rasual made a bold decision not to enter the NBA draft after high school (#CourageOverFear). Instead, he decided to stay in Philly and attend La Salle University with his best friend Donnie Carr. Donnie was Rasual's first mentor, and the reason Roman Catholic gave him a chance to play was because of Donnie's relentless praise of Rasual's abilities to the coaches.

In the summer of 2002 Rasual was drafted into the NBA by the Miami Heat. "I didn't go in the first round of the draft like everyone thought I would (#EarthquakeMoment). I remember sitting there, and for the first time doubting myself. I thought, 'this isn't going to happen. I'm not going to be drafted.' And I asked God *WHY?* And as soon as I said that, they called my name. I was drafted 53rd pick out of 58 (#ManifestThat!)."

In his tenth season in the NBA Rasual was let go by the Toronto Raptors, the first time he'd ever been released from a team. "The day I got home from being released is the day I met [my girlfriend] Leah. Everything happens for a reason," he told me.

But the reality was that he was over thirty years old, and the prior year he'd not played all that well. It was the year of the lockout and the first time he'd ever taken it easier while he waited for the lockout to be over. That decision showed in his performance, and for the first time ever the calls from other teams didn't come in. For eleven months he worked out, this time determined to stay in peak condition, waiting for that call. But when it finally did come, it was a shock.

"My agent wanted me to go play in the NBA Development League [also known as the D-league], which was very humbling (#EarthquakeMoment). At the time I was reading a book that talked about how sometimes God puts you back through 'development' so that you can learn new lessons and grow. So I did it. It taught me how to share my story and mentor kids, which added greater substance. Raven, my daughter, was living with me at the time, and that was the first time we'd been able to spend good quality time together, which was a huge blessing. She was my reason for not giving up. I wanted her to see how hard I was working to get back in the league, and that hard work pays off (#RelentlessPursuit).

"During that time I really learned who my true friends were. Donnie is still my best friend and a brother to me, but during that time my phone stopped ringing off the hook from other 'friends'; many people disappeared. When you're in the league everyone wants something all the time, and I realized that it was time to focus on myself and my family (#ChangeYourCrew)."

That summer Rasual played in the NBA summer league, something he hadn't done since he was a rookie during his first two seasons. This time he was a thirty-four-year-old veteran competing against eighteen-year-olds for a chance to make a team. All the odds were stacked against him. Yet he was invited to the Pacers camp and miraculously made the team on a nonguaranteed contract (#Winning!). But they didn't give him a contract after that. And then in 2014 the Washington Wizards brought him on for a one-year contract (#ManifestThat!).

"Those months out of the NBA were such great development for me. It helped me see that I needed to focus on how to become successful *after* basketball. I realized that I needed to be ready to transition into being a businessman (#HBRLife). My good friend and mentor Cuttino Mobley transitioned into a businessman, and has taught me how to look ahead to the future. Now I spend a lot of time talking to people who are successful in the corporate world, even though I'm in my thirteenth year in the NBA. I'm learning how to invest and build companies and a whole new skillset. I'm using the same tools and mentality I learned in order to be successful in basketball to become successful outside it."

RASUAL'S ADVICE TO YOU

"Once you have your dream, believe in it (#BelieveIT). Don't allow anyone to tell you that you can't be successful. Use those negative words to push you to become even more successful.

"Confidence comes from work. You need to enjoy the process and even the pain. But you will start to see results, and that gives you confidence (#FakeIT).

"You need to be in love with process. Be okay with all the work you will put in to get to your dream. Put all your focus and energy into it (#ItsTheJourney).

"Never give up on your story before it's over. Because you never know if yours is a storybook ending if you give up in the middle (#RelentlessPursuit).

"I heard a story once about a swimmer who was crossing the English Channel, and halfway across heavy fog set in. It was so dark that she couldn't see anything but the stroke of water right in front of her. When she'd finished, people asked her why she didn't give up. She said, 'because I didn't want land to be just one more stroke away.'"

Tragically, Rasual was killed in a car accident in January of 2018. His wife, Leah LaBelle, was in the passenger seat. They were returning from a fun evening of bowling with friends. It's believed that they both died instantly, together.

JAYSON HAWKINS'S STORY

I was introduced to JaySon "Belico" on Facebook by my niece. She said she knew a rapper in Southern Oregon who had just broken the *Guinness Book of World Records*, and that I should check out his hustle. By now I knew that the #HBRMethod worked for my specific goal of running a marathon, but I wanted to see if he'd also used it to become a world record holder.

"I was talking with my son one day, and he said, 'Dad, wouldn't it be cool if you could be in the *Guinness Book of World Records*?'" JaySon told me when I asked him how this idea came about. "My son had always been really into those books, so it made me stop and think. I'm a rapper in a part of the country that's not really a hotbed for rappers; this gave me a chance to showcase my talent in a new way. But the biggest motivator for me was to make my son's dream come true (#DreamIT) and show him he can do anything he sets his mind to.

"I looked up how many live performances [in 24 hours] held the record, and it was sixty-two by a band from overseas. I figured '*hey, I could do that!*' So I reached out to the *Guinness* book people, and a few months later they got back to me. They said they'd just closed the book for 2015 but that I could try to beat the record for 2016."

So JaySon went to work. He sat down and went through his original song list; there was enough material to perform sixty-five live sets in twenty-four hours. He timed every set exactly down to the minute, ten minutes for each one with a two-minute break in between, and scheduled four different venues for his performances. Then he found the two required professional timekeepers and filed all the necessary paperwork with *Guinness* (#TheHustle).

"When I put it out there (on social media) and told my friends what I was doing, I got a lot of haters (#SayIT). People were like, 'You're crazy dude. You can't do this!' People from my small town don't do this kind of thing and some of them didn't get it. But I just had to ignore the haters, and focus on the support that my friends and family, and especially my son, gave me (#ChangeYourCrew). We believed it was possible (#Believe-eIT). Once I'd made that decision there was no turning back. I wasn't about to fail (#RelentlessPursuit)."

On the day of the performances JaySon was joined by his team, the timekeepers for *Guinness*, and his crew who'd help document everything to make it official. "I hit my goal of sixty-five live sets in twenty-four hours, which beat the record. So I'll be in the book that comes out in December (#ManifestThat!).

"I'll probably cry when I see my name in that book, and get the certification. It's something so huge that no one can take away from me. I will be a part of history. And my son was so proud of me (#HBRLife)."

JAYSON'S ADVICE TO YOU

"Once you put it in your brain to do it, you gotta just DO it. And don't listen to the haters (#DoIT)."

JaySon "Belico" Hawkins is a rapper and promoter who lives in Medford, Oregon. Follow his journey on **Twitter:** @ belicoblackop

KITHE BREWSTER'S STORY

I discovered Kithe from an Instagram photo that Morgan Stanley Executive Director Kimberley Hatchett posted wearing one of his amazing collection pieces. About a week later I saw him on *The Real Housewives of Atlanta*, and I immediately sent him a message asking if he'd be interested in sharing his story for this book. Little did I realize that I'd sent it in the middle of spring Fashion Week, which is one of the busiest times of the year for Kithe, and it took nearly five weeks before he saw my message and replied. That whole time I was convinced I'd get him for this book. I just knew he'd be perfect, and I actually added his name to my list of participants applying the #HBRMethod to make it happen. So the day I got his message saying he'd love to be part of this project, I was over the moon, yes, but surprised? Not so much (#ManifestThat!)!

When he called for our interview I was nervous, to say the least. As with all my interviews, I tried not to research him first. This is a man who's normally interviewed by top fashion magazines, not a single mom from Oregon who mispronounced his name in our intro! But Kithe was beyond gracious and forgiving of my embarrassing faux pas, and so we began . . .

"I guess it started when I was quite young," he began. "I had an obsession for clothing and how I looked when I was a young kid. I would produce fashion shows and talent shows at home, and that was my version of a 'lemonade stand.'

"I was a performing arts student, studying dance and theater growing up in St. Louis. I moved to New York City after graduating from high school to pursue my dreams in dance and Broadway, and continued to explore what it was I really wanted to do. My Uncle Robert lived in New York with his boyfriend; they owned an upscale clothing showroom, where fashion editors would come to get clothes for their photo shoots. He allowed me to live with them and gave me a part-time job in his showroom, which enabled me to make the move to New York.

"I became increasingly interested in fashion, and it was clear that I had an instinct for it. I continued to work for my uncle Robert in the late '80s and really started to blossom in that regard. I took a seasonal job over Christmas break at Henri Bendel, and here I was, this black kid from the Midwest working in this high-end fashion store. One day I got an opportunity to fill in as a personal shopper when my coworker went to lunch, and in walks one of the wealthiest women in New York. She bought an astronomical amount of cashmere from me, everything I suggested. Later I learned that she had raved about me, and over the next few weeks I began helping other celebrities as their personal shopper.

"After that I decided I wanted to be a fashion editor and celebrity stylist, and to really be serious about it I needed to go to Paris. So I put together a portfolio book, full of my strongest ideas, even though I didn't have any 'tear sheets' (work published in a magazine), and I told everyone I was moving to France. When I told Uncle Robert this news he was very disappointed in my decision, which led to us not communicating for about three years.

"I gave up my life in New York and I moved with just $500 to my name. I [had] only a temporary place to live and no idea if I'd actually get a job (#CourageOverFear)."

Kithe stayed with a friend for the first few weeks, and spent all day walking around Paris looking for an agent to represent him so he could find a job as a stylist (#TheHustle). "I had no money, and was down to the last name on the list. By then I was so exhausted that I didn't even want to go; all the other agencies said I seemed talented but didn't have enough experience."

He thought about how far he had to walk to the last appointment; he was tired of being rejected, so he sat down on a park bench to think. He looked at the Eiffel Tower and considered giving up. He watched some children playing soccer in the park for a few minutes and then decided, *What was the harm in giving this last agency a shot?* (#RelentlessPursuit). When he got to the office the owner offered him a seat, and slowly she looked through every single page of Kithe's book. Then she looked through it all again, and said . . .

"I think you are amazing! I believe you will be one of the biggest stylists in the world (#Winning!)."

She took Kithe under her wing, introducing him to society in France. Within two weeks he booked his first gig as a correspondent traveling around Europe to attend fashion shows as an editorial writer and stylist (#ManifestThat!).

For eight years Kithe lived and worked in Paris. He started out sneaking into the big fashion shows because he wasn't on the guest list, yet he always found a way to make it happen. "I learned to dress the part. If I looked fabulous no one would question me! I looked so good that I could walk right past security into the shows with or without an invite (#FakeIT)!" In the early days he couldn't afford the latest designer trends to style his shoots, so he went vintage shopping, putting together pieces that rivaled anything on the runways. In all Kithe lived in Europe for fifteen years, while he traveled around the world and became a well-known fashion editor and stylist (#HBRLife).

In 2000 he moved back to America and was booked to style the cover of *Flaunt Magazine* with Julianne Moore, who was an up-and-coming star at the time. "The next day Julianne asked me to take her under my wing and become her personal stylist. It was an incredible experience. She was my first A-list actress as a personal client; I worked with her for three years helping to create her signature style (#ManifestThat!)."

When Julianne was nominated for an Oscar in 2000 she turned to Kithe to select the perfect dress for the red carpet. "By then I had such a good relationship with Chanel that they flew Julianne and I to Paris on the Concord. There were no agents or publisists with us, just Julianne and me on this jet (#HBRLife)!" He laughs. "Karl Lagerfeld (head of Chanel) himself designed an Oscar dress for Julianne; it was amazing! But being the fearless person I am, I also arranged the first-ever meeting between Tom Ford and Julianne. I remember sneaking Tom into our hotel at the Ritz because everyone was desperate to meet her and design that dress. One night I even snuck Julianne out the back of the hotel where Mr. Valentino had a car waiting to take us to his Chateau outside Paris for a private dinner. That's how badly designers wanted her!" Kithe laughs at the memory of how daring he was (#CourageOverFear). "It was those bold moves, which began the fashion obsession between Tom Ford and Julianne Moore."

"In 2010 I began dating Ryan, who was an exotic dancer at a gay club in New York," Kithe said. "He kept trying to talk to me but I told him I wasn't interested in having an 'exotic dancer moment;' but somehow our eyes always caught; it was clear we shared a strong connection. Once I got to know him, I realized that dancing was just his way to make money while he pursued his dream of becoming a writer."

In 2011 Kithe decided to take the bold step toward his childhood dream and create his own fashion line (#BigPictureDream). Fear always held him back in the past because he questioned his qualifications to create an entire fashion line and start a business of that magnitude. After all he'd never been to design school, and dropped out of college after one year.

"Tom Ford was my inspiration to become a designer," Kithe told me. "Because he'd made the transformation from editor to designer. I watched how he transitioned and that gave me the courage to do it myself (#CourageOverFear). Adversity is something that I've never been afraid of. You have to be willing to take rejection, be tough (#RelentlessPursuit), work hard (#TheHustle) if you want something bad enough."

In 2011 he met an investor who promised to help fund Kithe's first fashion line, but two weeks before his first runway show in New York Fashion Week the investor pulled out (#EarthquakeMoment). "I was forced to put all my savings into my company so we could keep going and do our first runway show. I built this business from nothing (#RelentlessPursuit)."

It was at his first trunk show in New York where Kithe met Kimberley Hatchett. She fell in love with his work and bought nearly the entire collection! From that time on the two have become great friends.

Not long after Ryan moved to LA, where he took a job in film production, and the two stopped dating. But as fate would have it Kithe took an opportunity as a costume designer for a film in LA, and the two began dating again. They fell madly in love. "We were really incredible together. Everyone who came around us commented on how beautiful we were."

One evening Ryan got down on his knee and asked Kithe to marry him. On December 23, 2012, the two were legally married in a beautiful ceremony in New York's West Village.

"In late June Ryan flew to LA." Kithe's voice got quiet for a moment. "He decided to take a last-minute road trip driving from LA to Las Vegas. His car broke down in the middle of the desert so he took a ride from a highway patrol officer to the nearest gas station. That was the last time anyone saw Ryan alive."

Ryan was missing for nearly three months. And for all that time Kithe looked for him. Worried sick, he even began to wonder if maybe Ryan just needed some space. But deep down he knew how strong their love was and that his husband would never just disappear on purpose.

Ryan's body was found in the desert by two joggers, just miles from where he was last seen. All his organs were missing, including his eyes.

His death became sensationalized in the media, adding to the shock and pain of Kithe's loss. "Not only did I have to see my husband's body in that condition, but I also dealt with the press, who made up stories about us. On top of all that Ryan's family did not accept me and tried to discredit our marriage.

"This has been the most difficult thing in my life. I couldn't control the pain of this loss. Eight months after our wedding he was gone. For six months after his death I couldn't get out of bed. I was just devastated," Kithe said with deep emotion in his voice.

I asked Kithe how he was able to move forward and find any meaning in life after losing Ryan (#EarthquakeMoment). "Because I knew he would want me to," he said. "It was the only thing that got me out of bed. I knew how much he loved and believed in me. He always said that our wedding day was the happiest day of his life. To be able to give that to him, that's what helped me to get up and face the world again.

"It's still hard. It will always be hard. But it's God that has gotten me through this. He's taught me to move through the pain and adversity. Ryan is my angel; he's always by my side."

KITHE'S ADVICE TO YOU

"Learn that if God closes one door then something better is coming (#BelieveIT). I pray and meditate, and I work really hard (#TheHustle). Nothing can stop me because I'm fueled by the joy of my work (#RelentlessPursuit).

- Keep in mind that no matter how successful you are, you need to be humble.
- Be able to finish a project when you start it.
- Don't be afraid to work hard (#TheHustle). Right now after a twenty-year successful career, I'm working harder than I've ever worked in my fucking life!
- You have to be determined, and passion is *everything!* Choose something that you love because you can pursue it without losing your life in the process (#BigPicture-Dream)."

KITHE BREWSTER is an American fashion designer and celebrity stylist. He has styled Beyonce, Drew Barrymore, Eve, Halle Berry, Naomi Campbell, Iman, Cate Blanchett, Heidi Klum, and the list goes on. He's also been part of Project Runway, appeared on the Bravo series *The Real Housewives of Atlanta*, and has worked with every major fashion house and fashion magazine on the planet! Follow Kithe's journey on **Twitter:** @kithebrewster **Instagram:** @kithebrewster

UPDATE: In May of 2015, a few months after our interview, I was in a New York taxi with my children headed to my best friend Lisa's birthday, where I'd hoped to meet Kithe for the first time in person. Kimberley and Dr. Janna Andrews were also joining us for dinner and I was excited for everyone to meet my kids. That's when I got a text from Kithe that filming for his documentary was running late and that sadly he wouldn't be done in time to join us for dinner. BUT he added "I'd love for you to send me your measurements so I could make you a dress for your red-carpet book launch party (#ManifestThat! on an #HBRLife kinda level)!"

I started screaming in the cab!

TODD WASHINGTON'S STORY

I met Todd in 2011 on the field when Kanen and I went to our first Baltimore Ravens game. He'd heard of Kanen's dream to meet Michael Oher from my friend who played on the team, and because he was Michael's coach, he offered to try and make my son's dream come true. He told Michael about Kanen, and a few minutes later that dream became a reality, as there was Michael, posing for pictures with my son and me. So when I reached out to Todd about this project he was happy to share his story in hopes that it will inspire you.

"My dream started when I was ten years old. That's when I decided I wanted to be a coach in the NFL (#BigPicture-Dream). My dad was a high school football coach in Virginia where I grew up, and every day I was at practice watching him coach. While other kids were out catching frogs and playing with their friends, I had a whistle around my neck.

"I was infatuated with the process it took to get to game day. My dad taught me so much about the game. I ended up getting a scholarship to play at Virginia Tech, and I had a great career, but I was still focused on becoming a coach. I wanted to be a graduate assistant (which is the first required step to becoming a coach at the college level), so I did all the necessary work to prepare myself to go into coaching once I graduated from college. But my coaches kept telling me that I would be playing in the NFL. Coaching has always been my first love. Playing was a distant second."

Todd was drafted by the Tampa Bay Buccaneers in the fourth round of the NFL Draft in 1998. He went on to have a distinguished career, playing for eight years in the NFL, including winning a Super Bowl with Tampa Bay.

But coaching remained Todd's passion and first love. "When I got to the NFL people thought I was crazy because I wanted to coach more than anything. I told all of my coaches what my dream was and that I was eager to learn the game. I was committed to learning everything I could about my craft and getting better, so I'd coach high school or middle school kids during the off-seasons, anything to practice and learn my craft (#TheHustle).

"When I was playing, I had so many 'friends' and teammates that you'd think would always be there for you, but as soon as I got released from the team, they were gone. Once that lifestyle was over, they were nowhere to be found. For a lot of guys, that transition is really hard because they don't have goals beyond playing. But for me, once I was done, I wanted to connect with my peers who had the same goals as me (#ChangeYourCrew). I realized that those old friends couldn't understand my new vision and they couldn't help me get there. I wanted to make connections that were already doing what I was aspiring to do, so I reached out to coaches and the guys I knew who were also trying to be coaches and I built a whole new network.

"But I realized quickly that I couldn't rely on anyone but myself to make my dream a reality. People who said they would be there, and help me out with the process, didn't. And the process was intense and sometimes really frustrating. But that didn't stop me because I knew what I wanted to do. So I just kept going. Nothing was going to stop me (#RelentlessPursuit).

"I came close to quitting. I began to second-guess myself. But I knew better. People told me I should just focus on coaching at the college level, but that was never my goal. I was so clear on what I wanted to do from the very beginning. If you make a clear goal there is no reason to ever settle for second best.

"But sometimes you have to do what you gotta do in order to reach your goals. I got my first interview at the University of San Diego. It was a long time coming, but I was ready! I was happy to accept the job and start building my coaching career."

Todd coached at the University of San Diego for three years, but knew the time was coming when he needed to follow his true passion of getting back into the NFL, this time as a coach. He knew the opportunities would be better on the East Coast, and he once again began the process of sending emails and making calls, just trying to get an interview.

And then the Baltimore Ravens called.

"I interviewed for twelve straight hours with the Ravens," Todd said with a bit of a laugh. "The process was no joke! But I was offered the job of assistant offensive line coach." He'd reached his lifetime goal; he was now a coach in the NFL.

"My first day on the job I found out that the head offensive line coach had been suspended for two weeks, which meant that it was just going to be me for our season opener. It was September 11 and we were opening the season against the Pittsburgh Steelers (the Ravens' biggest rival), and there I was on the sidelines, with the flag covering the field and the National Anthem being sung, and I almost lost it. This was the moment for which I had worked my butt off my whole life, to be standing on the sidelines before the game coaching the offensive line. We went out there and beat the Steelers 31 to 7. I will never forget that game! I even got a game ball. It felt like the Universe and God had given me a taste of my ultimate dream, as confirmation that the path I walked has prepared me to step up for that moment."

Todd is currently going on his fifth season with the Ravens and coached the team to a Super Bowl victory in 2012.

"Having gone through the full journey and challenges of being a player is what ultimately prepared me to be the coach that I am today. It has given me the ability to connect with players on a level that I would not be able to do if I hadn't once been in their shoes. It gives me credibility, and helps me get the most from my players."

Knowing how driven Todd is, I knew he must have dreams and goals that reach far beyond what he's already accomplished, so I asked him what his dream was for the future.

"I am the *assistant* offensive line coach for the Ravens. When I made my decision to be a coach, it wasn't to be an assistant. My first goal was to get a job coaching in the NFL. But that was just my short-term goal. My next goal is now to be the second black head O-line coach in the NFL. However; my ultimate dream is to one day be a head coach (#BigPictureDream).

"It's not enough to reach only one goal, because once you do, you start the next level of your journey. You can't look at it as though you've 'made it' because if you do, then you get complacent and fall off your game. This is a very cutthroat business, and you have to be on top of your game at this level, all the time. You can't afford to be content.

"I tell my players all the time that they can't be satisfied, because there is always some place they can improve and get better. You get rewarded for your work (by achieving a level of success or money), but it's all about *what have you done for me lately?* There is always someone out there who is better than you, always someone trying to take your job. It's coming to the table with your ultimate best, every time. You can't get lazy. You have got to stay hungry.

"This job isn't easy. During the season, 18- to 20-hour days are normal. Going weeks without a day off is normal (#TheHustle). And that's why as a coach the highs are higher when you win and the lows are lower when you lose. It's all about preparation for the next game, the next season, the next job. It never stops! In every stage you have to build your foundation as strong as possible. I know it's shaping me, and molding me for the next opportunity and because of that I know I will be ready when that time comes. You have to be willing to start at the bottom, and do the best job possible with what you have, and humble yourself to put in good work no matter what. If you do, you will be ready for anything."

TODD'S ADVICE TO YOU

"Make sure you surround yourself with people who have the same goals (#ChangeYourCrew). I grew up in a small coastal town in Virginia where crabbing was a way of life, and my father used to tell me; 'if you look at a bushel of crabs and you try to take one crab out, there will be four or five other crabs hanging on, trying to bring it down.' So you can't afford to be around people who have the potential to be negative around you and bring you down.

"Know what your dream is (#DreamIT). I ask my guys all the time what they want to do outside of football, what their goals and aspirations are after they are done playing, and that's how I can tell if a guy is driven or not. If all they wanted to do was play in the NFL, then they aren't driven to be successful past that. The average playing career is three years, so knowing what they want in life beyond playing is vital (#LifePlan)! The guys who can answer that question without hesitation are the guys who will have a bright future."

TODD WASHINGTON is the former assistant offensive line coach for the Super Bowl–winning Baltimore Ravens. He achieved another lifelong dream when he was chosen to coach the offensive line for the 2014 Pro Bowl.

BOB OWEN'S STORY

I first met Bob Owen in 2010. I had recently been promoted to the role of Executive Director, after just three months in a junior sales role with a start-up software company. I was "green" in every way, terrified I'd not be able to live up to the challenge and opportunity I was given, yet determined to figure it out and succeed. My role was to sell our software to the top 100 global law firms, the ones who represent companies like Coke, Ford, and all the big brands we love. I didn't know much, but enough to understand that if I was going to be successful I needed to make relationships with those at the top of the food chain—the rainmakers, the big dogs, the ones who made the decisions and had the power to influence the masses. In a law firm that role belongs to the partner. So I cold-called Bob one day and asked him to meet me for lunch so I could tell him all about my amazing software.

I think he was probably a little taken back. I had broken the rules; I'd skipped the middlemen and avoided the normal chain of command and gone right to the top. I'd had the audacity to ask for an hour of his time, something he couldn't spare. I'd done what few before me had the balls to do, and I think he was curious.

I'd intended to wow him with my limited knowledge of a world in which he was an acclaimed expert, and I'm sure my nerves were hard to hide. Yet we sat across from each other eating French onion soup on a rainy New York afternoon, and talked about . . . *life*. Fast-forward to three years later, and we were back sharing life stories and lessons over lunch in Manhattan. I'd just started doing interviews for this book and was dying to hear his story, knowing that like all the successful people I've come to know he must have a good one. I wanted to know how he had become one of the most sought-after litigators and industry experts in his field and built such a successful lifelong career. I was curious if I'd find the same themes in his story as I'd found in the others I'd been working on for *#HBR*.

So I asked Bob to tell me his story . . .

"I honestly think a lot of who I am was formed when I was six years old. I was in the first grade, when I walked home from school to find my mother at our neighbor's house, our things packed. My mother told me we were leaving my father for my own good and moving to St. Louis. That instilled in me an obligation from a very young age to make my mother proud, and to make her sacrifice worth it. She had an ability to get the best out of me, because she expected it. She wouldn't pay me, for getting A's in school. She always said 'I expect you to get A's.' I was conditioned to please, because I wanted to make her proud."

In the fourth grade Bob's teacher recognized his exceptional academic potential and gave him an IQ test to see if he'd qualify for the "gifted students" program, which he did. "It was a source of pride, and it raised my self-confidence. It taught me that I could do anything. It produced an environment of high achievement because the expectation was there, and I knew I had to meet it."

When Bob was nine years old his mother married again, to a man named Bill Luebbers. "I was a shy, scared little boy when I was nine, and the distance I have traveled since then I lay at his feet. Bill Luebbers was a volunteer in my life, in the truest sense of the word. He didn't have to become my father, but he did. He became Scoutmaster and helped not only me but a lot of other boys in our neighborhood. He was a great role model of what was possible when you worked hard, and treated people with respect. He was a strong, good-looking all-American kind of guy, and he was wonderfully kind.

"He gave me the book *How to Make Friends and Influence People*, and I learned through that how to turn my need to be liked into one of my biggest assets. Growing up in the '50s with a single mom and divorced parents was hard. It created in me an intense desire to be liked, one that could have been a real weakness, but he taught me how to turn weakness into strength. His impact on my life is immeasurable."

Bob was accepted into Northwestern University in Chicago, and promptly went to work to pay for his education. "I had no money to pay for school and neither did my mother, so I'd worked hard to get a good scholarship. But even then I still needed money to eat, so I took several jobs." Throughout his college career Bob worked a variety of different jobs including: bussing dishes, selling clothes, working as an office and shipping clerk, working in a psych ward, and working campus security (#TheHustle).

As if school and multiple jobs weren't enough, he was elected to the student senate and edited the school newspaper.

"I come from three generations of trial lawyers," Bob said. "Law school was always my goal, and my reason for working so hard. I had a legacy to live up to." He aced the law boards and set his sights on Penn Law.

"I remember calling the admissions officer at Penn Law and telling him I'd been given a scholarship to NYU and Georgetown Law. I told him I needed to make a decision and wanted to know if I was going to be admitted. He put me on hold and grabbed my file; a few minutes later he came back on the line, asked me a few questions, and said 'Okay. You've been admitted to Penn Law' (#LiveIT) (#SayIt)."

After second year of law school Bob went to Washington, DC, to volunteer in the Senate office of Stuart Symington. One day the staff lawyer quit, and Bob found himself in the right place at the right time (#ManifestThat!). His hard work had not gone unnoticed, and Symington hired him as the office's new attorney. "It was quite an experience, being a young lawyer, with a Senate badge, on the floor of the Democratic National Convention."

When the summer ended Bob was offered a job with the prestigious global law firm Sullivan and Cromwell in New York City. "I never thought I'd move to New York. I'd grown up in the Midwest, but it was a great position and everyone said I'd be crazy to turn it down, and so I took it. But I was secretly afraid of public speaking. I'd spent all this time preparing and working to become a trial lawyer, and here was my opportunity; it was everything I'd wanted. Yet I was scared to death of public speaking.

"Back when I was in the seventh grade I'd fainted when trying to give my first speech, and had always had a near crippling fear ever since. But I knew it was time to face that fear and find a way to get over it. I could have taken another position, one where I didn't have to speak, but I didn't want fear to limit my opportunities and guide my decisions (#CourageOverFear). The best way to push past it was to put myself in a situation where public speaking was inevitable."

To help conquer this fear Bob signed up for a public speaking class and began studying how to become a quality speaker (#TheHustle). "I had a wonderful teacher who encouraged my progress and helped me find my confidence. One day I confided to her my story of fainting in front of the class in seventh grade, and she kindly smiled and said, 'That's what happens when people forget to breathe. They pass out.' All this time I'd gone through life thinking I was basically allergic to public speaking.

I'd let that fear almost paralyze me; it had the potential to derail all my plans, but the whole time it was just the fact that I'd made a rookie mistake and forgotten to breathe. I would have never learned that had I not chosen to take action to overcome my fear and turn my weakness into an asset."

That decision opened the door for one of Bob's finest achievements, being asked to teach at the prestigious National Institute for Trial Advocacy program in Boulder, Colorado. At first his fear of speaking threatened to derail his lectures, but the more he pushed through it, the more he realized how much he actually loved teaching and mentoring young lawyers. "I turned that 'luck' of being asked to give one lecture into a real opportunity that changed the trajectory of my career," he said. Bob wound up being asked to join the faculty and taught in the program as an adjunct professor throughout the 1990s, and that achievement remains one of his greatest senses of accomplishment.

It wasn't long before Bob's winning mentality and work ethic got him noticed at his firm, and soon he was next in line to make the prestigious title of partner. But when the firm passed on promoting him to partner, Bob found himself in unfamiliar territory. It was the first time he'd let himself down and faced "failure." In the past his hard work and intellect had created opportunities, but this time he'd not reached his goal (#EarthquakeMoments). That forced him to make a decision—go to another big firm or go out on his own and open a private practice. He chose to take a chance and spent twenty years successfully running his own firm. It was a risky move. He was leaving behind a great career and income to pursue the unknown, even more so because by now he was married with small children.

"That decision required me to step up and find a way to make my practice successful. I needed to provide for my family.

It was a fantastic experience because it taught me how to run a business as well as how to be a great litigator."

I asked him if there was a moment in his life when he felt like he was *living his dream*, and he smiled. "I remember when I had my practice a few years and was sitting at my desk in New York, and the thought came to me: *Wow! You did it. You were this poor kid, raised by a single mom from the Midwest and here you are, making it in New York City.* That was a great moment I'll never forget."

When Bob's three kids grew up and went off to college, he rejoined Big Law at a global 100 law firm. Today, he has not only achieved his dream of making partner, but Bob is the *partner in charge* of the firm's New York office. He works out of a beautiful corner office in Manhattan, lives with his wife in their Westchester County home, and spends weekends at their vacation getaway in Maine (#HBRLife).

I asked Bob if his life has become the plan he'd originally designed it to be. "I was always focused my entire life on the consequences of the choices I make. I made them deliberately and with care. I have always been aware of the goals I have set for my future and made all my choices to align with those goals (#LifePlan). When I was younger I benefited greatly from surrounding myself with people I could learn from and look up to, and copy people who could challenge me (#ChangeYourCrew).

"My key to success has been that I love what I do. I get happiness from the earned accomplishment of my work; it's a source of joy every day. I revel in that happiness."

BOB'S ADVICE TO YOU

"Never be afraid to aim ridiculously high. Never be afraid of that. If you haven't failed, you're not trying hard enough. Never let fear of failure hold you back. Don't sell yourself short, and never tell yourself you can't do something."

BOB OWEN is the partner in charge of the New York office of Eversheds Sutherland. He is the proud father of three grown children; he is enjoying being a grandpa and has been married to the love of his life for nearly forty years. He is an accomplished speaker and sought-after expert in ediscovery. He is proud to say he is a fourth generation trial litigator. Follow his journey on **LinkedIn:** Robert D. Owen

STEP 4: #WRITEIT

"Ninety-five percent of the successful achievers I have interviewed practice writing down their goals, plans, or vision for success on a regular basis."

—Joel Brown, *Entrepreneur Magazine*

#HBRSoundtrack: "Written in the Stars" —Eric Turner

#LIFEPLAN

To create the life of your dreams, you must have deliberate direction. You can't expect to achieve success without goals and a plan, and you can't expect to change your life without knowing what you want it to become. A #LifePlan is your personal written blueprint for success, your road map. It is a holistic look at your new life and what it will take to get you to your goals.

EXAMPLE

Imagine an old mansion. It's been deserted for years. The floorboards are rotting away; the ceiling lets in the winter rain; its windows are cracked and broken. It's a total eyesore. This is your life, right now. It's the reason you picked up this book. You're tired of being an *eyesore*. But when an architect with a trained eye looks through this house, they see something different, something beautiful. They don't see the surface mold and dry rot; they see what it *could be*. They see its potential. Their trained eye can imagine what the house looked like back in its glory days, and can see what the recreated version will become.

In this old mansion, we walk together into every room and we draw out a new plan for what each will look like when we are finished. We bounce ideas off each other, we get excited about the vision together, and we put it down on paper. And when we are finished we have a blueprint for extraordinary!

As a coach, I am like that architect. I help people see their potential and then show them how to reach it. The rooms represent each area of your life: your finances, your physical appearance, health, relationships, family, career, passion, you name it. Every aspect of your life is represented in this "house." We even include the front and back yards because my method is holistic. It's not about manifesting a "thing" off a "vision board." It's about changing your entire life, and the lives of your family members. It's about spiraling up into success, happiness, joy, abundance, wealth, and fulfillment, instead of the alternative.

When you look at the blueprint for your newly renovated mansion, what's the first thing you ask the architect? *When will it be done?* And, *How much will it cost me?* You already understand that taking something old and dilapidated and transforming it into something magnificent is going to take time (#ChillOut) and hard work (#TheHustle). It will cost you something. BUT you *believe* it can be done (#BelieveIT), because you see the plan in front of you and that sparks your imagination. Now you can picture yourself walking into that beautiful home after a hard day of work, and you want that home, dammit (#CreateAMovieInYourHead)! You don't know how on earth you are going to make it happen, but I'm telling you that it's possible, and you're loving the plan and starting to buy in (#ChangingTheVoicesInYourHead).

Then I build you a model of your reimagined home (#FutureBoard). When you see it, you're excited; you're the way you used to get when you were a kid, full of imagination and wonder as I walk you through the beautiful mock-ups of each room. You can see it all now, as clearly as I could in the beginning. Now you *really* want that house! You can picture your family there, your entire life, thriving in that house. Now you *know* it's possible and are willing to do whatever it takes to make it a reality (#RelentlessPursuit).

But along the way you might realize that your new, shiny house is looking strangely out of place in the old, rundown neighborhood, and after doing some research you find that those other junky houses are actually lowering the value of your new one. You are forced to make a difficult decision—put the extra work and money into relocating to a neighborhood that is surrounded with houses just like the one you're working so hard to recreate, or stay and lower your value(#ChangeYourCrew).

Your #LifePlan works the same way for you that the blueprint worked on the house. The #HBRMethod will walk you through all the steps you'll need to create your own individual renovation plan, and then I'll show you how to make it a reality. All it will cost you is the price of this book and some old-fashioned hard work and patience.

It's important to note that the timing of your progress is not fully within your control (#ChillOut). Just as a contractor is never "on time," there are always unexpected "surprises" or setbacks with a remodel (#EarthquakeMoments). But those are simply delays in the process, not an end to the journey. Your desired end result will become your reality as long as you see it through to the end (#ManifestThat!).

EXAMPLE

After my husband left in 2008 I took a long hard look at my life. I realized that I no longer had any pride left whatsoever. My life was undeniably shit. I got pity looks from the few people who would look at me, and even my family didn't know how to help me pick up the pieces. It's like passing a massive car accident on the freeway, the kind where belongings are strewn across lanes of traffic, everyone is standing around scratching their heads, or driving by rubber-necking, but no one is doing anything. They are silent bystanders, because what can they really do? It's not their job to stop and pick up the mess. It was my job to pick up my mess, and I had to take full responsibility for it.

Little by little I began to realize that since I was starting from nothing at thirty-four years old, I might as well dream *fucking huge!* I mean, what would it hurt? I'd already lived through the worst-case scenario and knew that rebuilding the life I once had would no longer cut it. I wanted something better. WAY BETTER. So I sat down and mapped out what I wanted my new life to look like.

In my new #LifePlan I wanted to be a successful business-women, a real boss chick. I wanted to be the kind of woman who wears suits and stilettos to work and has the respect of her peers. She would travel for work and feel important, beautiful, and fulfilled. She was in good physical shape and took good care of herself. She smiled all the time and people were drawn to her. She did fun things with her kids on the weekends (even when it felt overwhelmingly difficult), cooked for them during the week, and was present in their lives. She invested time in her friendships and had a close-knit circle. She made time to pursue her passion and help others.

That was the woman I aspired to become.

I wanted to live the type of life where I could take my kids on vacation. I'd never taken real vacations growing up, or at any point in my life, so that goal was critically important to me. I figured if I could be the type of woman who took her family on vacation that would be the ultimate proof that I'd "made it." And if I could do that, it probably meant that I'd be wearing nice clothes, and driving a nice car, and have things like a checking account and a 401k. But all that would be the side effect of my success, not the motivation for it. I'd be able to take my son to football and basketball games. I'd find a way to share my story and hopefully inspire someone. That was the type of life I craved. I was completely unwilling to settle for anything less. When I started out, THAT was my #BigPictureDream.

I knew that woman needed to holistically jump a few levels on the class, social, and economic ladder in order for this to happen. She needed an upgrade in every area of her life. After all, what sense does it make to only wish for "things"? If all I wanted was a Mercedes, wouldn't I look pretty ridiculous buying my groceries with food stamps while driving a brand new Benz? I knew from the beginning that I needed to BECOME that woman so that life would make sense. I had to start with what I could control, and that was changing ME.

I took the time to really think about this woman I was creating. What did she look like? What type of friends did she have? What were her hobbies? How did she carry herself? Who did she date? What type of mom was she? What type of friend and coworker was she? What mattered to her? If she was a true boss chick, what did her life look and feel like?

That was my wish. But this was my reality: I was a woman with three very small children and no family support, who'd not worked in over two years. I'd been a waitress most of my life, aside from the few years I'd sold mortgages or web conferencing after leaving college my junior year to have my son. How the hell was I going to become THAT boss chick?

I honestly had no idea *how* I was going to make it happen. I just knew it was my only option. Plus, I had the *desire*.

YOUR HUSTLE: CREATE YOUR #LIFEPLAN

Have you ever stopped to actually plan your future life? What will it take for you to succeed?

Success is personally defined. It only matters what it means for YOU. Not "success" as defined by society or the media. Not what it means to your friend who always seemed to get the "lucky breaks," or for your coworker or neighbor. It's subjective, and it's what you decide it will be.

Your #LifePlan is the foundation for all the steps and exercises that will come in the following chapters because it is your personal written plan for your future. This plan is forward thinking, based on the life you WILL to create, not the one you currently have. It's basically as if you're creating a "dream life" out of thin air, starting with a clean slate. This simple exercise will get you thinking about what you want that life to become, and will be your blueprint for success.

The #HBRMethod does not focus on material THINGS. It focuses on EXPERIENCES. This is the reason I want you to start planning your new life by focusing on how you want it to *look* and *feel*. Base it on what is most important to you for your long-term happiness and well-being. The mission is to raise the bar on our entire life, not just achieve one or two goals related to a few specific areas. It's to find success in your career, achieve financial independence, have mutually fulfilling relationships, be healthy, love yourself, and be the best version of you that is humanly possible, which is your #BigPicture-Dream.

PART 1. YOUR FUTURE LIFE

In part one we are thinking about what our future life will look like in every area, and then writing a detailed "story" description of each area in our journal.

Imagine yourself five years into the future. You're looking down at yourself living your "dream life"; what do you see?

To help, ask yourself these questions:

Who do I want to become? What does my best self look like? What type of man or woman would I be if I could wipe the slate clean and start fresh with clear and deliberate direction?

Remember successful people spend time doing things they love, with people they love. They take care of their physical appearance. They have money in the bank for things like last-minute dinner invites from their friends. They have careers they enjoy. And most successful people strive to achieve balance by incorporating faith, mental and physical health, and a devotion to giving back.

Ask yourself what your future life looks like in each of the categories below.

Career Example (mine): *I am a successful author, with a bestselling book. I've built my coaching business and have traveled the world sharing my message of hope and tools for change. I've been interviewed by all the major TV shows and my book is a* New York Times *bestseller. My #HBRLive events draw thousands of people around the country and people are changing their lives and learning how to live their dream. I met Oprah!!* ☺

Be as detailed and specific as possible. Write down a paragraph "story" for each.

- Career
- Family/Relationships
- Physical Appearance/Health
- Finances
- Passion/Hobbies/Leisure
- Faith/Mental Well-being

PART 2: TANGIBLE GOALS

Now look over your list. Write five goals/milestones that you would like to achieve within the next five years for each category.

For example, for the "career" section, include specific steps you'd like to take to get a promotion, change careers, further your education, start a business, or retire. Be as specific as possible.

How could you begin working toward those goals today? For example, if one of your goals is to start your own business, you could write down several action items that are needed, such as making a business plan, registering a domain name, getting a website, and doing research. The list goes on.

Do this for each category on your list, and allow yourself to brainstorm as thoroughly as possible. Let go of any confines of your current reality. Remember, it is not about making it all happen *today,* so don't get discouraged. It's supposed to contain a blueprint for your future as well as action items to make it a reality.

The role of this exercise is to help get you thinking about what your goals are, what your ideal life will look like, what categories of your life you'd like to devote your time and energy to, and what's most important to you.

Note: Your plan will change over time and grow with you. In the chapters to come, we will return to this list, so keep your notebook handy.

#HBRSTORIES

STEPHANIE CANNADAY

SADIE LINCOLN

JUMANNE ROBERTSON

VICTOR MATTHEWS

MIA SAENZ

TAVIO HOBSON

STEPHANIE CANNADAY'S STORY

I met Stephanie at lunch for my corporate job one afternoon as the deadline for my book was fast approaching. In addition to discussing the business at hand, we also talked about our backgrounds and experiences in corporate America. By the end of lunch, I was asking if she'd consider being my final interview for this book, and I'm honored she accepted.

"I knew from a very young age that I wanted to be a lawyer, and more specifically a corporate lawyer," she began (#BigPictureDream). "I'm not sure how I knew this, because I didn't I even understood what a corporate lawyer was, but it has always been my dream. I think God put me on the right path at a very young age.

"My grandma jokes that I said I was going to be a lawyer as a little girl, before my feet even touched the floor when I was sitting at the kitchen table (#SayIT). As far back as I can remember I had a vision of where I was going and faith it could happen, even if I didn't know how I was going to get there (#BelieveIT).

"I was raised in a very small town in rural Virginia. It was a great place to grow up, but there were not many corporate law opportunities. By the age of six my father was out of the picture completely. The maternal side of my family raised me, and no one from that side had been to college. I knew at a young age I needed to blaze my own trail independent of what I'd ever seen, to make my dream happen (#DreamIT). Irrespective of the seemingly limited opportunities, the lack of any pedigree, or how unattainable my goals seemed, I always had faith that God would help me accomplish my goals and I maintained the vision for my future. I never once thought it was not going to happen no matter what the circumstances were.

"Growing up, I was very blessed to have talented and successful friends who were intelligent and quite ambitious (#ChangeYourCrew). They were a big influence on me. I watched them succeed, thrive, and prosper, and I also observed how other people reacted to them and I wanted that. I thought, *that's how I want people to see me.*"

Stephanie worked hard to put herself through school. For several years, she worked full time, went to college full time, and prepared to attend law school. "For several years, my daily routine was: get up early in the morning and drive 40-45 minutes to school, go to class for several hours, go straight to work for seven to eight hours, drive 40-45 minutes home, work until early in the morning on my classwork, and then get up the next morning to do that all over again (#TheHustle). While most of my college friends were doing their relaxing or socializing, I was working to pay my own way through school. There were years of sacrifice, daily hard work, long hours, and dedication (#RelentlessPursuit).

"I got through it by having faith that I could accomplish my ultimate goals (#BelieveIT), never losing sight of my vision (#CreateAMovieInYourHead), knowing I had a larger plan (#LifePlan), and focusing on the task at hand (#TheHustle). Once each task was completed, I moved on to the next one. Every time I encountered an obstacle, delay, setback, or hindrance, I would focus on the ultimate goal (#BigPictureDream) and work through it to accomplish each task along the way. I also never lost faith that God was guiding me and He would keep me on the right path.

"My goal from day one was to become an in-house corporate lawyer (#BigPictureDream), but many companies don't hire inexperienced attorneys for their in-house legal department. So when I graduated from law school, I created a plan (#LifePlan) and wrote it all out (#WriteIT) as to how I would eventually accomplish my goal of becoming an in-house attorney. That plan had various steps; first I'd need experience, which meant I'd have to practice at a law firm. Additionally, I'd need to work on corporate accounts or get corporate law experience to build my resume(#ItsTheJourney). I put specific goals and timelines around each phase of my plan to remain focused and prevent me from getting discouraged. And then I just executed. It required a lot of additional sacrifice and hard work, but I knew it would help me accomplish my ultimate goal.

"From the beginning I understood that I was creating my own destiny. I knew it was a process; there were hurdles and obstacles I had to overcome to get where I wanted to go. But my strategy and vision kept me so focused that I didn't even think of quitting (#RelentlessPursuit)."

When Stephanie first started practicing, she was doing non-corporate law work to gain experience and to receive a paycheck. She was practicing some family law, which was not an area of the law she was passionate about. "I didn't like it at all," she told me. "It was so emotionally draining. I'd come home from work every night and wonder, *Did I go to law school to do this?* I'd question why I worked so hard to just end up doing something I really did not enjoy and had not planned on doing. But on those days I'd have to remind myself that it was just a necessary stepping stone, and that it was only temporary (#ChangeTheVoicesInYourHead)."

Stephanie faced significant rejection in her quest to obtain her dream job. The application process was long, arduous, and brutal at times. She applied to many different open positions in both corporations and law firms. "I applied to so many different open positions for a very long time. I either heard absolutely nothing, or got rejection after rejection. I remember applying for a corporate position and promptly received a rejection via email. Then, I received another in the mail from that same company for that same position. In all I got four rejection letters from that company! It was very clear they didn't want me (#EarthquakeMoment)!

"But you just have to go back to your plan and keep moving forward (#RelentlessPursuit)."

Stephanie's plan worked, and she was eventually offered a job with a law firm in South Carolina solely practicing corporate law (#Winning!). "When I took the job I told myself I would only be there for two years (#SayIT). That was the amount of time I thought I'd need to gain the appropriate amount of experience to move to an in-house position." Stephanie was in that position for exactly two years. "That position gave me the experience to obtain a job as inside counsel for a corporation. In all, it took about ten years of lots of sacrifice, hard work, and focusing on the ultimate goal to get to where I wanted to be (#ManifestThat!)!"

Stephanie is now the Associate General Counsel for a large corporation, and has been living her dream in Southern California for the past seven years. "My vision came true far bigger than I ever even imagined as a little girl," she said. "And of course I have further goals and things I want to accomplish that I'm working towards. I know that using the same approach, while trusting God to lead me in the right direction, will allow me to realize these dreams as well (#HBRLife).

"I am a true testament [that] faith, coupled with hard work (lots of it), will enable you to realize your dreams and accomplish your goals.

STEPHANIE'S ADVICE TO YOU

"Faith plus hard work is the approach that has worked for me. You are in control of your destiny, so dream big (#DreamIT)! Don't let the magnitude of your ultimate vision scare you; break it out into smaller steps and tackle them one task at a time. Allow your faith and the vision of your ultimate goal get you through hard times (#LifePlan)."

STEPHANIE CANNADAY is the Associate General Counsel for Optum Services, Inc., living her dream in Orange County, California. Follow her journey on **LinkedIn:** Stephanie Cannaday.

SADIE LINCOLN'S STORY

I learned of Sadie by doing my very favorite workout, Barre3. I have been an avid fan of their studio classes for the past few years, and when I had the idea for #HBR I started looking for strong boss chicks to show us that we can live our dream too, just like boss boys do! It just so happens that the studio I took classes at was Sadie's very first studio and the headquarters for her company were in my hometown of Portland, Oregon, so I knew I had to find a way to get her on board! So I cold-called their marketing team, and it wasn't long before I was on the phone with the woman who was helping to reshape my body, asking her to tell me her story.

Nine years ago, Sadie and her husband Chris were living in Oakland, California, in a beautiful home with a view of the bay. Sadie had a thriving career as a member of the executive marketing team for 24 Hour Fitness, working directly with the CEO. It was an ideal career, one anyone would love and aspire to have. Sadie's husband, Chris, also had a successful career. They had built the "perfect" life. They had a child, two excellent incomes, and by all accounts they were "living the dream."

"But it wasn't us," Sadie told me. "It wasn't who we really were as people; that life didn't fit us. I'd discovered yoga when I was pregnant with my first child and fell in love with it. . . . I always knew I wanted a big, sexy career, but something that would allow me to be present with my children. And something that would be a family business."

Chris and Sadie had looked at options in the past to start their own business, but the right venture had not come along. Sadie had always had a passion for group exercise, and had been an instructor for years, yet the gym atmosphere never really appealed to her. "It felt too big, masculine, and lonely," she said. "I loved the warmth of yoga and its balance of ease with effort, but my body was ready for something different." She tried all types of exercise, studios, and classes—even other Barre programs—but nothing seemed to have the combination and balance she was looking for.

And then one day, in 2006, after having their second child, Chris came home and pulled a folded spreadsheet from his pocket. On it was a plan he'd quietly been working on, running the numbers and weighing the options. "My husband is the opposite of me," Sadie explained. "He's the analytical one. I act on optimism. I believe it will work out, so I jump all-in. I've always been that way; Chris is a perfect balance for me."

On the spreadsheet, Chris had mapped out a plan (#LifePlan) for them to sell their beautiful home, sell the second car, live minimally, quit their jobs, and move to Bend, Oregon. Chris's plan would allow the couple to take one year away from their corporate life and raise their small children at home together.

"I was so moved when Chris came to me with his plan. As a wife and mother, I thought it was incredibly beautiful that he wanted more than anything to find a way for us to raise our children at home together. And then I thought, *Well, I don't want to move to Bend!* So we settled on Portland. We decided to live minimally, renting a small home, and selling what we didn't need, and then we packed up our car, our two kids, and the cat, and drove to Oregon."

Chris and Sadie decided Portland would be the ideal place to follow their dream of becoming entrepreneurs. They went to work writing the business plan for Sadie's dream group-exercise studio—what would eventually become the national franchise brand, Barre3. She incorporated moves from over twenty years of teaching group and gym exercises, and brought inspiration from many different disciplines. She designed a studio to feel welcoming and warm, and put a child-care center in the lobby, so moms like her could get a nongym workout.

"We put every penny we had into Barre3, all our savings," Sadie told me.

"I never feared that it wouldn't work or that we'd lose everything we had," Sadie added (#BelieveIt). "Not for a moment. I never thought of quitting (#RelentlessPursuit). I always knew it would be BIG. We started the first studio in downtown Portland six years ago, but we did it with the vision (#CreateAMovieInYourHead) that it would be a franchise. We believed it would take off, but didn't know how big, obviously. From the beginning I had courage. I wanted to create something totally different, something done my way. Yet you always have those voices that say, 'Who are you to think you can create a new form of exercise?' But you just have to put that to the side and move forward with courage (#ChangeTheVoicesInYourHead)."

Since that first studio was opened in 2008, Barre3 has grown to have studios in twenty-three states, with seventy studios in the United States and five international locations. Barre3's Portland-based headquarters employs twenty full-time women, all of who were once clients. Over time, the women have organically grown into their individual roles in the company. Sadie recently launched a book tour for the release of her new book *Love Your Lower Body,* with the editors of *Prevention* magazine. She's appeared on QVC, Bloomberg TV, and has been featured in *Prevention* along with countless other media outlets. She's even launched the new Barre3 online workouts for those of you unlucky enough to not have a studio close by. And, oh yeah, she's trained several big-name celebrity clients!

With all this success, I asked Sadie: What was the moment when she felt like she was living her dream (#ManifestThat!)?

"I have that moment all the time, honestly, especially in the downtime. Like when I'm in the office with my team, drinking tea. I'm surrounded by these amazing beautiful women who have helped take this vision and brand to an extraordinary place," Sadie said. "And last year on our fifth anniversary, my team organized a free public-park class and asked me to teach it. We had no idea if anyone would show up; we'd never tried anything like it before. But over three hundred people came— clients that have been coming since the studio first opened. It was the most magical moment, looking out at all those people doing Barre3, and my mom and daughter in the front row. My daughter even got on stage and helped lead the class with me. It was just so unbelievably amazing." This year, over six hundred people came to her class in the park (#HBRLife).

"The best part of this whole experience for me has been validating that my intuition was right. That something which worked for my body could also work for thousands of others. I'm not a workout guru; I'm just a mom, trying to get her workout on."

SADIE'S ADVICE TO YOU:

"Have courage. Be fearless. It's a practice, learning how to make decisions that are not fear-based. When we operate from a level of fear it closes so many opportunities. But make sure you are buttoned up; know what you're getting into and do your research. Have a plan. Explore your options and ask lots of questions.

"And make sure you have balanced people around you, people who support you but can give you a different perspective

(#ChangeYourCrew). And always enjoy the moment; celebrate the joy of the moment (#GetGrateful)."

SADIE LINCOLN is the founder of Barre3 Fitness and author of *Love Your Lower Body*. She lives in Portland, Oregon with her husband Chris and their two children. Follow her journey on **Twitter** @barre3sadie **Instagram** @sadielincoln **Website**: www.barre3.com

JUMANNE ROBERTSON'S STORY

I connected with Jumanne on Twitter. He'd been following my tweets for #HustleBelieveReceive and I could see he was also living his dream, so I asked if he'd be willing to share his story.

"I started playing football when I was in eighth grade and I loved it right away, even though I was older than most of the other kids. In high school I played really well but didn't have the grades to make the big college recruit lists, so I wound up going to a junior college in Arizona. There came a point where I was finally being recruited by four-year universities and had several offers to play Division One ball, but I hadn't focused on my academics and was thirty-five credits short of being eligible to transfer. Everyone told me it was impossible to make up that many credits in one semester, but I wouldn't hear it. I found a way to hustle and get it done. Even though my school's semester limit was twenty credits, I enrolled in another junior college and took the additional fifteen at the same time (#TheHustle).

"When I saw the opportunity, I told myself if it was humanly possible I was going to take advantage of it. At the time, I was living on my own in a little studio apartment, taking the bus to school every day, waking up at 5:00 A.M., and being in class from 8:00 A.M. to 10:00 P.M. five days a week for four months (#RelentlessPursuit).

"It paid off though; I was able to accept a scholarship from Utah State University and start my first year as a junior. It was beyond amazing (#ManifestThat!)! That year we actually went to a bowl game, and my senior year we also went to a bowl

(#HBRLife). Not only that, but I was able to graduate with a degree in sociology from a four-year university."

After graduation, Jumanne wasn't drafted, but he did get invited to the Carolina Panthers' training camp. "I dreamed of getting invited to an NFL training camp and when it came true it was just out of this world—the realization of a lifetime dream (#ManifestThat!)! It was such a blessing, even though I was released; my family and I were still happy (#GetGrateful)."

Six months passed after graduation and there were no calls from prospective teams. "I had a fiancé and a young son and it got scary because I didn't have a job or income." Jumanne said. So he moved his family to Michigan in hopes of getting a job, but couldn't find any work that wasn't either in a factory or a coffee shop.

"Then one day I randomly got a call from a coach from Portland, Oregon, who asked me if I was still interested in playing football (#ManifestThat!). I took a risk and moved to play for the Portland Thunder in 2014. I only played for half a season before I got injured and then released (#EarthquakeMoment)."

Again Jumanne was faced with the decision to get a "real job" or continue pursuing his dream to play football. "My goal even beyond playing football was to be a coach," he told me (#BigPictureDream). So he began applying for every assistant high school coaching job he could find, but he received no leads and no callbacks.

"I finally decided to apply for coaching positions in Arizona, and was offered a position as an assistant high school coach. I absolutely love it! It's a lot of responsibility, but I can't imagine doing anything else. One day I plan to coach college football and eventually in the NFL. I've always been the guy to prove my haters wrong. If someone said it couldn't be done, I am going to find a way (#RelentlessPursuit)."

JUMANNE'S ADVICE TO YOU

"Sometimes you need to realize that the dream you've been pursuing isn't panning out the way you thought it would, for a reason. It's hard to accept at first, but you need to believe there is something else even better that you'll be more passionate about that fulfills you in the same way (#ItsTheJourney)."

JUMANNE ROBERTSON is a defensive back coach, a former professional arena football player, and a Utah State alum. He lives and coaches in Arizona.

VICTOR MATTHEWS'S STORY

I was introduced to Victor by Kimberley Hatchett, on my birthday in June 2014. We met him for drinks on a New York City rooftop bar with a fantastic view of the Hudson River, and we immediately clicked.

His story is the perfect example of following your passion at all costs, and why it's so important to have a clear #BigPictureDream.

"I've been a painter since I was a child. I started doing art as a kid in Brooklyn; it was my favorite class in public school. When I was in about fourth grade, I realized that I liked the quiet time of working and being alone. My mother was a portrait painter and so was my uncle, Sunny Little, so I grew up surrounded by artists and art.

"When I was in the seventh grade, my mother gave me a small art studio in our house. It was this little room where no one but me was allowed to go, my own quiet space with an easel, and paints. We didn't have much room, living in New York, and she didn't have a lot of money, but she was always a big encouragement for me.

"I am a self-taught painter; my degree is in commercial illustration, because my mother wanted me to go to college and get a degree I could use to earn a living. She didn't want me selling my paintings on the sidewalks of Brooklyn. But I just wanted to make art (#BigPictureDream); I didn't know anything about fine art. I never learned 'how to be a painter' from school (#FakeIT). Instead I learned techniques from other painters. I learned how to stretch canvas from Keith Haring. I learned how to have patience from Brice Marden. Francesco Clemente taught me how to use watercolors, and I learned how to work with bees wax from Ross Bleckner.

"I didn't have any money when I started out as a painter (#MoneyAintAThing!). So to get by I'd go get a job at a restaurant and work for a few weeks (#TheHustle), long enough to buy paint, white bread, and macaroni and cheese. When I'd run out of money for supplies, I'd paint on the wood I found around the city."

In 1987 Victor took a big risk. He began painting murals on buildings in the Soho neighborhood of New York City, in the middle of the night. He'd paint all night long, finishing just as the sun rose. Those murals got Victor noticed, and in 1988 he had enough paintings to have his own gallery show in Tribeca.

"It was the first time I'd sold a painting in my life. It was a great feeling to be earning money from painting rather than having to work odd jobs to be able to afford to paint (#ManifestThat!)." But most of his paintings were left unsold after the show, and he realized he had nowhere to store them. "I had to destroy the rest of those first paintings," Victor tells me. "There are very few remaining paintings from that first show in existence today."

In the years that followed Victor rebuilt his collection of paintings and began doing gallery shows around the world, in places like Berlin, Venice, Amsterdam, Switzerland, New York, and Los Angeles. Today Victor's works are on display in museums around the globe and sought after by private collectors such as Russell Simmons, Ellen DeGeneres, Donald Trump, and even the President of Botswana.

"I always knew I wanted to be an artist (#BigPictureDream). I know I was born to do this. If you feel that you are true, and have something unique to say, then you keep going no matter what. If you don't then you shut up, and I didn't want to shut up. I kept on searching for the reason as to why I paint the way I paint, and I'll keep searching. The journey is the satisfaction. I've never done anything else in my life; this is who I am," Victor told me when I asked him if he's ever considered giving up on his dream.

"I do everything myself. I make my own pigments, and stretch my own canvas and mix my own paint. And I get up at 5:00 A.M. and paint until 1:00 P.M. (#TheHustle) and then I take a nap. Siestas are important. I'm not as fast as I used to be, I'm not as young or as nimble, so I had to adjust. I love to paint in the early morning when the world is still asleep, and it's quiet. But to do that a siesta is needed; that way I can be refreshed going about the rest of my day. I had to put a routine in place, and be disciplined about working every day. So I get up and work.

"I just want to wake up every morning and paint, and to be able to do that every day is living my dream. I think of my success as just being able to do what I love to do. I'm painting right now as I talk to you," he adds with a laugh. "That's my dream, to be able to do what I love every day."

I asked Victor what his plan was for the future and he said, "In twenty years I hope I'm still breathing, and I hope people are still appreciating my work. I also want to help other young artists, and give back to the younger generation, teach them that they can follow their dreams."

VICTOR'S ADVICE TO YOU

"Have courage. Take advantage of the opportunities that come to you and the kindness of others. And only be around people that support your dream, and always follow your heart."

VICTOR MATTHEWS is an American painter/sculptor/ artist whose collectors include: JayZ, Russell Simmons, Robin Thicke, Donald Trump, and Ellen Degeneres. Follow Victor's journey: **Instagram:** @victormatthews_

MIA SAENZ'S STORY

Mia and I connected on Facebook in 2013. She'd seen my story on my blog and invited me on her radio show and then to be part of her annual women's online seminar as a featured speaker. So when I began writing this book I knew Mia's story would resonate and inspire you, as it has me.

"On my forty-fifth birthday I was 300 lbs," Mia began. "It was 2008 and I was so sick that my organs were shutting down and doctors told me that I had just two years to live.

"I hadn't always been overweight; in fact, when I was younger I had an incredible body. But I never felt comfortable with the attention I got for my body because I was molested for six years as a child and in high school I was raped. All of those things caused me to gain weight as a way of covering up and an attempt to keep men away (#EarthquakeMoment)."

Things got even worst after Mia was involved in an accident at a large retail chain where five boxes fell on her head and she had to be rushed to the hospital in an ambulance(#EarthquakeMoment). After the accident her weight continued to escalate to dangerous levels. "I was on eleven medications at that point and relying on a wheelchair to get from one place to the other; I spent twenty hours a day sleeping and the rest just sitting on the couch, as movement was difficult," Mia told me.

The turning point came when Mia was on vacation with her family in San Francisco. "We were on the BART (Bay Area Rapid Transit) and it stopped in a tunnel under the water and

I had a total panic attack, because I realized my whole family would die before they'd leave me on the train. I was physically unable to climb from the tracks up to the platform walkway. I started to see that my weight was not only affecting my health; it was affecting my family's well-being also."

Something clicked for Mia on her forty-fifth birthday. She chose to allow herself to envision what her life could be like if she were healthy and no longer battling her weight (#DreamIT). "I envisioned my dream life that day (#CreateAMovieInYour-Head). I envisioned myself thin, happy, and sexy. I thought about what it would be like to live with someone who I loved and who loved me, instead of the marriage that seemed lifeless. I thought if I could live and not die [from being overweight], how amazing would that be?! It was the best gift I could have ever given myself to visualize my dream life.

"On that day I made a concrete decision to thrive instead of survive (#BigPictureDream)."

Mia made the decision to change her life on her birthday and spent the next four months building a plan to make it happen, including getting out of the chair and building her inner core strength (#WriteIT). She told herself that on January 1, 2009 she would start her plan and never look back (#SayIT).

"I decided that the word 'no' was not going to be in my vocabulary anymore (#ChangeTheVoicesInsideYourHead). I refused to give up (#RelentlessPursuit). That morning of January 1, I got myself up with joy. I was determined to get back to living life instead of staying on the couch; my choice had been concrete and sealed into my thoughts. I was totally focused on creating my new life, which stopped my cravings because all my focus was on my goal. I cut out all options to 'fail,' and within six weeks I was losing weight so fast that I knew I was going to realize my dream (#ManifestThat!).

"Then something changed in me. I had a newfound glow inside and people were drawn to me, and I began feeling beautiful. I told myself, 'You are beautiful. You are fit,' all day every day. I committed to talk nice to myself (#MottoForLife).

"And when you see the vision of your new life, nothing else matters. My drive was to succeed to my goal and beyond; it was the only thing that mattered to me (#RelentlessPursuit).

"I lost 140 pounds in seven months without surgery (#ManifestThat!). I worked out twice a day and changed my eating habits to healthy ones (#TheHustle). It was a complete life transformation (#HBRLife). I always knew even as a child that I had a purpose and passion, but all my life could never find it. That's when I decided I wanted to be of service to others I knew that I'd found my passion."

Mia became known as the Passion Muse, sharing her story as the host of her radio show, KeyNote Empowerment Speaker, and became a well-recognized transformational self-love coach and author. In 2013 Mia married her soul mate. Not only was she able to manifest losing the weight like she'd envisioned, but she also manifested the man (#HBRLife). And in 2015 she started *BellaMia Magazine*. "I wanted to create something that taught women how to love themselves. Our motto is 'Every Woman is Beautiful.' We are teaching women to love and appreciate their bodies and themselves where you are right now."

MIA'S ADVICE TO YOU

"Losing weight is like anything else; it's all in your mindset (#ThinkIT). You have to stay on your game all the time. If you take your focus off your goals the results go away (#TheHustle)."

MIA SAENZ is the Editor-in-Chief and Publisher of *BellaMia Magazine*, a leading self-love coach and media host. She lives with her husband in Southern California. Follow her journey on: **Twitter:** @thepassionmuse **Facebook:** Mia Saenz **Website:** www.miasaenz.com

TAVIO HOBSON'S STORY

I met Tavio when I took Kanen to my friend's annual charity basketball camp, where he was coaching. Since then I've watched firsthand as Tavio has hustled harder than just about anyone I know to reach his dreams. He's truly an inspiration to me.

"My story began before I was born," Tavio told me when he called for our interview. "My grandfather was raised on a farm in Arkansas in an era when most people of color were not taught to read and write. But his parents believed strongly in the value of an education and taught him to read the Bible. When he was drafted by the military in World War II, he was placed with all the black men and an officer asked if anyone knew how to read and write. Having that knowledge is what kept my grandfather out of direct combat because those skills were so sought after. He was committed to making sure his kids were also educated so that they could have similar advantages.

"My grandfather was one of eleven siblings. He moved his family across the country to Seattle in search of a better life, hoping there would be greater opportunities for people of color than what they knew in Arkansas.

"I grew up in a home with my parents, siblings, and grandparents. My grandfather has always been such a strong example of leadership in my life. Even though he wasn't a high school graduate, his children were, and I was able to graduate college. In 2015 I earned my master's from Georgetown University, even though it meant making constant cross-country trips for a year to get it done."

Tavio was raised in Seattle's inner city, and watched his family struggle to keep the bills paid. "We didn't have a lot, but it never felt like we were missing out. There wasn't a high value placed on material things; instead, education was the most important thing to my family," Tavio said.

His parents separated when he was very young, and he continued to live with his mother and grandparents. "Sports is what kept me focused during that time. My mom always said, 'You gotta go to church every Sunday and keep your grades up if you want to play sports.' Playing sports kept me from getting into trouble the way some of my peers did.

"As I started finding my passion, I looked around and I didn't see a mechanism for kids of color to stay on the straight and narrow. Growing up my dad ran a nonprofit for several years, and I worked for various youth development programs throughout my life, so I had been around it. My mom volunteered at the church working with kids, and I was fascinated by the idea that people could impact and change a community. That's how I got the idea to start my nonprofit A PLUS Youth Program (#DreamIT).

"My goal was to start with what kids are passionate about, and then give them everything else. If you are able to engage them through activities they love like sports, then they are more inclined to stay on the straight and narrow. I started with a basketball program because that's what I knew and was most passionate about. I'd just finished playing at Sacred Heart University, and rather than focus on the next level in that sport, I was ready to move on and make a positive impact on my community back in Seattle (#BigPictureDream)."

Tavio's nonprofit began to quickly grow, offering the kids in Seattle mentorship, positive role models, leadership skills, teaching self-advocacy, and financial literacy. "A quality education is the ultimate equalizer in our society," Tavio told me. "We not only offer sports programs for kids, but we teach them the life skills that will create lasting success (#HBRLife)."

By the time Tavio was twenty-five, he was the Executive Director of his flourishing organization. "I never thought I'd be doing what I'm doing at such a young age. I've been fortunate to have the support of people in my community who enabled me to pilot this program and get it started.

"I've learned so much along the way. We started with twenty-five kids in our pilot program, and from that we were able to turn it into a full program after the first year. The community's support has been amazing, and we had donors lining up as we transitioned into a fully staffed organization."

Tavio brought in a trusted staff to help him grow and scale his organization. "We looked strategically into how to build a sustainable program and came up with a plan for the next eighteen months, then five years (#WriteIT).

"I have always tried to hire people who are smarter than me, who could replace me in my job. That way I know I can trust their judgment because they are smart, capable, and I value their opinion. Without that team you can't get where you want to go (#ChangeYourCrew). When I started A PLUS I thought my contribution was being really good at basketball and mentoring kids, but I needed a team to help build the business platform and help me take it national. Start with what you're good at, and then start building your team," Tavio said.

A PLUS has expanded to serve over fifty schools in fourteen different school districts. The organization has received sponsorship and support from an A-list of sports superstars including Magic Johnson, Steve Ballmer, Brandon Roy, and Pete Carroll, among others.

"I feel so fortunate to be doing what I love every day, and working with people who are as passionate and motivated to make a difference in kids' lives as I am. It's an inspiring environment to be a part of. I feel so humbled to be given the responsibility by parents to help their child."

Since Tavio prided himself on hiring people that were smarter than him, he felt comfortable with his succession plan that enabled him to accept a job with the LA Clippers as a Corporate Partnership Manager. His next chapter in life is yet to be written, but he is determined to achieve similar success with the Clippers that he had with A PLUS.

TAVIO'S ADVICE TO YOU

"My hustle is this ... I very rarely sleep (#TheHustle). All the things that need to get done can't be accomplished in a forty-hour workweek. When you're trying to establish something, you've gotta be prepared to do the work needed to achieve balance. Balance is earned. You've gotta be willing to live an unbalanced life until you get to the part when you can afford the luxury of balance (#RelentlessPursuit)."

TAVIO HOBSON is the founder and former Executive Director of A PLUS Youth Program based in Seattle, Washington. He served as the Corporate Partnership Manager for the LA Clippers. He's a former college basketball player at both Boston College and Sacred Heart, and received his Executive Masters in Leadership at Georgetown University in 2015. Follow his journey on **Twitter:** @TavioHobson and **Instagram:** @TavioHobson

*CREATEAMOVIEIN
YOURHEAD

STEP 5: #SEEIT

"What you imagine, you create." —Buddha

#CREATEAMOVIEIN YOURHEAD

Now that you've identified your dream life and written it out, it's time to vividly imagine it becoming a reality. Call it "visualization" or "daydreaming," but every successful person I've ever met has credited their ability to create a visual movie in their mind as being a key part of their success. In fact, it is something they do naturally as part of their daily life; it's simply *who they are*. The dream is not words, or a fleeting idea to them; it's an actual living, breathing part of their life.

EXAMPLE #1

When I was a little girl I loved creating movies in my head. I didn't watch TV at all growing up, so the first "movies" I saw were ones I created. I had a very unusual and difficult childhood, so "daydreaming" was a way to escape the reality of my life. It was about the only thing that made me feel in control. In my "daydream" I could choose to exchange my difficult reality for the positive narrative I built in my mind. I spent hours each day on these mental movies, filling them with elaborate details, each time adding new elements to the story. The amazing thing is that it may have taken me thirty-four years before I began to see those dreams come to life, but my life today is basically exactly what I "daydreamed" when I was a kid.

The power of visualizing your future cannot be overstated. You will see it appear in almost every story featured in this book. People from all walks of life, pursuing all types of dreams, used this same tool to create their future before they lived it.

#CreateAMovieInYourHead takes the concept of "daydreaming" to the next level. To get the best results, it's important to be deliberate and focused on your #BigPictureDream. You have already started this process by creating your #BucketList and #LifePlan. The #BucketList was meant to get your imagination stimulated, which automatically puts your mind to work creating your movie. In that exercise you were given free rein to imagine many different, pleasurable, exciting, and happy moments that you want to experience in your life. It was less of a "plan" and more of a way to get you excited about the possibilities the future holds for you, sort of a super awesome checklist for your life. When you created your #LifePlan you began to make a life that would include and allow for the experiences on your list.

This is the next step—channeling that creative, happy, imaginative plan into mentally living your dream.

It's taking the time to imagine a moment, one you want to live out so bad that it's almost an obsession. You think about it constantly, in excruciating detail. You know everything about that experience. What you're wearing, who you're with, what the day is like, what it will feel like, the emotions you'll experience—all of it is crystal-clear in your mind. And each time you think about it, you are playing that movie. Over time more and more details emerge as you build it out. When you allow your mind to go to this special place you can't help but feel a sense of joy and hope for your future. That feeling reinforces your dream, bringing you back for more, and that is what speeds up the process of you manifesting it into a reality.

That "feeling" is the *magic ingredient* in manifesting. It comes from the core of you, an authentic, pure place that is reflective of what makes your heart happy.

The #HBRMethod is based on the idea that we are creating our ideal, best life. One that lives up to our potential, fulfills our desires, brings us joy in every area, and makes us better. It is NOT focused on material "things" or money. I believe this key difference is what enables the #HBRMethod to work so effectively and quickly.

For example: if your motivation is to get a new car or a fancy house, this will not work. But if instead your motivation is to be the type of person who's successful in his or her career, and achievement of your dream has led you be able to afford a fancy house and new car, then we are on the right track. It may seem like a small difference, but it's actually HUGE. I want you to start creating the movie in your head that sees the #BigPictureDream and your successful life. That life and success will naturally create a lifestyle that enables and sustains the material objects you desire; they are the reward for your hustle.

EXAMPLE #2:

If you hand a lottery ticket to someone who's been broke their entire life, has no ambition, and never expected anything from life, what will happen to that person a year or two after winning the lottery? They will have blown all that money on the fancy house and car, right? They based their idea of happiness on what money could buy; it's not long before they are right back where they started. Broke with nothing.

This is why we don't focus on money. The difference between that person and the one who works for their dream is that the latter has vision, a plan, and desire. They know what success will look like, and they want it BAD. They have done their research, planned it out, lived those moments over and over in their head, and every time they wanted to give up, that vision is what kept them going.

EXAMPLE #3

If you ask a professional athlete if they play their sport just for the fancy cars and cool things their new money can buy, most honest ones will tell you "no." Money was not the reason they spent their entire childhood sacrificing and working harder than everyone else. Or the reason, in college, they stayed in to study plays, practice, or rest when all their friends went out partying. Or the reason they spent years, and most holidays, away from their family and friends trying to make various teams across the country as they pursued their dream. No, the cars and designer things are a side effect of, and validation for, successfully achieving their dream.

Their goal from the beginning was to earn a living for doing the thing they love. That desire to put on a uniform for the first time and take the field or the court as a professional player is what keeps them hustling and working when doors slam in their face and the odds are stacked against them. It's a life change they are working for, and the ability to say they *made it*. They do everything within their power to make sure they are prepared for opportunity when it comes. They believe it will and they move toward it every day.

When they want to quit they rely on that vision, that movie to keep them going. They play out a moment that motivates and drives them, such as the first time their name is called by the coach to enter the game as a professional; or winning the Super Bowl; or capturing a championship. Those moments are clear as day in their mind; they want it so bad they can taste it and they are willing to do whatever it takes to make it a reality.

Lucky for us, we don't have to be athletes to get the benefit of visualizing our dream. And even if you've never been a natural "dreamer," you can learn how to start right now.

YOUR HUSTLE
PART 1: Set Up

Think back to your #LifePlan and imagine yourself five years from now. In your new life money is irrelevant (#MoneyAintAThing). You are successfully living out your personal passion/dream, and the following are all GIVENS:

- You are HAPPY
- You have your dream job.
- Your friendships and social life are thriving.
- Your family is thriving and happy.
- You travel and take time to enjoy the things that bring you the most joy.
- You know how to relax and treat yourself to the finer things in life, rewarding your hard work.
- You are spending time cultivating your passion.
- If you are single and want to be married or be in a committed relationship, then that is also a reality.
- If you don't have children but want them, they are there too.
- You give and receive love.
- You are physically healthy, taking care of your body and mind.
- You are financially free.
- You give back, mentor, and make the world around you a better place.

PART 2: Create Your Movie

So now the real fun begins! It's time to get to work, time for you to make a customized mental "movie" of your #LifePlan. This exercise will bring your dream to life.

Whenever it comes to mind, try to expand it. Dream up more fabulous details and allow yourself to feel EXCITED! Who cares if your "rational" brain is telling you this will never happen? Pretend those thoughts are just a text from an annoying ex—"read" and IGNORE!

Make this mental fantasy your go-to *happy place*. When you slip into this mental movie let all the stress of how or when you are going to get there evaporate. Remember being a kid on Christmas Eve? You likely weren't worried about if or how Santa would come in the morning; you were just excited to know he WOULD be there. You probably imagined what it would be like to wake up in the morning and see the presents under your tree and it made you so excited you could hardly sleep. Let this movie of your #BigPictureDream keep you up nights with excitement in your chest.

Sit someplace quiet, without distraction, and close your eyes.

Choose a day, an average old day, in your future life. Start with the first thing you do in the morning, and walk through the entire day—work, school, kids, home, and so on. Try to imagine with intense detail everything about that day.

Before you answer each of the following questions in your journal, I want you to imagine the answers first. Take your time with this exercise. Let your mind really wrap around each question; let it create and awaken your childlike imagination.

So, it's five years into the future and you're looking forward to a very "average day."

Who are you?
- What kind of man/woman are you in this new life?
- You have become the best version of yourself in these five years, so what does that mean?

- You are successful and happy, so what does that look like?
- What do you physically look like? Note: You look different/better in the future, but in what ways? What do you ideally want to look like? (Would you want to be in better shape? Have better style?) Think of people you admire who are successful; how do they dress and present themselves?

Where do you live?
- City?
- State?
- Country?

What does your home look like? Picture all the details of it, inside and out. How does it look and feel first thing in the morning? Or when it's filled with friends and family for the holidays? Or when you're barbequing with friends in the summer? What's your favorite room in the house and why? What does that room mean to you?

> **Example:** Mine would be the kitchen. It will be light and airy, a mix of country chic and modern charm. I'll always be cooking in that kitchen, for my crew. It will be the room in the house where everyone wants to hang out, talking, helping, drinking wine. That room will radiate love and togetherness and make me happy to wake up every morning.

- What kind of car do you drive?
- Do you have animals?

What are you doing that day?
- Are you cooking breakfast for your family in the morning, before they leave for work and school? Or are you just coming back from vacation? Or headed

to work? What will an "average day" look like for you? What types of activities fill your days?

- Who are you doing it with? Is your family with you? Extended family? Best friends? Significant other? Children? Spouse? What do they look like in five years? How have those relationships grown and matured over time?

Where do you go for vacation?

- Have you traveled, and if so, where have you gone? Where are you planning to go and with whom?

Where do you work?

- You have your perfect job; so what is it?
- Do you work from home? Or in a fancy office?
- Are you a boss, or your own boss?
- What do you love about your job?

What is your relationship status?

- Are you married, divorced (hey, maybe that's your goal; no judgment, believe me!), in a committed relationship, engaged?
- What does your significant other look like? Where do they work? What do they do? What type of person are they, and how has your relationship grown (if you see yourself with the same person in the future) over time?
- If you are not currently in a relationship, what EXACTLY are you looking for in a potential mate?
- Do you have children? How many? What ages?

Continue to map out every area and category of your life. Grab your journal and write down the answers to each of those questions, using as much detail as possible. This movie will feel very unrealistic to you at the moment. The more unrealistic, the better—as long as it's aligned with your true self.

Write down in your journal how completing that exercise made you feel. Was it liberating? Exciting?

Did you notice your new movie isn't about getting "things" for the sake of having *things?* It was about experiences, moments, and memories.

#FUTUREBOARD

"Vision Boards" are all the rage lately. Spend a few minutes online to Google them, and you'll find hundreds of "experts" trying to sell you an audio book claiming the secret to manifesting. But the majority of people who've made a board, or followed those teachings, don't have success in manifesting their dreams. That's because most boards are nothing more than a pretty collage hanging on the wall (or tucked away in a closet). In my opinion, you can't have a "vision board party" or even a workshop without first laying the foundation for why we make these boards in the first place.

I choose to call it a #FutureBoard because to me that is just one more way you can apply #SayIT and claim your future. It's not a "dream board" or a "wish board" or even a "vision board." I think names mean something, and it needed to represent the true power it holds, which is the power to create and predict your future.

The homework that preceded this chapter is so critical to making a winning #FutureBoard because the whole board is built on the work you've already done in your #LifePlan and #CreateAMovieInYourHead. By the same token, it's not enough to have done all the homework up to this point and think that you can skip this step. Many of my clients feel uncomfortable doing this exercise and think it's unnecessary, or too "girly girl." They feel silly actually making a physical board with their future life on it. They are afraid of what people will think when it's displayed at home or work, and I get it. I was embarrassed and afraid, too, but me taking action and pushing through that fear and finally displaying my board was a huge reason it manifested so quickly (#CourageOverFear).

This exercise is not negotiable! YOU MUST MAKE A #FutureBoard. The physical act of getting the supplies, picking out pictures, and then applying them to your board are all critical elements in manifesting. It's the progression from a thought to its represented physical equitant, and each of those physical actions sets the Universe in motion to make it your reality. You will also notice that when you're finished, this life that felt "crazy" in the beginning is starting to feel like your future.

Stop reading until you are able to do this chapter's homework. Here is what you will need to complete your #FutureBoard:

1. Internet access and a Pinterest account.
2. A cork board roughly 2x3 feet (medium size), available at all office supply stores.
3. Pins or tacks to hang your pictures and clear tape.
4. Access to a color printer.
5. Access to Microsoft Word or similar blank-text document.
6. Nails and a hammer to hang your board.

This board is the visual representation of the life you are creating, so the key is to find pictures on Pinterest that best depict that life. I love Pinterest because you can find beautiful images of anything! You can also find great motivational quotes to add.

Break your board out into the following categories:

1. FAMILY LIFE AND RELATIONSHIPS

Here you'll want to represent what your *movie* already created around your family life. If your future life has kids and a spouse, find photographs that represent your life together. This section can also represent your social life with friends and extended family.

For those of you who want to find love, be married, and/or have kids, this section is especially critical. Be sure you take the time to identify what you want in your mate and fine photos that represent those qualities. I often print out great relationship quotes, or make my own list of qualities, typing and formatting them in Word (or a similar program), then printing them to add with the photos.

Tip: the better you can identify what you want, the more you will draw it to you.

Photo Example: If marriage is your dream you can put a picture of a wedding ring, a bride/groom/wedding couple, or a wedding thank-you note. The goal of using photographs is to trigger your mental movie so that when you see the images every day your brain will automatically recreate the movie and get you excited.

2. WEALTH AND FINANCES

What elements did your movie include when it came to "things money can buy"? What does "financial freedom" mean for you? "X" dollars in the bank? Retirement at a specific age? Investment accounts? Good credit? No debt? A new car? A boat? What would you be able to do if money were not an issue?

Photo Examples: Because we are focusing on experiences, if you're putting up a picture of a new ski boat, for example, it's not necessarily about the boat itself, at least not yet. The #CreateAMovieInYourHead needs to focus on the memories you'll make with your family on the boat. Because manifestations happen in levels, your first one (#MoneyAintAThing!) might be a day out on the lake skiing on a friend's boat. That will be a total #ManifestThat! moment where you are filled with gratitude and joy. Then level two might come down the road when you actually buy a boat (#HBRLife).
See the distinction?

Note: Be sure you have a movie for each image that's focused on what that moment will be like to live out.

3. HEALTH AND WELL-BEING

It's so important to feel good about yourself from the inside out, and to focus on your physical well-being. When you exercise on a regular basis you have more energy, clearer focus, higher confidence, less stress, and even more reason to be joyful. Make a section of your board that is devoted to being active and healthy.

What do you enjoy doing when it comes to physical fitness? Tennis? Running? Yoga? Walking the dog? Whatever it is, find images that represent this part of your life, and who you WILL to be in five years. They should be the "ideal you."

This is also the section for faith, meditation, or whatever you do to renew your spirit and gain strength. I believe we all need to find something that speaks to us, whether it's prayer, faith in God, or the Universe; something that gives us direction, guidance, hope, and peace. For me I draw strength from several different practices: prayer, #Hustle-BelieveReceive—which has really been my belief system the past six years—and yoga, which is very centering for me. But whatever you believe in, make sure that it's represented on your board. Nurturing this helps our plan be a holistic lifestyle change that propels us forward.

4. TRAVEL AND LEISURE

I believe that everyone should travel, even if it's just outside your town or state. Travel has an amazing ability to open your mind to new possibilities and helps us stay grateful. It reminds us to live in the moment and be open to new experiences—all things that are core to the #HBRMethod. You don't have to go across the world to experience the benefits of travel; just go someplace new and look at life through fresh lenses. I'd like you to start making travel and vacations a part of your life, and have at least six "must-see" global destinations on our #FutureBoard. Try to match them with items you put on your #BucketList.

Even if you can't leave your hometown right now, commit to exploring something new about where you live. Make time to relax and enjoy the finer things in life; after all, that's what successful people do—they work hard and play hard.

5. CAREER AND PASSION

Where do you see your career in five years? Will you work in a big office? Downtown? A studio in your backyard? What's your ideal career? What does someone who's successful in that career look/act like? It's also a great idea to start thinking about people you might know in that career who could mentor you.

If your passion isn't one you can turn into a living, than it's still one you can foster and make an important part of your life. We are happiest when we are doing what we love, so make sure your passions are represented on the board as well. What is your passion? What would it look like if it had prominent placement in your life? What activities would you do? Look for images that represent your passion at its height of success.

Note: If you do not currently have a solidly defined passion that's okay! Think of your entire #LifePlan as your passion for now. And add photos of items from your #BucketList to this section.

INSTRUCTIONS

Once you have found beautiful photos that represent your new life, it's time to put them on your board. On Pinterest you can save the photos to print them individually, or I like to copy and paste them to a blank Word document. That way I can adjust the size of different pictures so my board will have visual variation.

When all your pictures are printed and cut out, begin arranging them on your board. Be sure to have several photos for each category representing multiple experiences for each. For example, in the "Travel" category put a few pictures with different desired destinations. Arrange each category of your board and begin attaching the photos. Fill in any gaps with either written or printed quotes, mottos, or mantras that inspire you.

When you are finished, your board should be completely covered (and have way more photos than words). It should energize and excite you every time you see it.

Tip: I always pick pictures that are pretty specific; that way when I manifest that moment I can take pictures proving that I created my future. Check out my Pinterest "Reality Board" for lots of side-by-side comparisons between my #FutureBoard and the depiction of me living out the moment as predicted on my board.

NOW HANG IT UP!!

You can't get away with just making it, but not displaying it. IT MUST BE DISPLAYED! Put it at your desk or somewhere you'll see every day. The more you are around it, the more its power affects your subconscious.

You don't need to devote time looking at it; you don't need to meditate on it or give it voodoo magic! It just needs to be around you. That is its "magic." It's something you see daily whether you notice it or not; over time it stops being "unrealistic" and starts looking like your future. That transformation just naturally happens over time. You start thinking, "I can't wait to go to Disneyland with my kids!" Then you start daydreaming of what that day will be like, the looks on your kids' faces when they see Mickey. Then one day you find yourself talking about it like, *when we go to Disneyland we're going to do X!* Now you AND your kids are excited, and you've decided at some point (one you might not even remember) that you are now planning a trip to Disneyland. All those little transitions are what makes your board come to life. It's that quiet progression, that slow turnaround in your brain, where you go from thinking "I can't" to "I will. I'm just not sure when."

And when you go you snap a photo of your family in front of the **Welcome to Disney** sign, which had been hanging on your board, you now have your own side-by-side reality board! Then the whole day that you are walking around Disneyland, you have this strange feeling of déjà vu as if you'd already been there living out those moments . . . and then you remember the *movie* you created of this day.

NICOLE FRENCHMAN'S #FUTUREBOARD

A few months ago I got a message on Facebook from a woman named Nicole. She said she'd found my story and blog after Googling how to make a "vision board" that actually worked, and totally related to my story. It turns out that when she was five months pregnant with her second child (her son was three years old), she also found herself suddenly a single parent with nothing, and having to start over.

I called Nicole to ask how she'd been able to make it through that experience and find success.

"One day my boyfriend came home from work and said, 'I don't love you anymore, and you need to move out,'" she told me. "It was the most devastating thing I've ever been through. To make it worse, I didn't have a job and had to move in with my dad (#EarthquakeMoment)."

After her daughter was born, Nicole decided to make a #FutureBoard and find a way to support her children. She put pictures of Disneyland and the Golden Gate Bridge on her board, along with a photo of a new car because hers was falling apart; then she went looking for work (#TheHustle). When a friend offered to help Nicole get a job, she jumped at the opportunity. But it wasn't easy; every day she fought the urge to give up, especially on the really tough days.

"I remember one day a customer was yelling at me, I didn't have money to buy lunch, and I went on my break and cried. I thought *how can I do this?* I wanted to quit. But then I thought of my friend who was very successful at the company, I thought *if she can do it, then so can I.* I just kept telling myself over and over again (#ChangeTheVoicesInYourHead) that if someone else could find success here, then I could too (#MottoForLife). I chose to change how I thought about it and decided I wanted to be successful (#ThinkIT)."

A year later Nicole was named to the company's Presidents Club and recognized as the number seven rep in the entire company (#ManifestThat!). They flew her and her son to Florida for an all-expenses-paid trip to Disney World (#MoneyAintAThing)! During the course of that year she moved out of her dad's place and got a home for herself and her children, as well as the new car (#ManifestThat!).

"You know what is really amazing?" Nicole's voice is filled with the thrill that comes when you are manifesting your dream. "My dad recently relocated to San Francisco, so I'm taking my kids to see him and the Golden Gate Bridge next month (#ManifestThat!)!"

We chat excitedly for a few minutes about how things work out, how at first manifesting seems like a natural part of life and you almost don't even realize that *you* made it happen. "I didn't even really think about my board, Sarah. That's the crazy thing! I just had it on my wall and printed more pictures of Disneyland and put them on my fridge. I didn't obsess over how I'd make it happen or worry about it. It was like a goal I was working towards, a reward for my hard work that someday I'd experience."

And that, my friends, is how a #FutureBoard that is based on the life you want to create comes to life.

Facebook: Nicole Frenchman

#HBRSTORIES

JOSUE LOUIS

ANDREA WEINBERG

MARC ANTHONY NICOLAS

JANNA ANDREWS

JaTARA WRIGHT

JOSUE LOUIS'S STORY

I first "met" Josue through Instagram in 2013. He'd commented on one of my #FutureBoard posts and told me how much my story was inspiring him to pursue his dream of becoming an Olympian. A year later when I was in New York, he met my friend Lisa and me for drinks, and I learned more about his story. Since then I have coached Josue, and we've become great friends. He was even kind enough to accompany me to Victor Matthews's gallery opening in LA.

This is his story.

"My parents migrated to the US from Haiti in 1980 to build a better life for their five children and to create the American Dream. Much of my ambition and work ethic comes from my parents and watching how hard my dad worked to have his own business.

"Growing up, we lived in a two-bedroom apartment, the seven of us and my grandma. My dad worked three jobs and my mom worked two. Even as a child, I knew that was not the life I wanted. It was hard watching them struggle like that; my dream was to be able to take care of them one day. That was my motivation (#BigPictureDream).

"When I was twelve, my father was able to buy his own limo and taxi business, and it just made me believe that anything was possible (#ManifestThat!). My parents taught us that an education was the key to becoming successful, so I focused on school instead of a social life. My older brother was a huge track and football star and I was always under his shadow. So I chose my own path and went into the arts—dancing, acting, and singing.

I wanted to be a Disney kid (#DreamIT), and for about seven years I was solely focused on dance, shows, and recitals; it was my life. My dad had been driving me to and from dance, but told me he couldn't do that any longer because it was conflicting with his business, so I had to give it up.

"On my 14th birthday, I remember locking myself in the bathroom because I just wanted to be alone. I was so depressed and felt lost without performing and dance (#Earthquake-Moment). I channeled that disappointment and frustration by following my brother to track practice at seven A.M.; he let me work out with him and encouraged me to keep it up. Then in middle school I won my first medal, and for the first time in a long time I felt a sense of accomplishment.

"I set goals for myself before the season started and began knocking them down in football and track. And then I noticed that if I said something it would happen. I started to see the power my words had to predict my future (#SayIT), which made me even more driven to win."

One day his dad came home from work and said, "I'm going to buy a house. It's gonna have a pool, and you'll have your own room so you can invite your friends over to the house (#SayIT)." But Josue watched as the bills continued to pile up and didn't know how his dad could keep that promise. "I saw them struggling with my brother's student loans and I was determined to get a scholarship so they didn't have to pay for college," he told me.

In Josue's senior year of high school, his father came home and said, "Guys, I bought a house!" "I'll never forget going to see the house for the first time and the look on my mom's face was so amazing! We walked outside, and in the backyard was an in-ground pool. For years and years he'd been putting his money aside to make this dream come true for us (#ManifestThat!)."

Josue got a scholarship for track and field to Temple University, where he also played football. Each year he set higher goals for himself, visualized not only making it to the top meets, but placing in the top six. He put in the work, training relentlessly (#TheHustle), and relied on his vision (#CreateAMovieIn-YourHead) to break records. And each year he exceeded his own expectations (#ManifestThat!).

"My goal now is to make it to Rio for the Olympic Games in 2016 as a decathlete (#BigPictureDream). I train six days a week, for three to five hours a day, and that's just the physical training on the track or the pit working on my technique. I spend countless additional hours working to keep my mind right, study[ing] tape of my meets and practices, always working to get better (#TheHustle, #RelentlessPursuit).

"Not making it to the Olympics is not even something I've considered. Not even once," Josue told me (#BelieveIT).

In 2014 he moved from North Carolina (where he was training after college) to Los Angeles, to pursue his dream of training for the Olympics. "I'd never even been to California, when I moved here. I didn't have a job or anything lined up, other than a new coach. For the first nine months I really struggled to get by. It was very hard to find a job that would work around my hectic training schedule. I existed on canned food, some days not knowing if I'd even get to eat. But I just kept telling myself *I'm in a better place and everything would work out* (#MottoForLife)."

But the reality was that Josue had no income to support himself while he worked for his dream. "So I pulled a piece of paper out and looked at my life in ten years (#LifePlan). It was the first time I'd ever listed my goals for my life after competing. I wrote down everything—my family and relationship goals, my financial goals, what career I'd like to have, how much money

I'd need to retire early—I wrote it all down (#WriteIT). I'd known for years about 'vision boards' (#FutureBoard) but had never made one. That day I went to the store, bought a giant corkboard, a bottle of wine, [and] some magazines, and sat down in the living room to make my board. The more I cut out those pictures, the more excited I got. Now, every morning I wake up and it gets me going for the day. In the center of the board are the words "define your legacy." That quote gets me goin' and reminds me what I'm out there working towards every day (#BigPictureDream). It made me *hungry*. It's helped my life be more stable and taught me to have patience; it's been a huge focus for me."

With his renewed focus and motivation Josue started thinking of ways he could make money while he trained and started going on auditions. His experience in the theater and dance from his childhood gave him an advantage, as did his training physique, so he went out for some modeling jobs. "My first gig was walking in LA Fashion Week (#ManifestThat!). Even though I really didn't know what I was doing, I walked in there and owned it as if I did (#FakeIT)!"

Since then Josue has modeled for Nike commercials and done several magazine and print ads (#ItsTheJourney).

"Right now (June 2015) I'm about a year away from the Olympics. I train like a monster. My international season just started, and I have the Pan American Games coming up this summer. I am excited for this part of my dream to be realized. With every meet so far I've learned how important my mental hustle is.

"People say all the time that 'practice makes perfect,' and they think it's just about physical practice, but if you don't have the mental side synced up to your physical, then you won't have a perfect performance. If my mind isn't prepared to be on the same level as my body, then my thoughts will sabotage my body's efforts (#ThinkIT). I could do everything physically possible to prepare myself to beat anyone in the world, but if my mind isn't telling me that, or if I don't really believe it, then my body won't perform (#ChangeTheVoicesInYourHead).

"I visualize every moment of competition before it happens, walking through every aspect so that I'm prepared (#CreateA-MovieInYourHead)."

JOSUE'S ADVICE TO YOU

"You'll never know what you're made of until you put yourself in the position to be forced to rise to the next level. Take the risk."

JOSUE LOUIS is the National Decathlon Record Holder. He holds numerous records, both from his days at Temple and as a professional decathlete. He is also a model training in Los Angeles. Follow his journey on **Twitter:** @josuelouis224 and **Instagram**: @zel_ish1

ANDREA WEINBERG'S STORY

Andrea is Nikki MacCallum's best friend. After I wrapped up Nikki's interview she told me; "You have to talk to my best friend, she's a handbag designer!" I was like, "Say no more, girl!" So I looked up Andrea's website and reached out to set up our interview.

"As a little girl my favorite toy was Polly Pocket; it was this little brown case with a whole world inside. I love things with functional design, and the idea that pockets could hide so many amazing things inside.

"As I grew up I developed a sense of my own style. My mom raised me to be very nonmaterialistic, and as a result I was never one of those girls in high school and college who carried an expensive handbag. But when I was working on my master's degree I thought it was time for me to step it up and get a really nice bag.

"So there I was walking around New York City with my expensive leather bag, caught in a surprise rainstorm. I was trying to protect my bag from the rain when I had an idea for a waterproof bag cover that would fold up small enough to keep with you. Kinda like a bag umbrella, but cooler!"

That was the idea that started it all for Andrea. But the more she looked into making the bag umbrella, the more she wanted to make a really cool waterproof bag that was her own design, one with lots of functional pockets (#DreamIT).

She was inspired by her friend Ian Velardi to start designing her bag. Ian had lost his job and started his own fashion line.

"He was such an encouragement for me when I told him my design ideas, I was so inspired by what he'd accomplished.

"My company would not exist if it weren't for Ian; he has guided me at every step along the way. When I started I didn't even know what a pattern was! He sat down and patiently walked me through all the steps.

"Having a mentor was *everything*. I didn't have it all planned out when I started; I just wanted to move forward. I wasn't afraid to ask for help. When I didn't know something I looked around for people I knew that might have the answer, and I asked for help. So many people have been amazing mentors and helped me along the way. I think the meaning of our lives comes from what we can give to others (#ChangeYourCrew).

"When I started working on creating my bag, I had zero background in manufacturing, clothing, or fashion design. I just started working and figuring it out as I went along. (#CourageOverFear) My company officially started almost two years ago, even though I began working on the idea five years ago (#ChillOut).

"At my very first art market I didn't sell a single bag. But a woman came by my table and said she'd think about it; as I was packing up to go home, she came back and bought the first bag I ever sold. (#ManifestThat!) I don't know what I would have done if she hadn't come back—doubt was really starting to creep in. But that kept me going.

This hustle is so intense. It's physical, emotional, and even spiritual, and it's every day (#TheHustle). It's lonely; it's around the clock. It's exhausting. I've had a full-time corporate job the entire time I've been hustling to build my company, and it can be overwhelming. But now I have an office and a full-time employee. The most gratifying part of this journey has been when I get messages from my customers saying how much they love their bag. That encouragement always seems to come when I need it the most (#GetGrateful). I remember a day when I was trying to figure out how to make ends meet and working out issues with the factory, I was so stressed and frustrated, and in the middle of all that I got a call from a customer who told me how much she loved her bag. You hold on to those positive signs.

"There is something in me that drives this passion for what I'm doing. I really believe that this is my way of giving my talents to the world. I truly love my products and believe they make people's lives better, and I've found my creative outlet. I am passionate about design and building my brand; I really love the whole process.

"It's easy to get discouraged if you are comparing yourself with others, so I'm constantly reminding myself that my business is on my path, not anyone else's. My goal has been to grow slowly and strategically. Right now I'm working on bringing in people I trust to help me scale my business.

"My dream now is to grow into a global brand that includes active wear and spreads the message to women everywhere, to be good to themselves. That is the core value at the heart of my brand, penetrating the market with that message. Life is beautiful and I want to help women enjoy life. Having that as my company credo forces me to live by the same motto. (#MottoForLife)

"I believe that every day we have a choice to be negative or positive. I try to call out negativity when I see it, even when it's in myself. I look at it compassionately and that often allows it to subside, making way for positivity (#ChangeTheVoicesIn-YourHead). I try to smile, help other people, and be cheerful. I choose to see things as not a coincidence. A gratitude practice is everything (#GetGrateful)! It's so easy to get down and frustrated; when I'm down I say three things that I'm grateful for.

"I've always visualized my success. I've had vision boards (#FutureBoard) on my wall in my house and my office for about eight years, and I've manifested so much from them! The first board I made had a photo of Palm Island in Dubai, a big plane, a Swedish Cruise logo, a sign that said 'California Dreamin,' and a woman in a suit. During my master's program I actually went to Palm Island and traveled the world, taking huge planes overseas, and took a cruise in Sweden; I spent a lot of time working in California, and became the woman in a suit working in the corporate world. It's basically all come true!

"When I made my board and I chose photos that pulled me and spoke to me.

"The idea that it's your future is so powerful (#FutureBoard)!

"When I first started I remember visualizing that my friend and I were in a room packaging up all my bags to ship to clients (#CreateAMovieInYourHead). About a year later that actually happened! I had this amazing moment where I remembered imagining it, and then I was living it (#ManifestThat!)."

ANDREA'S ADVICE TO YOU

"Make sure your movement is forward and not side to side. Sometimes when you only see your end goals it's easy to get discouraged, so focus on what's next. One step at a time (#TheHustle)."

ANDREA WEINBERG is the Founder and CEO of ANDI New York, a smart casual accessories line. Her bags can be found in Equinox, Madison Square Garden, and boutiques around NYC, Florida, and California, as well as on her website. Follow her journey on **Twitter:** @theandibrand **Instagram:** @theandibrand **Website:** www.andinyc.com

MARC ANTHONY NICOLAS'S STORY

I was in LA for meetings when my phone rang. It was a Southern California number, so I did what I never do—I answered the phone. I was surprised to find Marc Anthony, a producer for the CBS show "The Talk," on the other end.

He'd chosen me several months before to tape a small viewer segment for "The Talk." For some reason (everything happens for a reason), that day he remembered me, and wanted to see if I'd be interested in being on the show the next morning. Unfortunately I would be on a plane then, but before he hung up I took the opportunity to tell him about this book (#CourageOverFear). He immediately pulled up the website, and I asked if he'd be willing to share his story with all of you. I'm so grateful he is a part of this project, because his story blew me away!

"I was born in the Philippines to very poor parents," he began. "They left me with my grandparents when I was two years old to move to California. They wanted to start a better life for us but needed to find jobs and a place to live before they could come back for me. When I was four years old they brought me to America.

"I didn't speak any English when I came to California, and they really wanted me to learn it quickly. They had no money; we were so poor, living in a one-bedroom apartment in LA. My mom was a banker and a hotel maid, and my dad worked in a manufacturing company. They both worked so hard that they hardly ever saw each other. But they understood the importance of a good education and wanted me to go to a private school so I could get the best chance at the American Dream.

"They stayed committed to their dream of having me graduate from a private school, and enrolled me in an all-boys high school. I was bullied and teased as a teenager; I was kinda nerdy, and the boys in school could be really cruel. I was a quiet, shy, and introverted kid who tried to stick with my friends to avoid being pushed, teased, and bullied (#EarthquakeMoments).

"But it did make me stronger because those scars and flaws have made me who I am. And yes it did make me cry, and I was too scared to defend myself, but I always had the support of my parents."

Marc Anthony's parents wanted him to be a pharmacist. It was a respectable career, one that would provide stability and make them proud, and so he first became a pharmacy assistant. "I was promoted not long after I was hired, and by all accounts had a great job. But I was unhappy and so miserable," he told me. "So I decided to quit the pharmacy and become a waiter at a pizza restaurant (#CourageOverFear)." He laughed.

"I always wanted to live a life that I wouldn't look back and regret anything. I'd rather fail at something than not try it at all. People are miserable because they don't take chances or a leap of faith; they just take the safe road and that brings misery and unhappiness."

Marc Anthony's passion was working in TV (#DreamIT) and he began sending his resume around to all the networks. A few years into waiting tables and searching for a job in TV, one of his coworkers quit the restaurant to become a production manager for a reality show. "I asked her to think of me if anything came up (#SayIT), and a few weeks later she called. She said there was an assistant position open on her reality show and asked if I'd like to interview. I got the job (#ManifestThat!)!"

Though Marc Anthony was ecstatic to finally have realized his dream of working on a TV show, the job only paid minimum wage. And even worse, it was sixty miles each way to the shoot. Plus it required working extremely long days with just one day off each week (#TheHustle). "The job didn't pay enough for me to cover my rent, and the location was so far away that it didn't make sense to keep my apartment, so I began sleeping in my car (#RelentlessPursuit)."

Every day he worked from 5:00 A.M. to 5:00 P.M. on set and then headed to 24 Hour Fitness to shower and get cleaned up. Then he'd go back to his sleeping bag in the car. "The night-time was bad for me because it was not a good neighborhood. People were always on drugs or drunk, roaming around outside. I'd be awake all night in my car because it was so scary.

"I knew that ultimately my dream was to become a producer and talk show host (#BigPictureDream). But there were times when it was 2:00 A.M. in December and I was cold, those moments you're kinda like *what am I doing?* And there were times when I thought about quitting, but I had to compare my future with my past and I was not willing to go back."

Despite those difficult times, Marc Anthony was still so happy to be finally doing what he loved (#GetGrateful). He began working to build relationships with the producers, and realized that's what he really wanted to be doing (#DreamIT). "One of the producers said she loved my energy; when the reality show was finished she asked me to come to MTV with her and offered me a job in casting. When she eventually left, I got her job as the casting producer (#ManifestThat!)! I thought I'd stay there forever! I loved it! I mean how much cooler does it get than MTV back then?" He laughed.

But two years later Marc Anthony got the opportunity of his life. "I got a call from the *Tyra Banks Show*, [which] wanted me to interview for a job as a booking producer. I was obsessed with *Top Model* and couldn't believe how crazy the Universe works because I was so into Tyra Banks!" He got the interview. But he was worried because he had no talk show experience. "I'm so grateful that Tyra gave me a shot; I was jumping up and down.

"I called my parents and thanked them for giving me the chance to come to America, for allowing me to follow my dream, and for everything they sacrificed for me. My mom was so proud and happy.

"Tyra was a great role model; she gave me so much encouragement. She instilled positivity, which made me motivated to work hard for her." Marc Anthony worked on the show for two seasons, and before the third one started Tyra had an announcement for the crew. They were picking up the show and moving it to New York City. She told the crew that they could only relocate a few producers, "And she picked me!" Marc Anthony's voice was still full of excitement.

"I sold my car [and] left my parents and family to follow my dreams (#CourageOverFear). I needed to shake up my life and take the chance. And I loved it! It was the best time of my life."

But in the fourth season of the show, Marc Anthony's life took a dramatic turn. "I got a call that my mom had stage four breast cancer. I was shaking in my office and my mind was flashing back through my life with my beloved mom. I thought of all she had done for me and everything she'd sacrificed. I needed to put my career on hold and move home to take care of her.

"Every day I stayed by my mom's side in my childhood home. Thank God I was making those memories with her because by that time she didn't have much time left. She told me how proud she was of me and said, 'I will always be with you.' I watched her take her last breath because she saw my first breath.

She died in my childhood home with me next to her. When she died, a part of me died too."

After his mother's death Marc Anthony hit rock bottom (#EarthquakeMoment). "I didn't want to do anything or even leave my room. I became a person I didn't know. I was mad at the world and got to such a dark place. I finally had to open my eyes and realize that I was not living my life, and I wanted to wake up [and] live life again."

So he called the *Tyra Banks Show* in New York and asked for his old job back (#DoIT); they told him that all the positions had been filled. But a few days later he got a call that a producer left the show and they offered him his job back (#ManifestThat!)!

When the *Tyra Banks Show* was canceled after five seasons, Marc Anthony knew it was time to start looking for a new job. He'd spent several years in New York and had loved it, but he was ready to go back to LA.

"I heard of a show getting created by Sara Gilbert and they called me in for an interview. When I got there, Sara herself interviewed me. She asked, 'why should I hire you as our very last producer?' I took everything out of me and laid it on the table. I told her that I wanted to be part of a show that I could be proud of and promised to make her proud.

"I was freaking out when she offered me the job on the spot. I called my dad and he said my mom would be so proud of me."

Marc Anthony has been nominated for an Emmy Award four times as a producer on *The Talk*.

"That was a crazy moment when I was first nominated. It's when I realized that all the sacrifices I made, even the bullying, had all led up to this. Going to the Emmys and being on TV as one of the youngest producers to be nominated, that was just crazy! And when my name was called I almost died! I am definitely living my dream (#HBRLife)."

In 2014 the Lifestyle Network was looking for new content and Marc Anthony pitched them an idea he had for his own show. "I wanted to be the first Filipino host of a celebrity show. (#DreamIT) I went to CBS to ask permission to do my own show and they said, 'Is this one of your dreams?' I told them it was, and so they were very supportive (#SayIT)."

Marc Anthony's show, *On Your Marc*, was picked up by the Lifestyle Network for six episodes the first season, and thirteen more for the second season. It is now (2015) in its third season.

"You can live two dreams and at the same time. I am just loving every single day (#GetGrateful). I would not trade anything for it. I'm going to let my light shine, and never let anyone take that light.

"I wanted to give a tribute to my mom on my show, so my tagline is 'believe in yourself,' something she always told me.

"If it happened to me, it can happen to anyone (#BelieveIT)."

In June, 2015, Marc Anthony made one of my major dreams come true! It was the most full-circle #HBR moment of my life! I'd flown to Los Angeles for work and texted him to see if he could grab lunch. I wound up arriving in Studio City two hours early planning to work at Starbucks across the street from the CBS lot. But I got a text from him that he'd left a pass for me at the security gate so I could come watch the live taping of his show *The Talk* (#ManifestThat!).

I was ecstatic! Words can't give this moment the justice it deserves. I tried to live in the joy of every second as Marc Anthony let me stand with the producers and camera crew while the show went live on CBS. One year before I'd submitted a fifteen-second clip that aired on the show, and here I was in person getting a full backstage, all-access VIP tour of the show and being personally introduced to the producers. It was surreal, to say the least. All I can say is that you never know what can come out of the little decisions you make, and that extra effort you put in can change everything (#TheHustle). When opportunities come, jump on them! And relish the joy they bring (#GetGrateful).

You can watch my video of that moment on YouTube and see the pictures on my blog post "CBS The Talk . . . A Dream Come True."

In 2016, Marc won his first Emmy Award as a senior producer for The Talk on CBS. In 2018, he won his SECOND! #ManifestThat!

MARC ANTHONY'S ADVICE TO YOU

"Don't let anyone put a ceiling in your sky (#BelieveIT). Be authentic and be yourself. Stay true to who you are because people will try to change you. Don't ever change for anyone.

"And remember dreams don't work unless you do (#The-Hustle). If you have a dream of being an actress or singer and you're just sitting at home, it will never work. I was willing to be homeless and sleep in my car to make my dream come true. Be willing to do whatever it takes (#RelentlessPursuit).

"I've had the same friends for ten years because when you find success people will try to ride your coattails (#Change YourCrew). I had to cut so many people from my life because they were not positive. They say it's lonely at the top, and it can be, but not if you surround yourself with a few people who really love and support you."

MARC ANTHONY NICOLAS is a producer for the CBS show *The Talk*. He is also the host and creator of the Lifestyle Network show *On Your Marc*. In 2014 he was nominated for his fourth Emmy Award, and was named to the "2013's Most Influential Filipino Americans" list by the *Philippine News*. Follow his journey on **Twitter:** @marc_nicolas and **Instagram:** @marcnicolas7

JANNA ANDREWS'S STORY

I met Janna at her charity event Kicked It In Heels, in New York City. I'd been invited by Kimberley Hatchett, and it was the first red carpet event I'd ever attended. I knew right away that I wanted to hear Janna's story, and she didn't hesitate when I asked if she'd be willing to share it with us.

"I've wanted to be a doctor since I could walk," she began. "I remember watching *The Cosby Show* as a child and being inspired by the parents who were a doctor and a lawyer, and whose daughter was going to Princeton. That became my dream, to become a doctor and go to Princeton (#DreamIT).

"My mother was my first mentor. She was a single mom who never put limits on me and always supported my dreams one hundred percent. She worked very hard to support me, and always said she would pay for my education, even when I told her I wanted to go to Princeton! I grew up in a community with little racial diversity, and I didn't realize until later in life how much that shaped me.

"I was fortunate in that school came easy for me. I put in the work (#TheHustle) and was accepted to Princeton (#ManifestThat!)."

After Princeton, Janna's mother kept her promise and paid for medical school at Temple University School of Medicine. "I chose Radiation Oncology, which is a very specialized field. I remember being told that I should have chosen primary medicine instead so that I could 'help my community' (meaning the African American community). I was really taken aback by that because the assumption was that black people don't get cancer.

"I was fortunate to complete a fellowship at UCSF under an incredible mentor, Dr. Mack Roach, chairman of Radiation Oncology at [the] University of California in San Francisco (#ChangeYourCrew). He gave me his complete support, which was the first time I'd had that type of professional backing. He has been a godsend in so many ways. He was very community-oriented and ran a nonprofit, in addition to having a high-profile career. I learned from watching him, how important it is to give back. He taught me that to whom much is given, much is expected."

After her residency Janna was offered a prestigious position as head of the breast cancer program for Indiana University. "Professionally, it opened many great opportunities. During that time I worked with the governor and the Congressional Black Caucus to help educate disadvantaged minorities about their health."

Janna maneuvered and politicked to serve on the residency acceptance committee at Indiana University, were she felt it was important to champion the cause of encouraging minority women into joining the field of Radiation Oncology. "I realized how important it is to have more minority representation in medicine. While I served on the committee I made sure we reviewed ALL applications. It was such a white male-dominated field that diversity wasn't part of the agenda. Being a voice for that community in an extremely competitive field was a responsibility I took seriously. During my tenure we accepted [two women, one of whom was a minority] because of their outstanding qualifications. That was an amazing feeling to be able to help make their dreams a reality."

It was around that time that Janna's mother was diagnosed with breast cancer.

"My mom was very stoic, and didn't talk about her diagnosis. Once she finished treatment I noticed that she became very angry about being labeled a 'cancer survivor.' She had always considered herself to be a healthy woman before being diagnosed, and didn't want cancer to define her.

"I wholeheartedly believe that having a positive attitude affects every aspect of your life, your health, and your outcomes (#ThinkIT). I've seen some of the most beautiful stories of survival from people facing their mortality with a positive mindset. Letting go of what they think the outcome should look like and attacking their diagnosis with a positive attitude makes a world of difference."

Janna noticed that there were not many organizations that dealt specifically with the role of cancer *survivor*; most focused on prevention. She also noticed that there was a stigma around breast cancer, and that after women had fought it, they often seemed lost and unable to regain their footing. During the fight all their attention had been on beating cancer, where before all their attention had been on taking care of everyone else. During the fight they did whatever the doctors told them to do, but once it was all over they seemed to lose their sense of purpose and direction for themselves.

"When I decided to move back home to New York, I didn't love the first job I took. I had unfortunately found myself in a very toxic and unprofessional work environment. I got [to] a place where I was beginning to dislike my job and medicine in general, and I started to think of other ways that I could move these obstacles out of my path so that I could be of service. That is when I came up with the idea for Kicked In Heels (#ItsTheJourney), an organization that supports and educates breast cancer survivors.

"My dream (#BigPictureDream) is that we can help remove the stigma and teach women how to reclaim their life after cancer. We want women to feel beautiful, sexual, and comfortable in their skin, in spite of this obstacle. It's a diagnosis that affects the entire family, and I'd like to open up that dialogue. I want women to embrace survivorship and thrive."

JANNA'S ADVICE TO YOU

"Be fearless. Be willing to take a chance, even if it means you might fail (#CourageOverFear). Set your mind to your goal and regardless of what anyone thinks go after it. If you fall, get back up (#RelentlessPursuit).

"Success is not finite. I always have a goal and a next step (#LifePlan), and I always know what I need to do to reach it (#TheHustle). Keep your success target moving (#HBRLife); when one thing is accomplished add something new.

"How you define yourself is not about one moment, it's about the LIFE you've lived(#ItsTheJourney)."

DR. JANNA ANDREWS serves on the Congressional subcommittee for radiation oncologists as well as the Health-care Access and Training Subcommittee that focuses on recruiting and retaining minorities into radiation oncology for the American Society for Radiation Oncology (ASTRO). *The Network Journal* named her one of their "40 Under 40" achievers in 2012. Follow her journey on **Twitter and Instagram**: @ jannaandrewsmd **Website:** www.jannaandrewsmd.com

JaTARA WRIGHT'S STORY

I came across JaTara's story, thanks to my Facebook post looking for successful people who'd beaten the odds. She messaged me that her story had defied many odds and that I should also reach out to Dan Felix, a personal mentor of hers.

When JaTara and I spoke I'd just quit my corporate job and was just getting the idea for this book. I wasn't sure what I was doing, but I knew I needed to hear the stories of people who'd taken the same journey and become successful.

JaTara had a great job in corporate America. She'd been mentored by the best, and despite being in a male-dominated corporate environment, she was flourishing as one of the top performers in the company.

JaTara and her then husband were thrilled when they learned she was pregnant, but she was only six months along when her baby was born. As a result, the doctors told her that her baby wouldn't make it through the night (#EarthquakeMoment). But she sat up all night holding her tiny daughter, and praying for a miracle, and God had answered her prayers. Yet still her daughter faced an uphill health battle, with several heartbreaking diagnoses, which required special attention.

After her daughter was born it wasn't long before her "perfect job" showed signs of being less than ideal. The more the duties of taking care of her daughter interfered with work, the less understanding work became. The strain of everything JaTara faced took its toll on her marriage, and when her daughter was eight years old she divorced. Now as a new single mom she was trying to do it all—balance her daughter's care with a high-pressure job, but it quickly became clear that her only option was to resign.

"As a new single mom with bills pilling up, I didn't know what I was going to do at first. But I knew I needed to be home and available to care for my daughter (#CourageOverFear). I'd spent years in corporate marketing and it was something I loved, so I decided to start my own business. The first year was really a struggle. My goal was to not lose anything, not lose our home or car or my daughter's care, and I made it. Just barely, but I made that goal.

"My daughter is my 'why.' She is the reason I refused to give up, and why I was so determined to become successful at this. She has been through so much already in her seven years. She's faced so many struggles, I just wanted to work hard and make a better life for us, one that I could control (#BigPictureDream). But every day I was walking in faith, waking up with an attitude of expectancy (#GetGrateful). I just knew it would work out (#BelieveIT).

"My driving force is always my faith; I know God created me for a purpose. I understood that there would be obstacles on the journey, but I always trusted Him, knowing He had a plan. Every day it was a challenge; I knew what I needed to do on a daily basis to make it happen (#TheHustle). I woke up every day knowing that God would provide and that the opportunity would come to me."

At the one-year mark since she quit her job, that opportunity came, bringing with it big clients (#ManifestThat!). Today JaTara is the CEO and Founder of her company Innovative Marketing, with a team of people working for her. She hopes to grow her presence to 100 reps across the country, empowering people to change their life as well (#HBRLife!). And the best part is that not only is she living her dream, but also she's able to be home and available to her daughter while she does.

JaTARA'S ADVICE TO YOU

"It's either play the victim or be victorious. It's either make excuses or make money. I've always felt that if you don't like something you make a change; if you are unhappy you have got to take control of the situation."

JaTARA WRIGHT is the Founder and CEO of Innovative Marketing. Follow her journey on **Facebook:** ms.j.tarawright **Website:** www.imagrowth.com

STEP 6: #DOIT

"The dream is free. The hustle is sold separately." —Unknown

#HBR Soundtrack: "Work" —Iggy Azalea

#THEHUSTLE

This is the chapter you've been dreading. It's the one that demands that you work for what you want. It's no wonder this step is missing from most "success" teachings; it's the scary one. It's the one that no one wants to talk about. It's not sexy. It says you can't just wish for something; you need to go make it happen. In our *I-want-it-yesterday* society, this is not what we want to talk about.

I get it.

But if you're on your hustle like everyone in this book, this is your shit right here! #TheHustle is the action that backs up everything we have learned so far. It's the chance to actually get out there and start making your dream a reality. It's all those little things we hustlers do to take our dreams from an idea to an experience.

#TheHustle is *everything*.

EXAMPLE

When I was training for my marathon, my hustle was getting up every single Saturday for six months to do my distance runs with my training group. It was not getting wasted on Friday nights with my friends. It was making sure I drank water all week and ate right. My hustle was getting my girls out of their cozy beds at six A.M. To take them to the sitter's. It was the nearly two hundred training miles I ran before I actually ran 26.2. It was the hundreds of dollars I spent on running gear and baby-sitting. It was running in the rain, in ninety-degree heat, alongside highways and on hotel treadmills. All of that is #TheHustle. It's the work you must put in *every freakin' day* if you plan on achieving your goals and manifesting your dreams.

But the beautiful thing about #TheHustle is that every one of those things, though difficult, also feels so insanely awesome when they've been accomplished. Sure, there are a million times when you want to quit and give up, but actually *doing* what you love, working toward your goal, feels so good.

As you read the stories in this book you will notice that #TheHustle comes up in every single one. I wanted to show you each person's hustle so you'd have dozens of examples of what it looks like for various dreams. There is not one person featured who had a dream, envisioned it, talked about it to their friends, and then woke up one day living it—not one. Every single one of us was willing and ready to get our hands dirty and work for our success. We are committed to doing whatever it took to make it happen.

And then someplace along the way, something amazing began to happen. The work faded to the background, and our passion took the lead. In the beginning it was our sheer hustle that kept us up nights working on our dreams when everyone else was sleeping. But over time our passion is what kept us awake even when #TheHustle was trying to get some shut-eye. Somewhere along the way our hustle became *who we are.*

#TheHustle is gritty, it's hungry for what's next, and it's never satisfied. It's tough. It gets us through when we really want to give up; it's our tenacity and work ethic.

#TheHustle is not for the lazy.

Success is not for the lazy.

You can't lose weight by dreaming about being thinner. Eventually you will have to get up and move your ass. You'll need to become physically active and change your diet; it's just how it goes. There is no replacement for putting in the work if you want lasting results over time. But the beauty of #TheHustle is that once again, over time, the person that started out hating going to the gym and eating healthy, can easily turn into a gym rat. #TheHustle transitions quickly into a passion and instead of it being something you *have to do*, it becomes something you *can't wait to do*.

MENTAL HUSTLE

I bet you didn't realize that you've already put in some serious hustle toward your dream, did you? But you have. Every homework assignment that you've completed so far while reading this book, that's #TheHustle. Every time you #ChangeTheVoicesInYourHead, that is your hustle. Every time you choose to speak positivity into your life instead of failure, you are hustlin', my friend!

The mental hustle is just as important as the physical. But I believe that what makes the #HBRMethod different than the Law of Attraction or other success teaching is that you learn how to do both. They go together. One will not work without the other. You can't just think and wish for something and expect it to happen, any more than you can work your butt off for something that you don't believe will work. Both of those scenarios end in failure and disappointment. But the combination of the two is limitless.

If you're not entirely sure what your dream is yet, or you're still struggling with your physical hustle, keep working on your mental one. Go back and read your completed homework. Keep applying the tools you are learning, and always keep thinking outside the box. It will come to you.

TAKING PHYSICAL ACTION

I believe success and the #HBRMethod is something that can be self-taught, even if you are not by nature a "hustler." Having said that, I also think that some people are wired with a degree of hustle from a very early age. That was me. I've always been "street smart" and a "hard worker." I've had the ability to hustle harder than anyone I knew, my whole life. I was never satisfied with "getting by." I wanted more and had an insane work ethic.

As a kid I would crochet blankets, scarves, and hats, then sit outside supermarkets in winter for hours trying to sell them while my parents ran errands. Or I'd pick veggies and flowers from our garden and set up a roadside stand trying to peddle them to our neighbors (who all grew their own gardens). I could be out there all day long and three or four cars would pass down our gravel road. In high school I waited tables at night and worked doubles on the weekends to pay for school clothes for my siblings and myself and to help my parents pay the bills. In college I did the same, working two jobs, often four or five double shifts a week between classes.

#TheHustle is just what I've always known. I knew from a very young age that without hard work you'd get nowhere in life.

It is all about doing every conceivable thing within your power to make it happen. Hustlers will take two or even three jobs if they have to get where they want to go faster. They will work nights while they study their craft during the day, or vice versa. In short they don't let anything get in the way of getting just one step closer to their goal.

But I have found that this step is not natural for many people. Even if they want to put in the work, they normally have no idea how to get started or what they should do. When you're starting from scratch sometimes it all seems so daunting, especially when you're focused on your #BigPictureDream, because it looks like so much work to get from where you are today to your five-year #LifePlan. Those are long-term visionary steps, whereas #The-Hustle is right now. It's all about *today*, about aligning your life to make room for your dream to come true. It's about preparation, and being ready. It's the difference between envisioning a new job, putting its description in your #LifePlan using #ThinkIT and #SayIT, vs. actually taking the next step and going out and putting resumes all over town.

It's the action that backs up the dream. It's the baby steps that close the gap between were you are now and where you want to be.

EXAMPLE

When a football player has the dream to one day play in the NFL, they don't sit back and rely solely on that #BigPictureDream. That is their long-term goal, and they count on #CreateAMovieInYourHead to keep them going when the struggle is real. But their hustle, on the other hand, is present in their day-to-day life. It's eating right, it's daily workouts, and it's studying plays. It's going to training camps or coaching kids; it's anything they can think of to stay active and be prepared. They know when the call comes in saying it's time to go, they need to be ready. They control what is within their power, and let the rest go (#ChillOut). They don't control the timing of that call coming in. They don't even control if it ever will. But they do control their dream, their faith in that dream, and the work they must put in to be ready (#HustleBelieveReceive).

THROWING SPAGHETTI AT THE WALL

Let's be honest—sometimes it feels like you're just throwing spaghetti at the wall waitin' for somethin' to stick. But at least you are taking action, and that is what the Universe is looking for. It wants to see if you really want it, and it rewards your hustle.

EXAMPLE

If your dream is a better job, then your hustle is searching the job boards daily and applying to everything that remotely sounds interesting; eventually one will call and want an interview. It's updating your resume, and your LinkedIn. It's talking to recruiters. It's telling your friends you're looking for a new job. It's reaching out to your network to help you. It's following up on every application and writing thank-you notes after every interview. And it's following up again. It's even taking a job that doesn't seem "perfect" at all, because it's what you need to do at the moment. Then it's busting your ass at that job, whether it's great, or you find out it sucks. It's making the most of every opportunity and realizing that it was put in your path for a reason, and you won't know that reason if you quit.

CAREER ADVICE FROM A PRO

Jessica Robinson is the Director of eData Practice Support at the global law firm Morgan Lewis. She oversees a team of twenty-five people, servicing twenty-nine locations worldwide. She has helped grow her division to become one of the most respected leaders in the industry. She also teaches a legal project management course at Georgetown University in the continuing education program, giving back and mentoring the next generation of leaders.

I asked Jessica to give us some career advice. Her vast accomplishments, achieved through determination and hustle, moved her quickly up the corporate ladder. I thought she'd be the perfect person to shed some light on what it takes to have a successful corporate career.

"Be the best at what you're doing, where you're at," she told me. "Even if you don't like it, still do your very best because you can learn in every situation. Constantly be learning; there's no reason you can't have new ideas and make things happen in *any role*. Find ways to be exceptional.

"Don't get hung up on a job title; just because you're in a low-level position doesn't mean that's all you can do. Step up in that position (#TheHustle). Get noticed. A title doesn't define you; always do more than your title would suggest (#ItsTheJourney).

"Being a woman with an executive role in a global law firm has allowed me to exceed expectations really quickly. I don't set my bar by what other people think, and I don't let their ideas of me define who I am. Learn what your assets are. What most people would consider a hindrance, turn that into your asset. Being a woman is an asset for me. Being black is an asset.

"If you're working in a profession you enjoy, you then need to become a brand. Find ways to be known outside your company network and bring value to your industry as a whole. Diversify your knowledge; become industry smart, not just company smart.

"My biggest lesson? Stop fighting battles that don't matter; learn when to fall back. And find ways to make life easier for your boss! That's how you make yourself invaluable."

IT AIN'T ALWAYS PRETTY

I thought I'd share a little about my hustle as I sit here today writing this book. It's one thing to dream of writing a book and it's another thing to get an agent, then get a book deal, and finally make it all a reality. Though I'm doing what I love, and this hustle is my shit, it's still ugly and lonely some days.

This is what the #RelentlessPursuit of your dream looks like in real life. It's the behind-the-scenes version. What does it take to write a book, launch a brand, and start a company, all while holding down a full-time "day job," AND be a single mom of three? This is a sample of my day. Maybe it will help give a little perspective on the hustle it takes to make your dreams a reality.

- **2:10 A.M.** My phone rang. It was my office manager in New York for my corporate job wanting to make sure we had everything lined up for the deal we'd spent the last 24 hours trying to close, which had a 9:00 A.M. EST deadline. I walked her through the plan and double-checked everything, lights still off, head still groggy, eyes glued shut.

- **5:55 A.M.** the alarm on my iPhone blasts next to my ear, and I tell Siri to call the number for my daily morning conference call with my New York sales team. This call happens *every single morning,* at 6:00 A.M. Today I have to lead the call, and I'm still so exhausted I have no idea what day it is. I rack my brain trying to clear it and remember what I'm supposed to say. I sit up in bed and open my eyes, hoping that will help. But there's no way to sound alert at this time of the day for me. Mornings are my nemesis.

- **7:00 A.M.** I wake my twin girls, pulling them out of bed. I pack lunches, make breakfast, and brew a pot of coffee. I push, I pull, I prod, and some mornings I yell. It's impossible to get these girls out the door in time, and I notice that I'm still in my robe when they are finally ready to go. I rush to throw on some sweats and drive them the four miles to school. I'm careful not to speed, as I've already gotten a ticket once, trying to beat the last tardy bell.

- **8:15 A.M.** I'm back home making Kanen breakfast and lunch and getting him off to the bus stop.

- **8:30 A.M.** Finally I'm ready to sit down and catch up on my work emails. My office is in my bedroom, and I feel claustrophobic.

- **From 8:30–12:00** I work, making calls, setting meetings, and following up on deals—grinding on my day job. In between I respond to coaching emails, Facebook messages, and I conduct interviews that can't be rescheduled for the evening.

- **12:00–1:00 P.M.** On a good day I get to go to my Barre3 workout. On normal days something comes up and I can't.

- The rest of the afternoon I finish up work, scheduling upcoming trips and booking meetings for them. I host or listen in on conference calls. I do all the things a sales rep with a national territory has to do to keep their job and make money.

- **2:30 P.M.** I leave to pick the kids up from school. On my way I check the mail. In it is a notice saying I forgot to show up for my speeding ticket court date, and what could have been a free online class is now a $600 judgment. I want to cry. Or kick a tree.

I've been carrying that fucking ticket in my purse for three weeks, with my to-do list a mile long, saying every day that I'd drop it off and take the class. But I'm always just one step behind the eight ball.

I start the car, and the light reminds me that I'm now two quarts low on oil instead of the one I was a few weeks ago. And oh yeah, my brakes need replacing and my car's warning message tells me I should drive it to the shop, that it's late for a service. I pound my head on the steering wheel and take a deep breath. I need to be in a good mood when I pick up the kids, so I try to shake it off. Some days it works, and others not so much.

- **5:00 P.M.** is dinner, then practice, or dance class, or Kanen's basketball game, or homework, depending on the day.
- **8:00 P.M.** sharp is bedtime, because on most nights I have an 8:00 P.M. coaching call or book interview.
- **From 8:00 P.M.–1:00 or 2:00 A.M.** I grind . . . and I hustle.
  - I have two months left on my book deadline, and 24 stories to write.
  - I catch up on social media, and try to keep my 900 profiles up to date.
  - I conduct book interviews.
  - I edit and rewrite the book.
  - I do coaching calls.
  - I respond to a coaching client's homework assignments.
  - I work on my business plan and my documentary movie pitch.
  - I research the best way to hire interns. Then realize I can't afford to hire one.
  - I review my list of 400 things that need to be done in the next six months before my book release.
  - I plan and stress about my book launch party.
  - I market.
  - I try to learn Photoshop so I can design my own logo. Then I resist the urge to throw my laptop in the street.
  - I pour a glass of wine. Then another.
  - I chase down the people in my book for edit notes and approvals, and I schedule interview times. (Coordinating

schedules with 51 uber successful people is harder than it looks).

- I respond to messages on Facebook, Instagram, Twitter, text, email, my blog . . .
- I blog . . . Or try to.
- I scream at my blog and wish I had a web designer because it's a technical nightmare.
- I create websites for my brands, and then recreate them.
- I plan my work trips to San Francisco, New York, LA, and DC alternating biweekly.

The days blur together. There is no night, no day, no rain, and no sunshine. Right now, in this crunch hour, there is only #TheHustle.

The only breaks are when my kids are home from school and the weekends with them, because I've made a vow to try to always be present with them. That time is sacred. The phone gets turned off. The laptop powers down. That is my sanity, because most days I wonder if I'm going crazy. Sometimes it feels like I'm hanging on by a thread; like if one of these balls I'm juggling falls, the whole lot will come crashing down.

When you work this hard, and in such an isolated manner (working from home all day every day), you take rejection harder. You notice when your friends don't respond to your text. You take it personally. #TheHustle can be very lonely. They don't say *it's lonely at the top* for no reason. You question if it's worth it.

But then you look backward, and there's no way in hell you'll go back to what you used to know. And then you look forward and it's everything that burns inside of you; you want it so bad the taste is always in your mouth.

You thank God every day for the small signs that come and they do come, even on hard days. They let you know that it's going to all pay off, that one day it will be worth it and that you are making a difference. Those rays of light fuel you like nothing else could. You hold on to them and keep moving forward.

No matter what you always keep moving forward.

How bad do you want your dream?

#COURAGEOVERFEAR

Fear is the enemy of success.

When you're on your hustle, opportunities will come your way as a result of all the hard work, but most of the time they will require courageous action. In my experience these opportunities never seem "too good to be true" or something so obvious and risk-free, at least not in the beginning phases of manifesting. Instead they cause fear and doubt to creep in and make you question everything, and it's your clear vision of your #BigPictureDream that helps guide your decisions in moments like these. That is why it was so important in #DreamIT to focus on the dream that was aligned with your true happiness, and with the core of who you are. Because that will continue to be your compass as you work toward and find success.

When opportunity calls, you will likely be faced with two options. One might make you sick to your stomach, but it also may give you butterflies. That's how you know it's the right choice, because it's aligned with your dream, even though it requires so much courage that you doubt your ability to make it. The other is the choice you make based on fear.

Maintaining courage in the face of fear is how I've been able to make tough decisions. Making those decisions has usually resulted in my greatest manifestations, or the realization of my dreams.

One of the ways I dismantle fear and anxiety is to immediately think of the worst-case scenario. I know that seems crazy, but it's because we are too afraid to really consider what would happen if the "worst case" occurred, that we allow fear to paralyze us. If instead you stare it down, take it apart, and say, *Okay, if that happens then I would be forced to do X. Can I live with myself if X happens? Will that outcome kill me?* If you can live with those answers then you know the only option is to move forward right through fear.

And if your fear is that of failure, just know this . . . failure is an illusion. There is no such thing. It is simply a necessary education on the way to achieve our dream. Failure does not exist; it is only the perceived judgment of others, as Jami Curl said. And who are those *others?* Probably haters, or people whose lives we are not trying to emulate anyway . . . I say put blinders on and keep it movin'; who cares what they think?

EXAMPLE

In May of 2014 I found myself at a very pivotal and scary crossroads. I'd spent the previous five months on #TheHustle to make my dream of sharing my story with the world a reality, but as a result things at my corporate job began to rapidly deteriorate after my appearance as a guest on *The Steve Harvey Show*. I had always known that following my passion (especially because it was so public), would eventually cross paths with my corporate life, and that time had come. It was one of those major life-changing moments when you have to decide between following your dream, stepping out on faith (quitting my job), or making a decision based on fear (staying even though I was unhappy).

I was terrified. Even though I'd done better financially in that job than I'd ever imagined, I was still a single mom, solely responsible for a family of four. I was sick for days wrestling with what to do. I knew the option of giving up everything I'd worked so hard to achieve was not one I was willing to take. I'd finally been able to see real progress, even meeting with the executive producers at HARPO and OWN TV who were interested in my story. Giving up was just never gonna happen. But on the other hand quitting my job was by all accounts ludicrous. I had enough savings to cover bills for four months without an income (something I was incredibly proud of), but after that . . . just the income from my coaching clients couldn't begin to touch my corporate salary and commission checks.

As if that pressure wasn't enough, I'd also tried for the past year to switch industries and get a job that was more aligned with my personal happiness, but all of them had fallen through. I knew if I quit my job, the chances of finding another one that would pay me even half as much was next to nothing; the job market is just that tough.

All the signs were pointing me in the direction of my dream, but fear was screaming in my face, "Don't do it! You're insane!" Yet deep down, I knew what I needed to do. That was the night I took my kids to see the Disney movie *Million Dollar Arm*. During the entire movie I felt as if the message of *follow your dream*, was directed specifically to me. When I got home it weighed heavy on me, with such a mix of fear and excitement that I decided to tweet about it, and that is how I met Ash.

I stayed up late that night and wrote my letter of resignation. I cried, and then I rewrote it. I stared at it in my Outlook and poured a glass of wine. I knew this decision would change everything. I set my laptop on the couch and turned on the TV to Oprah's Life Class, and the topic was, you guessed it . . . follow your dream.

I reached for my laptop and hit *send*.

As soon as I made that decision the most incredible blanket of peace engulfed me. I cried like a baby, rocking back and forth on the couch. I was suddenly so full of relief, like the world had just been taken off my back.

That moment, and those emotions told me I had made the right call.

The next morning is when I had the idea for this book and began setting up interviews. It seemed like every day was laced with magic and doors that had never been open to me swung wide. I busted my butt day and night to build up my coaching business and speaking business in hopes to start generating a real income. I hustled, searching for any media opportunity to get my message out there, and every day I was rewarded in amazing ways.

My old job actually offered to pay me out for an entire month after I quit, so I knew I was on the right path; things were just "magically" working out (really the "magic" was the result of my hustle the previous six months, and as well as my decision to act on courage, but it felt magical)!

Two months passed and though I was on top of the world, interviewing successful people who were reinforcing my belief that I could do this, I was starting to worry. My savings was quickly dwindling and my coaching practice was in no position to fill such a giant void. Even though I was getting increasingly nervous, I didn't doubt my dream or the process. I knew with total certainty that somehow it would work out (#BelieveIT).

That's about the time I got a call from a CEO in New York, for a company that was in the industry I'd been trying to get back in for the past year. He said a mutual friend had referred him to me and he wanted to offer me a job.

I almost laughed because the first thing that came out of my mouth was, "You realize I just quit my job, to live my dream right?" But he didn't seem to care. I couldn't believe it. This time the opportunity came *to me*, after the others I'd chased fell through. That was my cue to pay attention and hear him out. But I also knew that this time I wasn't going to put myself in a position where my dream and my "day job" couldn't coexist, so I told him; "Go Google me, and then take a few days to think about it. If you still want to hire me, I'm in."

He called two days later and offered me the job. As I write this today, in the late hours of the night, I am so grateful to have an amazing "day job" that supports my dream and enables me to pursue it. Not only that, but it allows me to travel (something I desperately wanted in my last job, but didn't have). It put me in the industry I loved and gave me the highest base salary of my entire career, three times what I made just four years before.

Acting on courage and not on fear is where the biggest rewards will lie. Once you've made your decision, peace will replace the fear and then the floodgates will open and your faith will be rewarded.

#CHILLOUT

This is going to sound crazy, but once you've committed to doing everything in your power (your hustle, and the previous steps), you need to let it go. We've talked a lot about controlling your thoughts, your words, making a plan, and creating its vision; all of those are "things" you can do daily to get closer to your dream.

But there is a piece that you cannot control. That piece is timing, and the way in which your dream will show up. As I've said before, your manifestation will probably come in a package you don't immediately recognize, that's why it's so critical to remain present and grateful so you won't miss it.

Be patient. Trust in the process.

You have no control over whether the person who interviewed you for your dream job actually likes you or not. But you can control how you presented yourself at the interview. If you're a writer you can't control when one of your stories will be published, but you can control how many submissions you send, and how good the quality of your work is.

Learning to let go of the pieces to the puzzle that you do not control will bring you peace. Your belief will kick in and remind you that one day your dream will come true. Demonstrating that trust while you are applying your hustle is what makes magic happen. On the flip-side, you will drive yourself nuts if you try to control those elements that are outside your zone. You'll start putting so much stress into *making it happen* in your specific way, and on your schedule, that you will actually be defeating the purpose. That is struggle. We don't like struggle. You have got to relax and trust the journey. Trust the process. Know it will happen when the time is right.

In the example above I was struggling to get another job for over a year. I did my hustle, but underneath all that positive hustle was a hint of desperation. I was holding on too tight, trying to solve my problem on my time. Once I completely let that go and decided to do my own thing, the perfect job literally called me. I had to get to a place where I just let it go, and decided that I'd accept whatever was meant to be.

Patience is key. One of the reasons I make sure to mention dates in my examples, is because I want you to see the timeline of #ManifestThat! It's not overnight. In my case, most have taken a year or two, from the time I defined my dream to the time I lived it. So remember that this is a lifelong process. It's not just a five-year plan; that was simply a starting point for the rest of your life.

Let the peace of knowing you're doing everything in your power replace the stress of trying to control what is not.

TIP

It is possible that you can practice all the steps and the end result will not be what you expected, at least not right away. When this happens you need to #BelieveIT with extra *oomph*, that the outcome is somehow in your best interest (even if you disagree, or can't see it yet). Trusting this will take so much stress off your back.

EXAMPLE

During the course of writing this book, there were some big-name stories I desperately wanted to interview. But people like Kevin Durant, Akon, and 50 Cent are difficult to reach, to say the least. I applied #TheHustle, searching all over the Internet for ways to reach them. I commented on their Instagram pictures, tagged them, and tweeted at them—generally just *throwin' spaghetti at the wall!* I knew that if there was any possible way that a no-name single mom from Oregon could get in front of these guys, I would find it. And sure enough, my hustle returned leads, and all the pitches at least got passed on to each of those big stars (#Winning!). I have no idea if they all actually saw them or not, but my goal was to get the pitch to them and I manifested that!

The part I could not control was if they would respond or agree to be interviewed. And it's something I let go of right from the start. I had total belief that if it was within my power, and MEANT TO BE, I'd make it happen. I'd do my part and let the rest go. If it didn't work I'd move on to the next.

You must set expectations that enable gratitude instead of disappointment. If I'd gone in with the EXPECTATION that Kevin Durant would be a featured story, and that anything less would mean I'd not succeeded, than I might have been inclined to give up on the whole project when I couldn't reach him. Instead I went in with the dream of featuring him, I did #TheHustle to do everything in my power to make it happen, but when it didn't I needed to realize it wasn't meant to be and move on to the next story. My ultimate goal was to write a book about successful people; it wasn't to write a Kevin Durant book. My #RelentlessPursuit was focused on what mattered—my end result—and my expectations were set in such a way that rejection would not set me back.

Control what you can, and leave the rest up to the powers that be. Trust the Universe/God to make the right final call.

ADVICE FROM A PRO:

Seneca Blue is the founder and Executive Director of Blueprint for Success, and a pro-basketball skill development coach. He recently launched his nonprofit organization nationwide *(Twitter/Instagram: @SenecaBlue)*.

"When you are building something and following your dream, you need to balance ambition with patience. My nationwide program launch was seven years in the making. It takes time. For a long time I thought I had to be the first one to the market with my idea, but in the end I realized I wasn't competing against other people; I was competing against myself.

"When I was in my hustle reaching out to find partners and sponsors, one was a CEO. I remember his assistant sent me an email saying they wanted to work with me, but that I needed to be patient and not bombard them. That was a good lesson for me. You have to know what the line is between being passionate and being overly aggressive.

"There is something in me that believes wholeheartedly that my dream IS GOING TO HAPPEN. (#BelieveIT) There are times when all doors seem to close, and you think there is nowhere left to go (#EarthquakeMoment), but you push through it, and that's when I see the rewards (#ManifestThat!). Whenever I start to doubt it I'll post something positive online and put it back out there, and keep going (#RelentlessPursuit).

"Make daily investments in your dream (#TheHustle). You need to be sure that your behaviors, words, actions, and daily activities align with your goals."

YOUR HUSTLE

Grab your journal and write down your hustle list. Think about your #LifePlan and your goals, then look at your life the way it is today. What can you do every single day to change your situation? There are a million things, but I need you to clearly identify twenty that you can start working on right away.

If you want a new job, what is your Hustle? *Hint: Start throwing spaghetti at the wall.*

If you want to be a writer, what is your Hustle? *Hint: Start writing!*

If you want to become a singer or an actor, what is your Hustle? *Hint: practice your craft and go on auditions!*

Whatever your dream is you need to hustle every single day to get closer to it. If you're not sure what it really takes to achieve the dream, do some research. Find out who's already accomplished something similar to you, and then learn all you can about the process they followed to get there. Most of us are not totally reinventing the wheel here; there is someone who's gone before you, and if you pay attention they've left a nice little map on how to follow in their footsteps—or at least great ideas on how to make it happen.

Identify those steps here (even if you're just guessing at this point, you can always refine it latter). Now start DOING it immediately! And don't stop until you've realized your dream.

TIP: Think outside the box. Push the limits. Get creative. These might sound like clichés, but for good reason, they are a critical part of how you become successful.

NOTE: If your dream at this stage is to change your life, then focus on your #BigPictureDream (the life you want)—what can you do TODAY that will get you closer to that life? Make a hustle list based on your #LifePlan. There is a ton you can do on a daily basis to close the gap in each category of your life.

#RELENTLESSPURSUIT

Statistics tell us that only the top 2 percent of the population are uber successful. Two percent! Why is that number so small, you ask? Because the other 98 percent don't have #RelentlessPursuit. As we've learned already there are many components to success, and each has its particular role in helping us achieve our goals and dreams, but without #RelentlessPursuit nothing else matters.

#RelentlessPursuit causes you to look at your goals, and say, *I will not stop until I've achieved them. Period.* It's that basic. Its strength comes from the moment you first made the decision to start your journey. That decision holds immense power. It holds you accountable.

#RelentlessPursuit is not sidelined by obstacles. It's not discouraged by how slowly things happen or don't. It doesn't care if the odds are a thousand to one, against us. It ignores the haters. It is that burning desire inside you that will not let you give up. It's that little voice that says, "Just give it ONE more try." It speaks up even when you've given it 200 tries and each time faced the back side of a door. It's the embodiment of *where there's a will, there's a way.* It is your will.

It's because of #RelentlessPursuit and that very last try that the door opens, when you've exhausted every other option and time was running out.

#HBRSTORIES

LAVASIER TUINEI

LISA MARCHANT

EDDIE PALMER

LAURA MUNSON

REGINALD FOREMAN

HOLY CUSTIS

LAVASIER TUINEI'S STORY

I met Lavasier ("LT" as he's known to friends and family) when I was living in Seattle and he'd just graduated from the University of Oregon. He was an undrafted NFL free agent at spring training camp with the Seattle Seahawks. He'd found me on Facebook, knowing I'd coached some of his former teammates. We've remained close friends since then. His story has always inspired me.

"My parents divorced when I was young, and I went to live with my dad when I was eight years old. That was when I held a football for the first time. As soon as I touched that football I knew I would love the game. I didn't want to put it down; I took it everywhere with me. I wanted to be just like my dad, who was playing in the NFL for the Chicago Bears at the time.

"I asked my dad to teach me how to play football, and he gave me a choice. He said, 'go to sleep tonight and set your alarm for 5:00 A.M.; if you still want to learn how to play in the morning, come wake me up and I'll train you.' The next morning I woke him up at 5:00 A.M. and we trained for two hours before school every morning all the way through high school." (#TheHustle)

Lavasier transferred schools his senior year hoping to get into a better football program, but the move backfired and he found himself ineligible to play. Without playing time there were no college scouts and no scholarships. It seemed hopeless (#Earth-quakeMoment). But his dad wouldn't let his son give up; he knew LT had talent, ability, and most importantly heart. So they drove together to colleges, and he tried to join one of the teams as a walk-on (#RelentlessPursuit).

He was repeatedly denied.

Then his dad had an idea—move LT to southern California to attend the same junior college that he'd attended and see if his son could get a chance to finally play. Things began to fall into place, and for the first time in a long time LT was back on the field doing what he loved, having fun, and turning in some impressive numbers. It wasn't long before Oregon took notice and offered him a scholarship after just one season of junior college.

But "bad luck" seemed to tail LT, and again his dream was put on hold as he worked out issues with his transfer and eligibility. It looked like his chance to play for Oregon was dead in the water.

"I felt like I was done. I couldn't see a way out; the doors had all closed. I was just broken," LT said. "I was devastated. Here I'd worked so hard, gotten this close, and was stopped by something out of my control, something the administration had done incorrectly. It didn't seem fair (#EarthquakeMoment).

"Staying and playing another year for the junior college was not at all what I wanted to do, but what choice did I have? I guess I could have quit, but that was never really an option. When you have a dream like this it's who you are; quitting's not an option. My dad always believed in me and I wanted to make him proud and show him I could do it."

A month later LT got the unbelievable news that Oregon had fought for him and he was cleared to join the team (#Manifest-That!). That spring training camp was a rough one. He'd never competed on that level, or played with athletes of that caliber before. He felt overwhelmed and under-prepared. "I sucked," he told me. "I was this skinny kid from a little school with no credibility. I was dropping every pass. It was a mess. At the end of practice I went up to the coach and asked him if I could redshirt my first year; I just felt there was no way I'd be ready to compete in the fall."

That summer after classes LT could be found at the practice facility working out or in his room memorizing the playbook. He learned the offense and did everything he could think of to be ready (#TheHustle). And when fall training camp came around he didn't drop a single pass (#ManifestThat!). By the third game of his first season he was named Oregon's starting receiver (#HBRLife).

In 2012, LT's senior year, he was named the Rose Bowl MVP. He was at the top of his game. Yet the draft came and went, and he was unsigned.

"I didn't know honestly if I would get drafted," he told me. "It's a statistics game at the end of the day, and I wasn't sure I had the numbers the NFL was looking for. When I didn't get picked up in the draft it was another major disappointment. But I still believed in my dream (#BelieveIT). I knew I'd get a chance to play in the league. I knew that a team would see my heart, my athletic ability, and take a chance on me.

"And then I got a call from the Seattle Seahawks.

"It's been a struggle. A mix of highs and lows. In the past three years I've been signed and released by the Seahawks, Bengels, Cowboys, and Patriots. It seems like every time I get my chance, I have an injury that prevents me from being a hundred percent. My body has worked against me, and I've pushed it beyond what it should have to endure, and played when it wasn't healthy. I've paid the price.

"But the lowest point came on a car ride home with my dad after I was injured and cut form the Bengels. He was so mad at me for getting injured and released. He said my career was over and that I'd never play football again. He told me I should quit.

"That broke me. Coming from someone you love so much and admire and credit for your success, that was devastating (#EarthquakeMoment).

"Now I have something to prove, to myself and to my dad. I know and believe I can make this dream happen; now I just need to prove it. And to my peers, at a certain point when you're chasing your dream and you see other people succeed, you can start to get down on yourself for not being where you want to be. It can be humbling; not everyone is going to get my vision for my life and I'm okay with that. I'm doing it because it's who I am, it's what makes me happy, and it's what I love. Sometimes you just need to tune out what other people think of your dream and just use it as fuel and motivation (#ChangeTheVoicesInYourHead).

"There's no doubt in my mind, I will make it happen." LT told me.

I asked him what his current hustle is and he said, "It's every day. Putting in the work needed to get my body healthy. I train three to four hours a day, six days a week, getting ready for that call from a team. It's also keeping my mind right; I rely on prayer a lot for that. And . . . I play dominoes! (He laughs). No matter how much you chase your dream it can never be all you do. Life is short; you need to enjoy it, have fun, let your mind relax, [and] save the next hustle for tomorrow."

LT did get the call from the New York Jets. He flew to New York and worked out for a few days with the coaches, hoping to make the team. But no follow-up call came. So he went back to his hustle, coming back to Eugene to continue training, in hopes the next call would come.

And in July 2014 it finally did. This time the call came from the BC Lions, in the Canadian Football League. LT packed his bags and moved to Vancouver, BC, excited to finally be a part of a team. For weeks he practiced, worked, and waited for his turn to play. But yet again, it never came. Instead he found himself in the all-too-familiar position of being cut from the roster.

But instead of heading back to Eugene to train like he'd done in the past, Lavisier made a decision that would change everything. He stayed (#CourageOverFear). He took a lease on a nearby apartment and decided to wait out the rest of the BC Lions season, even though he was no longer part of the team (#BelieveIT). He told the coaches he was staying in town and would be there if they needed him (#SayIT), and then he went out and looked for a "real job" to pay his rent. When he got hired at a temp agency he was grateful to be getting a paycheck. For several weeks he worked his temp job and trained himself, never questioning his belief that one day his opportunity would come (#RelentlessPursuit).

In early October 2014, it did. The Lions had lost several players to injury and found themselves desperately needing a wide receiver. The coaches remembered that LT stayed in town waiting for a chance to play, and they called him to come back to practice (#ManifestThat!).

LT was ready to go when he got that call, knowing this might be his last shot at his dream. He practiced hard, determined to prove himself to the coaching staff, in hopes they'd put him in the game (#TheHustle).

On October 11, 2014, just days after being called back to the team, and an hour before kickoff, he was told to suit up. He was starting. A few plays into the game, LT caught his first pass in a regular season game as a professional football player. The ball kept coming his way, and each time he was ready. Then the moment he had worked and bled for, believed in, and pursued against all odds, came—he scored his first professional regular season touchdown (#HBRLife).

LAVASIER'S ADVICE TO YOU

"Don't let anyone tell you that you can't do somethin'."

LAVASIER TUINEI is a wide receiver in the American Football League, and Rose Bowl MVP. Follow his journey on **Twitter** @lavasiertuinei

LISA MARCHANT'S STORY

Lisa is my lifelong bestie. We've been friends since we were two years old, back when our parents met on a quest to find God at a camp meeting. We've seen each other through everything in life, supported and pushed the other, and have remained closer than sisters through it all. Lisa went through a divorce not long after mine, and together we searched for how to recreate our lives and find our happiness.

Lisa was my first real #HBR test case. She'd watched me change my life, and our many lengthy phone conversations helped me define my beliefs and shape the #HBRMethod. So when she talked about her longtime dream of moving from Boston to New York City, I told her this was the perfect time for her to start using the #HBRMethod to manifest her dream.

I love her for embracing it fully, for trusting my coaching advice, and for doing the work every single day.

This is the story of how a timid girl followed her dream and found her power.

"I remember saying that my life felt so stale," Lisa began when I called her for our interview. "I had just gone through a difficult divorce and was trying to find my place, my happiness. I'd lived in the same area outside Boston since high school, all my friends and family were there and I was still working for my ex-husband's company. I just kept thinking that there has to be more to life than this! I tried dating and at first it was exciting, but still it felt like I'd maxed out my life there.

"I knew I needed to make a big change, and I was always drawn to New York City. The decision was bittersweet because in order to make this big change, I had to move away from my family and friends. But, the city made me feel alive again, and I knew if I didn't go I would be settling for a mediocre life.

"New York was the opposite of my life, and when I was there I felt this intense energy and excitement that I hadn't felt in a long time. The more I visited, the more I knew this was where I needed to be. I wanted to explore what my life could be if I started over in a new city, and my intuition told me that amazing things were waiting for me if I took this leap of faith."

During this time Lisa and I talked almost daily about her taking the leap of faith and just doing it! But Lisa is shy by nature and not the best at dealing with big changes, especially something as big as this. She'd been with her ex-husband for ten years and he'd taken care of her. Starting over alone in the toughest city on the planet was daunting, to say the least. But I could hear the passion in her voice every time she talked about New York, and I knew she could do it.

"I was so scared to make the decision!" Lisa laughed, knowing I remembered this all too well. "Even though I knew that's where my heart was, my fear kept holding me back and I just couldn't do it.

"Then one day something clicked; it was like a light switch went off, and I knew in that instant that I was more scared to stay [with] my old life then I was to move forward and embrace this new life. I remember I'd just gotten off the phone with you, and you told me I needed to step out on faith and take action, show the Universe I was serious. [You told me] that I needed to make the first move, [and] then everything else would start to fall into place. You said I couldn't sit around and wait for it to magically happen on its own; I had to give my thirty-day notice on my apartment and make the decision to go (#CourageOverFear).

"That was it! I knew right then there was no going back. I put in my notice at my job and apartment, and I threw myself into setting up my new life in New York."

Every weekend Lisa took the train to Manhattan to look for a job and an apartment. She'd spent years running her ex-husband's company and had a strong executive resume; finding a job couldn't be that tough. Surely finding an apartment wouldn't be impossible either. She was willing to use her life savings to make both things happen.

"I knew nothing about New York when I started this process; I was afraid of everyone and everything. Even the apartment brokers were shady; it was all way outside my comfort zone.

"Three weeks passed and I still hadn't found an apartment. I was doing all #TheHustle, but there was just nothing available in the location I wanted. And on top of that all the brokers said they would not rent to me because I didn't have a job in New York."

I remember having daily conversations with her during this time. I encouraged her to keep believing and to keep practicing #MottoForLife. I told her to keep focusing on her #BigPictureDream and above all to keep up #TheHustle.

"It was really scary and exhausting," Lisa told me, reflecting back.

"It was the last weekend before I needed to move out of my place in Boston, and I was once again in New York desperately looking for an apartment. On the last day of that trip, fear threatened to turn into panic. I'd seen nothing that would work, and had run out of brokers willing to work with me because of my job situation. It looked hopeless (#EarthquakeMoment).

"I was walking around my dream neighborhood, trying to not let doubt take over, envisioning my new life (#CreateAMovie-

InYourHead), when I came across a broker standing in front of an apartment building. I asked him if he was showing a unit, and he told me that he was waiting for a client, but that he'd be happy to show it to me while he waited. That unit was more than I was looking for, but he offered to take me back to his office to see if they had anything I'd not already seen."

Back at his office, the broker showed Lisa all the apartment listings he was working on, and none of them were new. "I remember looking at him and saying 'That's it? You really don't have ANYTHING else (#RelentlessPursuit)?' I refused to believe I'd hit the end of the road," Lisa said.

That's when the broker told her about a unit that wasn't even on the market yet, and was in no shape to be shown. "I told him, that's my apartment! I made him take me, and the second I walked in I knew that was it! It was the exact location I'd dreamed of, even on the same street I'd visualized. We went back to the office and signed the paperwork on the spot (#ManifestThat!)!

"Even though it was the scarcest thing I've ever done, and at times it looked hopeless, I never lost faith (#BelieveIT). When I first moved to New York I was over the moon. I'd never felt so alive and optimistic about the future and starting my new life (#GetGrateful).

"But then reality began to sink in."

Every day Lisa went out looking for a job. At first she applied to those in her career path, ones that made the most sense with her prior experience. But weeks passed and she wasn't even getting called in for interviews. So she broadened her search and cast a wider net (#TheHustle).

Still nothing.

"It got super lonely. I didn't know a single soul in the city, and I was putting in all this effort every day with no results. I was so confused because I knew I'd come here for a reason, and that I'd followed my heart, so why was it not working out? I mean, I was busting my ass (#ChillOut)! It got to the point where I was going door to door with my resume to restaurants, coffee shops, and retail stores (#TheHustle). But still nothing. I never dreamed it would be this difficult to get a job."

Six months passed and Lisa was quickly burning through her savings, and still had no job. "It took so much perseverance to keep going every day and fight for my dream. I made the commitment, so the option to give up and leave never existed for me. When I made the decision to come, I told myself I'd live in New York City even if I had to be homeless to do it. I was so committed to my dream that there was never an option to quit and go home (#RelentlessPursuit).

"I practiced positive self-talk daily (#MottoForLife), I talked to you, I listened to motivating videos—anything I could think of to keep my faith. There were days when I just wanted to cry and not get out of bed because it was so frustrating and I felt so invisible."

It was the eleventh hour when everything changed. Lisa had been living in the city for eight months without a job, and she had reached the end of her rope. Her situation was about to get desperate without an income, and again she canvased the city looking for work.

I remember her calling me one day, so excited. She'd gotten an interview, and a job offer from a wax salon. The wax salon offered her minimum wage. In her former position, she'd been an executive with an excellent salary. I was so proud of her for being willing to take the job, and do it with excitement and gratitude. I told her the Universe needed to see how bad she wanted her dream, and that her faith would be rewarded. That somehow it was a test. On her first day of work, two other companies called from her previous outreach and offered her a job. So in the span of a few days she went from no job offers in eight months to three!

Lisa quit the wax salon and took a job in real estate, which came with a nice salary (#ManifestThat!).

"This journey has tested me to the core. It's changed me in every possible way. It's made me a confident woman who's overcome more fears than I could even name! I learned how to fake it till I made it here, and that even perceived confidence is king. I learned that what I said really did affect what happened (#SayIT). Through everything I kept going back to gratitude. I'd walk around the city and be so thankful to be here, living my dream (#GetGrateful).

"I look at my life now and look back to what it used to be, and I'm not even the same person."

LISA'S ADVICE TO YOU

"You have to be 1,000 percent in, or you'll give up. If you're not fully committed, then you'll just think *It's not meant to be* or *It didn't work out.* The only reason it 'didn't work out' is because you quit too soon!

"There's no such thing as failure when you are pursuing your dream because even if the worst-case scenario happens it's not going to kill you. You'll still live and be able to try again, so anything short of that is winning.

"You've gotta be willing to do what scares you. As long as you're okay with where you are, then you'll never be anywhere else.

"No matter what your dream is, the #HBRMethod will change your life. I was able to use it to totally change mine, not just where I live but who I am.

"There are times when your faith will be tested, but just keep applying it and you will keep progressing.

"The #HBRMethod has given me tools to use on a daily basis. There is no way I would have been able to make these major changes to my life and achieve my dream without it. I lived it every day. And it worked! Even when you don't think it's working, it is. And from experience I know that everything's gonna be okay. The fear never fully goes away, but now I know that no matter what, it will work out the way it should in the end, and that brings me peace."

LISA MARCHANT is a marketing and communications professional, living her dream in New York City. Follow her journey on **Twitter:** @lmarchant17 and **Instagram:** @lisadmarchant

EDDIE PALMER'S STORY

I found Eddie and his story from an Instagram post by his close friend Jonathan Stewart, and after taking a quick glance at Eddie's pictures, I knew right away that I needed to hear his story. I'd seen a few posts that led me to believe he was living his dream, so I reached out. But I was unprepared for how blown away I'd be by the story behind the pictures when Eddie called for our interview.

In 2012 Eddie was a twenty-five-year-old successful college graduate with a great job in banking. He was one of the lucky few who left college and got the "perfect job" almost immediately, making great money and living in his hometown of Charlotte, North Carolina. He had a new car and a beautiful new apartment; by all accounts he was "living the dream."

But Eddie was *miserable*. He hated his job and the life he was building; it felt dry, fake, and stuffy. He remembered something a college professor once said: "What career would you choose because you loved it, even if you did it for free?" The only career that came to mind for Eddie was: "I would be a personal fitness trainer (#BigPictureDream)." It was the only thing he was truly passionate about.

"I was sitting at my desk at work one day," Eddie began when I asked him to tell me his story. "And I thought, maybe I need to move—maybe that will help. Then I thought, what would I do? Transfer jobs? I'd still have this same life, just in a different place. It didn't make sense. So I decided to take a trip to California, get away for a while and clear my head. I fell in love with Santa

Monica immediately, and when I got home I told my friends and family I was moving to California to pursue my dream of becoming a personal trainer (#SayIT)! I gave myself exactly one year to prepare for my big move and set a definitive date: March 11, 2013 (#LifePlan)."

For the next year Eddie put in his hustle. He worked two jobs and moved back home with his parents to save money for the big transition to California. Every single day for a year he went to the library, sitting for hours at a time at a little desk to read everything he could get his hands on about being a trainer, focusing on how to train women specifically. He studied, he researched, and he came up with a plan and a style of training that he felt would work well for women in California. Then he went to work getting himself in the best shape of his life, knowing that his body would be his calling card (#TheHustle).

On March 11, 2013, he packed up his small two-door car, selling anything that didn't fit, and pulled out of his parents' driveway (#DoIT). He was leaving behind his friends and family to pursue his dream in California. There was no job waiting for him when he got there, and no apartment lined up, even though he'd been looking for both for a while.

"Everyone thought I was insane." Eddie said. "But it felt totally logical to me. There was this voice in the back of my head that just kept saying, 'If you go west it will all work out.' I knew somehow it was all going to come together (#BelieveIT)."

When Eddie first got to L.A., he searched for work as a trainer to begin building his brand and client base. At first his savings enabled him to stay in hotels, and then as it dwindled, he stayed at hostels, stretching out every last dime. Then one day in October 2013, six months after acting on faith and moving to California, he found himself with no place to go when his shift at the gym ended. His income was not enough for the weekly rent at the hostel and his savings was gone (#Earth-quakeMoment).

That night he drove around looking for a safe place to park his car, where he wouldn't be harassed or carjacked, and wound up in front of the Santa Monica courthouse. The parking lot was well-lit with security cameras everywhere, so it was the safest possible place to spend the night. Each night for the next six months, that parking lot became his home. The nights got colder as fall turned into winter, and he'd steal a few hours of sleep until it was time to wake up and turn the car on for heat.

Each night his six-foot, two-inch frame scrunched behind the wheel of his two-seater car, and every morning he'd get up before sunrise and go to the gym where he worked and took a shower. Lying down was a luxury that didn't exist in his world, so in those early mornings he'd stretch out his long legs and aching back on the wood boards in the sauna (#Relent-lessPursuit). Then he'd go for a run on the beach before his twelve-hour day started, and think: *I'm living the dream! What is there to complain about? It's beautiful! I'm in the place I want to be, doing what I love to do.* I wouldn't let anything take away my smile. I'd never been so happy or felt more alive in my life." I could hear the contagious exuberance in his voice; it gave me full-body chills (#GetGrateful).

No one knew Eddie was homeless. He hid it from his clients and managers at the gym. He even hid it from his close friends, one of whom was an NFL star. No one even remotely suspected what he was going through on a daily basis—no one, that is, except his mama. She cried when he finally came clean and told her what his life was actually like in sunny California. She'd been suspicious about things getting harder for her son, and he was beginning to see that maybe someone should know, just in case something were to happen. She begged him to get a "real job," to go back to banking, or to move back home to North Carolina. But those options never existed in Eddie's world.

"Before I left for California, I told my friends and family that I was going to make it in California as a trainer, even if I had to sleep under the Santa Monica Pier," Eddie said with a laugh. "Of course I didn't think I'd literally have to do that, but that's how strong my commitment and belief in my dream was. I knew I was going to make it, period (#BelieveIT). Sleeping in my car was a blessing; I was grateful to not literally have to sleep under the Pier (#GetGrateful).

"Quitting was not an option, and going home was not an option; I never had a 'Plan B.' No one ever said it would be easy, and I never expected it to be. I knew the struggle was part of the process (#ChillOut). Every month since I moved here, I've hit a milestone, and that gave me the confidence to know I was on the right path (#Winning!). I knew it was all just a test to see how bad I really wanted it (#RelentlessPursuit). I never doubted for a minute that I'd reach my goal (#BelieveIT) of having an apartment to come home to, and own a successful business (#BigPictureDream)."

Before long, Eddie began to build his brand and a loyal client base. All his hard work studying how to get amazing, targeted results for women had earned him a reputation for being able to quickly sculpt model bodies, *literally*—swimsuit models, to be exact. "There was a fine balance between working at the gym and building my business, but at the end of the day I came to LA to build a self-sustaining brand, to work for myself and change lives," Eddie said. I could hear the excitement in his voice when he talked about his clients and the transformations he's helped them achieve (#ManifestThat!).

In January 2014 Eddie moved into his own apartment. "I've never been more grateful to come home and sleep in a bed in all my life," he said. Even over the phone, his gratitude and optimism were impossible to miss. "To be able to come home and watch TV, or just have a quiet place with privacy to unwind. Or a bathroom to go to in the middle of the night that didn't require freezing, and trying to find a tree (#GetGrateful)!"

On his one-year anniversary in LA, Eddie became his own boss (#HBRLife). His business is thriving and self-sustaining; he's living his dream exactly as he'd imagined and planned to live it (#LifePlan).

"Some days it's still just overwhelming. I'll be driving home from training a client and I'll just start to cry. The gravity of it all, that this is actually my reality, is almost too much at times. It's the greatest feeling in the entire world. I said it out loud (#SayIT), and everything I said I'd do has come to pass (#ManifestThat!).

"The day that one of my clients who I'd been working with for several months came to our session with her photos for *Sports Illustrated*, that was one of those moments when you think, *Wow, is this really my life?* Helping my client achieve one of her ultimate goals to be a swimsuit model in *Sports Illustrated* and know that she appreciated what I'd been able to help her accomplish, that was an amazing feeling. This is my calling, this is what I'm good at, and helping my clients get to their goals—it's still an unreal feeling. I am so blessed."

EDDIE'S ADVICE TO YOU

"You have to pursue your happiness. Otherwise, you have to sit and take what's given to you. I had to get my happiness. Now I wake up every day doing what I love and there's a tingle in my body—it's joy."

EDDIE PALMER is a personal trainer living in Santa Monica, California. Follow his journey on **Instagram** and **Twitter**: @ eddie_p365

LAURA MUNSON'S STORY

In 2013 I was walking through Barnes & Noble looking for ideas for the cover of my memoir when a book caught my eye. I didn't read the back, or the inside jacket, or have any general idea what the book was about. I simply bought it based on its cover (if you did that for my book, then the method to my madness worked!). The book was *This Is Not The Story You Think It Is*, by Laura Munson.

I went home and devoured it, then tweeted my review to Laura. To my utter amazement, she responded. Not only did she reply, but she was kind enough to engage me in my infancy as I dreamed of one day following in her footsteps. It is thanks to Laura that I eventually met my literary agent, Beth Davey. Beth was also Laura's agent, and mentioning that in my query letter is what got me on Beth's initial radar almost three years before we actually worked together.

So when I approached Laura about being featured in this book, I was humbled to hear her story firsthand.

"I have been writing since I was a little girl as a way to process life. But growing up, I wanted to be an actress and so I studied acting in college," Laura told me when I called her for our interview.

But Laura was torn because she realized that a career as an actress would mean that having a normal family life would be very difficult. During her senior year of college, she took a film class and began writing a screenplay that was supposed to be a thirty-minute short, but what she turned in was a feature-length film script. "The professor gave it back to me with a D- grade and told me that it was not cinema I'd written, but a manuscript! He told me to take it to the English department because I was a *writer*. So in 1988 I enrolled in an advanced writing class, and I became a writer!" she laughed.

When she graduated college, Laura's friends and family encouraged her to take a job in advertising—something that would pay the bills but still feel creative. "But I wanted to write books. Period. So I took odd jobs that wouldn't get me side-tracked, and I went out and studied my craft every way I could (#TheHustle)." Laura wrote fourteen novels, and with each one she learned more about how to be a writer (#RelentlessPursuit).

"My initial thinking as a writer was lethal, because the value I placed on myself was completely proportional to being 'published to wide acclaim.' I had this relentless notion that this was the only way to my happiness. But I began to realize that I was defining my happiness by something that was totally out-side of my control. And when I realized the insanity of that, I knew I had to flip my thinking. Instead of basing my happiness on the publishing world, I focused my attention on finding happiness from the work instead of the outcome (#GetGrateful).

"To help keep myself in this healthy mental place, I decided to write a 'writer's statement' (#WriteIT). It hangs in my office to this day, and reads '*I write to shine a light on a dim or otherwise pitch-black corner to provide relief for myself and others.*' I began to see my writing as something that grew from a place of service. It was no longer about me and my desire for accomplishment. It was about helping myself and other people come to a new place of awareness," Laura told me. "And maybe even healing."

It was when Laura followed that mantra and wrote her way through a personal crisis, that she found "wide acclaim" success in her memoir *This Is Not The Story You Think It Is*. The short version went viral in the popular *New York Times* "Modern Love" column and is now ranked #2 in all "Modern Love" essays ever published. The book quickly became a *New York Times* bestseller.

"It has been an incredible ride. Suddenly I found myself on the Wellness and Personal Transformation speaking and media circuits where so many people asked me the same questions: *How can I write my way through rough times? How can I get unstuck? How do I find my own voice? How do I give myself permission to tell my story?* I started to see that writing is a powerful transformation and even therapeutic tool and it was the one thing that I'd spent my entire life practicing with passion and loyalty. I thought, *Writing has been my lifeline. I can help other people use writing in their lives too, whether or not they care about being published.* That's how Haven Writing Retreats was born. I've now worked with over 300 people from around the globe, and Open Road Media named it [one of] the top five writing retreats in the country (#ItsTheJourney)!"

"The reason why people trusted me initially when I started my retreats was due to the book, but now it's more because of the Haven Retreat reputation. People see the value of taking this powerful stand for their voice and setting it free. I've seen this experience change lives over and over again. It's been the most amazing journey."

LAURA'S ADVICE TO YOU

"Go where the flow is. Follow what feels most natural to you (#BigPictureDream). Once you start moving into your natural flow, the doors start to open. When it starts to feel easy and not like a struggle . . . you are probably on the right path.

"Get out of your own way. Silence your inner critic (#ChangeTheVoicesInYourHead).

"Set yourself up for completion. Tune into yourself. Pay attention to where you are most creative, happy, and not fighting yourself. Then look at your lifestyle: what in your life is not helping get you closer to your dream? Does that clash with your creativity?

"You can ALWAYS find ways to make your dream happen (#TheHustle). Tell people your dream (#SayIT) and what you're working on. It's often a numbers game, so don't depend on one thing to 'hit.' (Remember my fourteen novels!) Instead, put five things out there and be happy when one 'hits.' Be disciplined about working towards your dream, and set up rules, tasks, and guidelines. Make it your job (#LifePlan).

"Look at who you are already being, and mine that! That's where the gold is. Allow your dream to evolve as you do (#ItsTheJourney)."

LAURA MUNSON is the *New York Times* bestselling author of *This Is Not the Story You Think It Is*. Her work has been published in *O, The Oprah Magazine*, the *New York Times Magazine*, the *New York Times, Redbook, More, Time, Woman's Day, The Week*, and many other publications. She is the founder of Haven Writing Retreats. She lives in Montana with her family. Follow her journey on **Facebook** and **Twitter:** @Lauramunson **Instagram:** @Lamunson **Website:** www.lauramunson.com

REGINALD FOREMAN'S STORY

I was introduced to Reggie by one of my Facebook friends from that initial post. I was blown away by his story.

"My mother had me at a young age; she was on drugs and moved around a lot, all over Chicago. Everywhere I went growing up, there was that negative inner city vibe and kids were always fighting and bullying each other. My mother was very angry and abusive, and my father was in the military living in Florida."

When he was about fourteen years old Reggie went to live with his father in Florida. "It was the suburban dream! The big house, nice cars. It was a totally different life. But my father was very strict, trying to take the ghetto out of me, which just made me rebellious. I didn't want to go to school or dress nice because when I did the kids at school bullied me. I remember one day being beaten up by four guys in the bathroom and I went to school the next day with brass knuckles ready to get revenge. 'You can't beat a man with fists,' my father told me. 'You have to use your mind.'

"He showed me that a different life was possible from what I'd known as a kid in Chicago. He taught me how to be proper, and the importance of an education.

"One day I saw a rolled dollar bill with coke in my father's truck. It was the first time I'd ever see that around him and I just couldn't believe it. He was this Bill Cosby kinda guy; I just couldn't imagine it was really his. He was the one who told me to watch who I was around because that was the type of person I'd become (#ChangeYourCrew).

"When I was fourteen my stepmom told me I should start designing T-shirts, and that stuck with me because there was still always something inside me that wanted to be 'big.' I knew I had a calling. I loved to draw, I'd spend all my time drawing, and she told me to make shirts with my designs (#DreamIT).

"I believe that there are people who come into our lives to water the seed of hope, or our dream, even before we've recognized it yet," Reggie said.

When his father and stepmother got divorced, his dad began to fall apart. He started doing more drugs and hanging out with drug addicts and prostitutes. Instead of being tough on Reggie he disappeared and stopped paying attention to his son. He even became a pimp, with hookers working the street corners.

"My father started to disappear for months at a time. I was nineteen working security at a strip club trying to pay the bills while he was away," Reggie told me. "One day a DEA agent came to the house to find my dad; at the same time the bank was foreclosing on our house. Everything just fell apart. That's when I started doing robberies for hire."

He needed to get a big job, one that would help save the house and pay back the mortgage, so he agreed to rob a house that was supposed to have a safe full of coke. "We ripped the safe out of the ground and brought it outside, but it was empty. By then we were so desperate that we robbed a lady making a bank drop from a retail store, but when we got home it was just receipts. There were so many signs saying 'this is not for you.' I wished I'd paid attention and listened to those signs, but desperation is a scary thing.

"That's when we decided to rob a bank. I attempted to rob it twice but each time something wasn't right; then on the third try it worked. I walked in with a ski mask, shot a round in the ceiling, and got everyone's money," Reggie said.

He was arrested for armed robbery and spent four years in prison. While there he gave his life to God and vowed to become a changed man when he got out. When he was released Reggie went to live with his aunt in the south, and for three years went to church faithfully, living out his commitment to God and working to rebuild his life.

"One day I walked downstairs and there were federal marshals everywhere in my house. They said they'd been looking for me for the past three years and said I'd been released by mistake. It was an unbelievable blow. In total I spent eight and a half years in prison.

"When I came out the second time, I was determined to utilize everything I could to better myself. I decided to go to school for graphic design and follow my passion for drawing (#BigPictureDream). My first shirt design was '*God bless my haters.*' I was selling them out of the back of my car (#TheHustle).

"I started getting up at 3 A.M., studying YouTube videos on how to make shirts, and how to build a business, and decided I was going to put everything I had into creating this company."

Reggie's company God Made Apparel has taken off. In 2014 he had his first fashion show for his men's and women's clothing line, and he's expanded his brand to children's and baby apparel as well. His clothing line is now sold in several retail stores and online.

Reggie's story proves that it really doesn't matter what your story is, or what obstacles you have to overcome along the way. If you are determined to change your life and live your dream, than anything truly is possible.

REGGIE'S ADVICE TO YOU

"It's not about who you've been. It's who you're becoming. If you are still breathing, then the chapters of your life are not over."

REGINALD FOREMAN is a fashion designer and founder/
CEO of God Made Apparel, and the author of *Live Determined*:
Don't Let Your Struggles Bully Your Dreams, his memoir. He is also
a speaker, writer, and husband. Follow his journey on **Website:**
reginaldforeman.com

HOLLY CUSTIS'S STORY

I "met" Holly on Facebook, and when she saw my post looking for people who were following their dream, she messaged me. When I learned what that meant for her, I had to hear about it! Her story proves that it doesn't matter what your dream is, or how "unrealistic" people think it might be, if you want it bad enough then it's going to happen.

"When I was about seven years old I remember going to an Oregon football game with my dad. I immediately fell in love with it! Everything about being in the stadium, the pageantry of game day, it was just amazing. I knew then that I wanted to play football. When I was growing up my favorite Oregon player was Patrick Johnson, and after a game my parents waited with me in the rain so I could get his autograph. I loved everything about how he played; he was such a huge inspiration for me.

"I went to college at Oregon and played recreational league basketball and softball, but had always wanted to follow my passion and play football. After I graduated I learned of a women-only league football team, and I signed up! I learned really quickly that I didn't know the game as well as I thought I did. [But] I'd always been the player with hustle, and football was the sport that rewarded my hustle like nothing else I'd ever done.

"To me, football was a metaphor for my life. I could go out on the field and exhibit strength I didn't know I had. I put all my energy into my game and it made me very mentally strong. During that time I was dealing with a lot of adversity, my childhood home burned to the ground, and my mother was in a horrible accident. But when you are faced with pain you can either run away from it or run through it. I learned how to channel that pain, and everything I was going through into my fuel on the field; I had the best year of my career that season."

HOLLY'S ADVICE TO YOU

"In order to be great, you have to do the work (#TheHustle). Your effort and your determination directly affect your performance."

HOLLY CUSTIS is a running back for the Seattle Majestics, a professional women's tackle football team. She has played for the past decade and lives in Portland, Oregon. Follow her journey on **Facebook:** Holly Custis **Website:** www.relentless21.wordpress.com

STEP 7: #BELIEVEIT

"All things are possible if you believe." —Mark 9:23

#HBR Soundtrack: "Believe"—Justin Bieber

BELIEVE. BUT HOW??

I am asked this question all the time, "How do I believe when this stuff seems so unrealistic in my life?" And it's a logical question. I am asking you to trust in something that is so outside the realm of your current situation that it probably feels impossible.

That is totally normal.

Our brain doesn't like change, and for its entire existence, up to this point, it's been allowed to run amok. Now that you are trying to retrain it with #ThinkIT and #SayIT, it is probably reacting with a shit-ton of doubt. That nasty little voice in the back of your head says, "This will never work for me!" But in both of those chapters you learned how to shut that voice up, and if you have been keeping up on your homework and daily journal, you are already further along the road of "believing" than you think.

Belief is something that is established and reinforced over time.

EXAMPLE

Imagine an empty five-gallon bucket. If you put a penny in that bucket it won't make a huge impact, right? Even if you fill the whole bottom of the bucket with pennies, you are going to look at it and say, "I'm NEVER going to fill this bucket with money!" (And with that attitude we already know you won't! Lol). But if every single day you keep adding pennies and nickels to the bucket, over time it will slowly start to fill up. Every time you choose to put one in the bucket instead of spend it, you feel proud of yourself. You see that it's starting to make a difference; along the way you started to believe you could fill it. And the fuller it gets, the more determined you become. You become more confident that you'll reach the goal, until one day there's no doubt in your mind.

That is how belief works.

Each time you #ChangeTheVoicesInYourHead and choose to put those positive coins in your belief jar, you are building belief. Each time you replace a negative thought with a positive mantra you are adding another coin. Applying #ThinkIT and #SayIT are the two best ways to build genuine belief, even if it feels fake in the beginning.

There are four stages of belief. The first is teaching yourself how to believe using #FakeIT. The second is reinforcing your faith in #CountYourWins. Third is protecting it by applying #ChangeYourCrew. And finally, the last is relying on it to survive your #EarthquakeMoments.

#FAKEIT

The best way to actively build belief in the beginning is to *fake it till you make it.* If you want to be a successful business person, you should start *acting like one.* You buy a suit and tie (or heels) and you wear it to work, or to interviews, and even around town. You fix your physical appearance so you look like a successful "business person." You start putting all your meetings in your calendar, and generally do anything you'd imagine doing if you already were a "success." You are acting as if that is already you.

Before you know it, you will realize that people treat you differently than they did before. People notice you. You walk with purpose, with your head held high, and you conduct yourself in the manner of an extraordinary success. The strangers at the coffee place, or the supermarket, make eye contact and smile at you where before you were invisible; now you get respect. None of them know that it's all an act at this point, and after a little while your brain won't know it is, either. And that is the transition from faking it to actually believing it. It happens over time with a combination of what you think, what you say, and what you do.

This is an amazing and simple tool to trick your brain into believing. You can apply it to whatever your dream or goal is, regardless of your circumstances.

EXAMPLE

When I took a sales job in the high-tech industry and moved to Seattle, Washington, in November of 2011, I had no idea what I was doing. I'd never done that type of intensely technical sales before. I'd never sold into that specific business sector, never called on clients in the Seattle market, and generally was in way over my head. I wasn't trained in all these things when I started either; I worked out of an office alone most days and had very little support. I didn't know how to even attempt to do my job. It was all so overwhelming.

I understood that every prospect I would call on would know ten times more than I did, and knew I just needed to suck it up and #FakeIT. I cold-called for meetings my first week and just went for it. Before every meeting, I'd use #MottoForLife to tell myself that I could do it, and then I'd imagine putting on a big overcoat of confidence. That image has always stayed with me. When I feel like I'm in over my head I imagine putting on my #FakeIT confidence, almost like a separate persona. I'd present myself as a confident and knowledgeable business woman. When I didn't know the answer to a client's question, or felt like the conversation was getting too technical, I'd ask more questions. I'd take notes and tell them I'd get back to them with the answers. I decided to focus on what I am great at, and that's building relationships with strangers. I can meet someone for the first time, and in a matter of minutes put them at ease and get them talking about their life. I would go back to that whenever I got stumped.

And it worked! In my first year (2012) I sold $1.8 million, on a quota of $1.5 million. The next year (2013) I sold over $2 million and had the most financially successful year of my life enabling me to triple my overall income from 2011 to 2013. And I still had no idea what I was doing (#ManifestThat!)!

You don't have to know everything to be successful. You just have to be willing to get out there and start doing it, even if you need to #FakeIT for a while.

#WINNING!

There is no better way to reinforce belief than to really celebrate your wins. Wins might include getting a returned email or phone call, when you've been throwing spaghetti at the wall all damn day!

No win is too small. Greet them with childlike enthusiasm and joy; this will speed up the timing for succeeding at the bigger stuff!

This is why it's so important to #GetGrateful, because it's your awareness and gratitude that will catch the smaller wins right away. Nothing that comes into your life is random. You created it and drew it to you. And nothing builds genuine belief like #Winning!

EXAMPLE

When I started conducting interviews for this book, I did not have a book deal. I had an idea for a book. I'd made the *decision* that I was going to write it, no matter what. So I went about finding all the stories you have been reading, and each time someone agreed to be featured I was #Winning!

I got so excited! I'd post it on social media, I'd tell my kids about who had just become part of the project, and then

I'd tell them the stories after each interview. Every story I heard reinforced my belief that one day I would get an agent and then a book deal. Celebrating those wins is what encouraged me to keep going even when doors closed in my face, and on days when I let doubt creep in. I'd go back to those wins and remember that if I'd gotten this far, it could only mean that I was on the right path.

Then when I sent my pitch to my dream agent and she responded to my email, I was #Winning! When she asked to have a call (our first ever), I was ecstatic. That was #Winning! All those little steps in the process that led up to the big #ManifestThat! moment are all worthy of celebration, and they are all examples of #Winning!

Read the post on my blog "How I got a literary agent" to see the video of the day my big dream came true!

#CHANGEYOURCREW

Reference: I use this hashtag to refer to both removing negative crew and/or adding a positive crew.

Oprah says, "Surround yourself with ONLY people who will lift you higher." It's pretty hard to believe that any of this is possible if you're surrounded by a negative crew. The people you've allowed into your circle have by default become your circle of influence. They are your crew.

You are either judged or elevated by the company you keep. They can be your greatest asset or your biggest liability. The wrong crew is a dangerous thing; they can sabotage or even destroy your success.

Positive people and negative people don't mix. You might think that it's your responsibility to change the negative individuals, to make them see the light and get on board, but let me tell you, either people get it or they don't. Either they are with you, or they are not. We can't try to fix people who don't want to be fixed. All we can do is focus on our journey and be a positive example for those around us. But if those around us continue to be negative, or start to drag you down, then it's time for them to go.

It's like trying to swim up a waterfall. It can't be done. You can't be successful at #HBR or anything else while you are surrounded by haters.

Most of the time we know who the "dead weight" in our life is, but many times we don't have the courage to remove them. Don't be surprised if the Universe does it for you. You can't live a positive life surrounded by negativity (#EarthquakeMoment).

#ChangeYourCrew has come up organically in almost every interview I conducted for this book. At some point in their journey most of these featured individuals had to make the tough decision to cut out people who no longer served them, just the way I did. It might seem selfish or wrong, but trust me, it's the only way. As you find success, either people will drop out of your life because your changes make them uncomfortable, or you will need to cut them out because their energy is toxic.

EXAMPLE

When I was starting out that first year, I realized that I couldn't get back on my feet, let alone be successful with the negative people who were in my life at the time, including family. I had so little energy after working and taking care of my kids, that I couldn't spare it on drama, or people who did not support me. So I cut almost everyone out of my life, for my own survival. For a while it really sucked ass. I was so totally alone and isolated (which is the reason I started blogging in the first place), but over time I slowly began to replace those negative people with a positive crew.

I also discovered that if I wanted to be successful I needed to know successful people, and learn from them. So I began building relationships with everyone I met who was living their dream, or pursuing their passion. I watched, I listened, and eventually I started to ask questions and really apply what I was learning.

When successful people like and accept you, it's an open invitation to knowing more successful people. It's almost like *Well, hey, if you know so-and-so, and they think you're an okay person, then you must be okay.* That is how you build a network. It wasn't long before I realized that almost everyone I knew in my personal life or in business was incredibly successful. In fact, I'm probably the least successful person I know! That alone gave me credibility when I began looking to interview people for this book.

A positive crew is an enormous blessing and asset in your journey to achieve your dream. Find a mentor or someone you admire and work on building that relationship. Take them to coffee or lunch and get to know them. Ask questions. I've found that accomplished people are very open to helping someone who's earnest and hard-working. They freely give their advice and are more approachable than you'd imagine.

DON'T LISTEN TO THE HATERS

"I've never met a hater whose life I wish I had." –Dwyane Wade

As you begin to find success you will notice that not everyone is happy for you. Haters' opinions are irrelevant. A hater can be someone in your crew, someone close to you, or just an online troll. No matter who it is, remember that words can only affect you if you ALLOW them to affect you. So brush it off. Trust me, they're not worth it.

Don't give them the satisfaction of a response, or the validation of an argument or defense. ALWAYS take the high road, even when that's the LAST thing you want to do. Don't be the one that makes a hater relevant.

Is there anyone who's not good for you that you've allowed in your crew? Are you prepared to make the difficult decision to move forward without them?

POSITIVE CREW

The power of having positive people in your life can't be underestimated either. You'll notice I use the tag #ChangeYourCrew
even when talking about people who are a positive influence
on our lives. To me it means that whether positive or negative,
the people we surround ourselves with greatly influence our
journey.

Be sure your crew is a positive one.

#EARTHQUAKEMOMENTS

It's easy to believe in yourself and the process when things are going great. The challenge comes when the shit hits the fan. And it will, trust me.

I know this is NOT what you wanted to hear, but this is the reality. Just because you've adopted the #HBR Method doesn't mean that it's going to be all roses and sunshine. There are going to be times when it feels like everything you ever worked for and all the progress you've made gets swept away with one stroke of "bad luck" or one unfortunate event. Those are the "Why me?" moments when you are shaking your fist at God and asking *how could this happen?*

Sooner or later you will face one of these earthquake moments. Not to scare you, but this way when they happen, it will be less likely to derail your progress.

There is a reason for everything we face in life, even when we can't see or understand it. Nothing happens without a purpose. These disappointments and setbacks are part of getting you to the next level, even though when it happens it's going to feel like the worst thing ever. This is where belief comes in, because if you believe as I do, that these obstacles are actually part of getting you closer to your dream, then you will close your eyes, grit your teeth, and endure it. You will fight to get through to the other side, and you won't lose faith no matter how dark it gets.

You know how rainbows always show up after a bad storm? They shine brightest when the sun finally breaks through the dark clouds, even just a little, after the rain has passed. That's exactly how this works. Once you make it through the storm without losing faith, you will see your dream waiting for you. It might take a few weeks, or months, or even a year after the dust settles before you really see the connection, but it will be there. One day you will be able to connect the dots and realize that what seemed like the biggest disaster is actually your dream in disguise.

NOTE: An #EarthquakeMoment can also happen in the form of tragedy or loss. In those cases I'm not suggesting that it's "part of your dream." It is, however, something very difficult to move through without the proper tools. These steps can help you get through anything, no matter how devastating.

HOW TO KEEP FAITH IN THE STORM

The only way to keep faith when you are faced with these inevitable tough times is to #GetGrateful. I know I sound like a broken record, but it's the secret sauce to everything. The same thing that was able to get this whole dream off the ground in the first place, and help you recognize your wins and opportunities, is the same thing that will carry you through the dark times. You have got to find a way to count your blessings, and remain grateful, *no matter what.*

This is not the time to quit, or to say that all of this is bullshit and doesn't work. News flash: every successful person has faced adversity. But successful people don't quit just because shit is not going their way. Instead, they fight through it and trust the process.

This is the time to go back to the basics. Go back to #ThinkIT and #SayIT. Start practicing the steps harder than ever before. That's where the strength will come from to get you through it.

EXAMPLE #1

I used this example on my blog several years ago, and that's where I got the term #EarthquakeMoments

Think of it like this. You live in a home that you've never really liked, but it does the job, and it's your home. All your memories are there, and your life is there. But your deepest wish has always been to tear that house down and build your dream home on the same piece of land. You've had this dream for years, but you have no idea how you could ever make this dream a reality. You don't have the resources or the know-how to make this happen.

Then one day an earthquake strikes, and the land beneath your home opens up and swallows it. That's the worst possible thing that could happen, right? It's the greatest disaster, the worst kind of "luck." It begs the question *"Why me, God?"* It's heart-wrenching, and you can't imagine how any good could come from something so awful.

But time passes, and finally the insurance claim on your old home comes through. Now you can start to see the possibilities; the option to build your dream house on that same property, like you'd always imagined, begins to register. And before you know it, construction is underway and your dream home is going up, in the very place where your old house once stood.

Sometimes our lives need an earthquake to make room for what is next. Sometimes we send out a wish so big into the Universe that it takes one look at our life and says, "How the hell can I deliver this wish to your current life? There is no room for it."

So it goes about making changes to allow room for your #Big-PictureDream to come true.

In the example above there was no way to build the new house without somehow destroying the old one. When we don't have the faith or courage to destroy our own house the Universe might send an earthquake to do it for us.

This is the reason why I've stressed from the first chapter that you have got to align your dreams and goals with your true passion, and your honest core. As long as you've done that you can trust the process when you are going through the darkness, because you know that something great is going to be waiting for you on the other side.

EXAMPLE #2

In the spring of 2011 when I was laid off of my dream job, I was devastated. It felt like my whole world came crashing down again, only this time it came with the sting of public humiliation. At that time my blog had really started to take off, and I'd manifested my first #FutureBoard. Things could not have been going better, and Facebook had been my witness.

The job I'd held enabled me to travel to New York and Los Angeles first class, and I'd been staying at the Ritz Carlton three days before I was suddenly laid off. It was like going from rags to riches, and back to rags all in about eighteen months.

I was scared and mortified.

But I refused to panic, or give up on the #HBRMethod just because I'd encountered a little "bad luck." So every single day, I said my #MottoForLife mantras all day. I thanked the Universe/God for the roof over my head, and the food on the table (#GetGrateful). Then I went out and turned my Hustle into overdrive.

After a few weeks of applying for every imaginable job, I finally got a phone interview. When the day came, I put my daughters (who were three years old at the time) down for their afternoon nap, and ran downstairs to answer the phone. Five minutes into the call I heard a blood-curdling scream, followed by the sound of a water pipe exploding. I dropped the phone and ran up the stairs to my girls' room, grabbing them as water gushed from the ceiling and ran down the stairs. By the time I got the girls out of the house and called the fire department, there was standing water in all three levels of our home.

What I remember most about that day was milling around a place that was, in an instant, no longer my home. I tried to wrap my head around what that meant for the kids and myself. The fire chief told me that our home was unlivable, and he handed me a card to call the American Red Cross. I just remember feeling so embarrassed and humiliated. I didn't feel right calling the Red Cross when just a few weeks before I'd been staying at a five-star hotel (though it had been paid for by my previous job). Still, it didn't seem right to take charity.

Yet the reality of the situation was that I'd been unemployed for over a month with no potential income on the horizon, and now we were homeless.

I'll never forget the elderly gentleman from the Red Cross who came to my house that day. He gave me the first hug I'd received all day. I instantly started crying. He handed me a debit card with funds loaded on it, so I could get dinner for the kids for the next week, and he reserved a motel for us to stay in until we could figure something out.

For four weeks the kids and I lived in that little rundown roadside motel, with no kitchen or bedrooms or tables on which to do homework.

That was the night I fully understood what it meant to #GetGrateful. I cried for hours after I put the kids to bed.

My girlfriend Sarah came over with a bottle of wine and poured me a glass in the Styrofoam cups from the bathroom sink.

I just kept saying, "How do I get through this?"

It felt so hopeless that first week. For a few days the dark side called my name with great force. Everything I'd worked so hard for was gone, overnight. The emotional devastation from that was almost worse than when my ex-husband left. I felt defeated, broken, and utterly alone.

I was back to starting over with nothing.

But what choice did I have other than to fight, trust the process, count my blessings, and hustle? I knew it had worked for me once, so it had to work again. During that time I took videos of what life was like living in that motel and posted them to YouTube. It was embarrassing yes, but it was real, and raw, and it was my life. I wanted to remind myself to be thankful and to never forget what it feels like to be knocked down so low you are begging to give up.

It was about eight months later that I got a message from the Red Cross on one of the blogs I'd posted while living in the motel. It said they were doing a national search for true stories and wanted to know if I'd be interested in submitting mine for a chance to be featured in a national PSA campaign. Out of thousands of entries, our story was chosen to air on thirty-two networks across the United States. The campaign was to raise awareness for the amazing work the Red Cross does helping families that face disasters large and small (you can view the PSA on my website under "press").

The PSA began airing for Giving Tuesday in December of 2011. That morning on my way to work, I stopped at Starbucks to grab my triple-shot latte, and there we were. There was a picture of my daughters, on the cover of the *New York Times* business section. It was our story, for the world to see, inspiring people in a way I'd never imagined back when I'd put the dream of sharing my story with the world (via the image of a microphone) on my #FutureBoard in 2009.

In May of 2012 I found myself standing in front of a thousand people—big money corporate donors—to give the keynote speech for the Seattle chapter of the American Red Cross annual fundraiser. I broke down in tears as my children joined me on stage and I held up a personal check, my donation written in the amount of that first debit card they had given me.

It took an #EarthquakeMoment for my dream of sharing my story with the world, via media and speaking, to come true. Those opportunities would have never come my way, had it not been for the tragedy of our home flooding and me losing my job. That was my reward for trusting the process and not giving up. And it's the only way my #BigPictureDream could fit into my life.

Trust the process.

EXAMPLE #3

When I was lying on my living room floor in a puddle of tears the night my husband left and my world fell apart, I had no idea that I'd actually been given a second chance at life. I had said many a prayer the year or two leading up to that night, for God to change my life. I prayed He'd see how unhappy I was and fix it somehow. In my heart of hearts, I felt my life had fallen so far short of the expectation I'd had for it when I was young, that I almost hated myself for allowing it to happen. I did not like the person I was and couldn't imagine living out my entire life in that unhappiness. But God/the Universe knew I would never take action to change my situation.

So it did it for me.

It tore my world apart in such a violent way that I had no choice but to sit up and pay attention. And thankfully it also put the ability in my heart to recognize that I'd been given a second chance, and it gave me the courage to create the life I always dreamed of.

It's been six years since he left, and I am honestly happier than I ever dreamed possible. I've created a life and a future beyond even my wildest dreams, and I am grateful every day for surviving my #EarthquakeMoment.

Without it, I would never be here right now. I would have never learned these lessons, or found my calling and my passion. It was my greatest blessing, disguised as the end of the world.

YOUR HUSTLE
Grab your journal.

- Try to think of a time when something bad happened in your life. Spend a little time tearing it apart and following the path your life took after that event; can you see where something positive came from that experience? Write about it.
- Write about where you are still struggling to believe. In what areas and why? What is holding you back? Can you identify any of the things we've discussed in your response?
- Pretend that response was written by a friend. What #HBR advice would you give them to address their fears and get them to keep moving forward?
- Write three wins you've had so far since you started reading this book and implementing the #HBRMethod through your homework. How did those feel? Did you celebrate them? If not, why not? If so, how?

#HBRSTORIES

NATASHA PESTANO RICE

CHARLES A. ARCHER

JOCELYN WADSWORTH

DONNA KRECH

MARTELL WEBSTER

NATASHA PESTANO RICE'S STORY

I first met Natasha in Los Angeles at the art gallery opening for Victor Matthews. I noticed her positive energy immediately; she has that quality about her. Her exuberance, excitement, and passion were hard to miss, and I knew she must have a great story.

A week later when she called for our interview, I sat at my laptop while she made a cup of tea, and I asked her to tell me her story . . .

"My drive doesn't have a beginning," she began. "Both of my parents were entrepreneurs. My mother is Indian from Fiji, and my father is Portuguese-Irish from Guyana. At the age of three my father was out selling papers to help earn money for his family, and at eighteen moved his mother and sister to Australia in search of a better life. My mother is a second-generation chef who moved to Australia, where she met my father and opened an Indian restaurant. They divorced shortly after I was born.

"From the time I could hold a crayon, my mother was teaching me how to cook, propping me up on the counter while she chopped potatoes and carrots, always showing me how to be a strong, independent woman. Food was a huge part of my childhood and represented love and family as I grew up. Learning to cook was in my blood from the beginning. It was a form of communication, and a way for me to express what I was feeling even when words failed me. To me, food is love.

"When I was thirteen I went to live with my father. He worked as a mediator, a voice for those without one. He'd grown up seeing the weak preyed upon and abused and he was determined to stand up for those who didn't have that ability.

"My father detested the idea of working for anyone; he always told me that it was no one's job to put money in my hand. That was up to me. I needed to find a way to make my own money and not rely on a job, because that could be taken away. So in the third grade I had the idea to sell my older brother's comp card (who was a model) to my friends, who were obsessed with him. I'd charge one price for just a picture, more for an autographed photo, and still more for him to walk us home from school. That was my earliest attempt at being an entrepreneur (#TheHustle).

"Growing up, my father worked every day to provide for us. Paying the bills was a struggle, and every dollar meant something. I've always had a strong work ethic and drive, seeing my parents work so hard to build a life for their children."

Natasha met her now-husband when she was just fifteen years old, and as you might imagine her father was less than enthusiastic about his daughter being in a serious relationship at such a young age. When she was nineteen, the couple moved to Miami to attend college. Her father came for a month-long visit, and it was the first time he'd given his blessing to his daughter's relationship.

Her father retuned to Australia, and two weeks later he was murdered.

"Part of me died with him," Natasha said quietly. I can hear the emotion in her voice. "I ran from everything that reminded me of him—my passion, my work, myself. I felt like I couldn't celebrate anything for years after his death. I couldn't touch anything that I'd been working on or creating before his death. Everything reminded me of him."

I asked Natasha how she managed to pull through this incredibly difficult time (#EarthquakeMoment). "After a few years I had to tell myself that I needed to be brave and go back to what made me happy. I had to push myself to get where I am today."

After her father's death Natasha returned to Australia to deal with the aftermath of his murder. Because of his high-profile position as a mediator, the press became relentless. "It was very difficult to deal with all that in addition to coping with my loss," she said. "For years there was no celebrations in my life, because every occasion that I should have been celebrating, I mourned him instead."

Natasha turned away from her passion for food, since it reminded her of her father. "I had to push myself, with my husband's help, to be where I am today. I made a conscious decision to follow my true passion for cooking (#BigPictureDream), and once I recalibrated my life to align it with my happiness, it was as if the missing pieces for success came to me. They just came into my world."

Natasha began to develop her own organic food line, and with the help of her husband/executive producer she created a two-minute "sizzle reel" of her cooking in their kitchen, inspiring people to cook at home. She'd never really thought of being in front of the camera, especially after the media became so destructively negative after her father's death. Her dream had always been to teach people how to make delicious and healthy meals for their families, and to share the joy and love it brings (#BigPictureDream).

"I realized that the camera also could give me a voice, and power to make a positive impact on people's lives. It helped me take my power back.

"But I went through a time when I didn't believe I was worthy, when I questioned if I deserved to have success (#ChangeTheVoicesInYourHead). To move through that I had to go back to my purpose—showing people how to cook and share that joy and love. It wasn't about being pretty in front of a camera; it was about helping people. When I connected those dots, then I knew I was worthy of the success I wanted to attain."

So she pushed past her fear and inhibitions and put it out there (#CourageOverFear). Her tape landed in the hands of the Food Network (#ManifestThat!).

Then one day the phone rang and it was media mogul Russell Simmons. He'd seen the sizzle reel of Natasha cooking and loved it. "He said, 'You know, we have beaches in LA!' He convinced [my husband and me] to move from Miami to LA and to work on a new cooking series he was developing. When Russell Simmons suggests something, you pretty much know it's in your best interest to do it!" Natasha laughs. Within the month they had packed up their car and headed west (#DoIT).

"The first time I met Russell was in his Los Angeles home, and I came bearing gifts. I founded SuperStart Your Life with my husband, and I brought my cold cereal line which comes in three flavor varieties. The first flavor is called *Passion,* because life without passion is death. I knew that from firsthand experience. Once you have found your passion then you can achieve *Success,* which is our second flavor. And when you have both *Passion* and *Success,* then you will taste *Freedom,* which is our final flavor." Natasha handed each to Russell while explaining their meanings. When she was finished Russell's business partner looked at Russell and said, "Where did you find her!?"

The next week Natasha and her husband were signing contracts to become business partners with Russell Simmons (#HBRLife).

"I had been lying dormant in mourning for so long that I needed to super-start my own life. I needed to take control and do it for myself. Now I can celebrate every single day in my life and be grateful for it," Natasha said (#GetGrateful).

NATASHA'S ADVICE TO YOU

"Work is life. Leisure is just enjoying the work you have put in. If you are able to work towards what makes you happy, that is an honor. I have never been afraid of hard work (#TheHustle).

"Remember that your journey is personal—it's yours. It's not the journey of your family, not your friends, not even of your significant other. Not everyone is going to like and support you. Sometimes it will feel like you are doing it alone, and that's okay (#ChangeYourCrew).

"I always imagine a canoe full of people, and you're trying to cross a lake. The lake is full of crocodiles and piranhas and you are rowing like crazy at the helm of the boat to get quickly and safely to the other side. You assume the people in the boat are rowing with you, but you start to notice the boat is quickly taking on water and starting to sink. You look back, and they are just sitting in the boat watching you work. You have a choice—drown with them, or get them out of your boat. It might sound harsh, but if they don't pull their weight, then they can't be in the boat with you. You might have to row it alone in order to cross the lake and get to your goal. But you never know what the future holds, and it's possible they could be there waiting on the other side one day.

"The struggle is real and you have to be willing to sacrifice everything (#RelentlessPursuit). Because if you don't, the person who does will take your dream from you.

"I'd rather struggle to achieve my dream than live without it (#RelentlessPursuit). If you don't have a purposeful vision (#LifePlan), you can't achieve anything.

"Ask yourself if you are serving others. If you're not, you will likely never be successful (#HBRLife).

"Believe in yourself and your purpose (#BelieveIT). When you believe it, people will respect you."

NATASHA PESTANO RICE is a third-generation chef and relationship expert. She is the founder of SuperStart Your Life—an organic food and lifestyle company. She is also a TV personality. She lives with her husband in Los Angeles and Miami, where they aim to inspire and motivate others to pursue their dreams. Be sure to follow and encourage her journey: **Instagram:** @NatashaPestanoRice **Twitter:** @NatashaPestano

CHARLES A. ARCHER'S STORY

I came across Charles as a result of a Janna Andrews Instagram post, of a photo taken at the book launch for *Everybody Paddles*, Charles's new book. I tracked him down because I wanted to hear how he'd made his dreams a reality.

"I was a child with very low self-esteem, extremely shy," Charles began. "Growing up in the lower middle class, I've seen what poor looks like. I knew from a very early age, maybe five or six years old, that the only way out of the economic situation I was raised in would be to get an education. The only successful people I knew as a child were doctors and lawyers, so that's why I decided to be a lawyer.

"But in the fourth grade I was held back a year. When all my friends were moving on to fifth grade but I couldn't, that changed my life (#EarthquakeMoment). The message it sent was that I had failed. Failure became the 'F' word to me. I didn't like it and I was going to do something about it. I would prove myself first as a student and then whatever followed.

"As a result I have been in school my entire life. I saw so much racism growing up, setting such low expectations of what I could and could not be, that I was determined to break the mold. I knew that I never wanted to rely on a paycheck. I wanted to be the opposite of anything people thought I should be (#BelieveIT)."

So Charles traveled the world. He set out to learn as much as possible about others and in turn help them. The education he has pursued to achieve this goal is truly outstanding. His legal degree helped him found and lead a large nonprofit organization. His master's enabled him to become a strong leader and accept the position of CEO. The PhD he's currently earning will help him write human and civil rights policy, which is his next frontier.

He started a successful nonprofit organization to serve people in need, and became a CEO and bestselling author. I think he's obliterated any sign of "failure" from his life (#ManifestThat!).

Clearly all his education has benefited his career in extraordinary ways. His legal degree helped him found and lead a large nonprofit organization. His masters enabled him to become a strong leader and accept the position of CEO. And the PhD he's currently earning will help him write equal, human, and civil rights policy, which is his next frontier.

"But after my PhD I'm done with school!" Charles laughed.

"I want people to understand that if you come from a sense of insecurity you still can make it. You can turn your fear and your haters into what motivates you. What I've achieved so far in life has only happened because I dreamed it (#BigPictureDream), and then I challenge myself to make it happen (#TheHustle).

"My dream has now developed into leaving a legacy—effect change and contribute to society. Anything less is unacceptable. Success is a moving target (#HBRLife)."

CHARLES'S ADVICE TO YOU

"Everybody matters. If I could go back in time, I'd tell my nine-year-old self that *I mattered*. That adversity did not diminish my worth. Your economic background, or whatever it is you lack, doesn't define you."

CHARLES A. ARCHER is a lawyer, advocate, speaker, entrepreneur, CEO, cofounder of the Thrive Network, and international bestselling author of *Everybody Paddles: A Leader's Blueprint to Creating a Unified Team.*

JOCELYN WADSWORTH'S STORY

Jocelyn reached out to me on Facebook some time ago after being inspired by my YouTube videos. She saw my initial Facebook interview post and sent me a message with a snippet of her story, and I immediately wanted to hear it all.

"I've wanted to be a writer since I was ten years old," (#BigPictureDream) she told me when I called her for our interview. "That's when I wrote my first book. Then I spent my teen years and twenties sending out query letters, entering writing contests, and trying to get an agent. I tried everything to get my book published, but ultimately with no success (#TheHustle)."

In the meantime, Jocelyn became a history teacher and wrestled with the notion that teaching might need to become her new dream. But as we know, our dreams manifest on their own timing.

"When I was thirty-three my two-year-old son was diagnosed with autism, and my entire world stopped spinning right there. I knew what suffering was in one awful instant. (#EarthquakeMoment). It felt like a death. At first you feel like there is nothing to be happy about or even a reason to smile anymore. Those thoughts can take you to a very dark place; they can absolutely ruin you if you let them (#ThinkIT).

"Suffering will heal or destroy you—your choice. Having a special-needs child meant my life was going to change, so what? If I had faith that everything I wanted for myself would come to pass, then this must surely be a way to get there, right? Did I really believe that? Or was I going to fight that optimism, deciding instead to live my life in this bowl of nasty, smelly, suffering soup?"

Jocelyn's son was thrust into a full schedule of doctor and therapy appointments. The autism diagnosis forced her to be a caregiver instead of a teacher, putting that dream on the back burner as well.

"What this whole thing did . . . was force me to be who I really am—a writer," she said (#GetGrateful).

That's when her sister, an established graphic designer, encouraged her to self-publish her book and let the public decide. She even designed a cover and formatted the interior. All Jocelyn needed to do was hit the "publish" button (#CourageOverFear).

So she took her life circumstances as a sign to go for it. She published her middle-grade fiction novel, *Wisher*, in July of 2013 to rave reviews. She has since released the audio version and the sequel is due to be released at the end 2015 (#ManifestThat!).

"What began as a devastating diagnosis has become the start of my new, more meaningful life. I think we need to look at our suffering and difficult times, and see what it's taught us. I stopped caring what people think. Having a special-needs child has helped me let go of the judgment of others and focus on what really matters. Nothing really bothers me anymore, and that has been a gift. It's taught me not to judge others, because you never know what it's like until you live that experience."

JOCELYN'S ADVICE TO YOU

"Experiencing suffering doesn't mean your life is over. Good can come from any situation and can ultimately lead to living your dream. Be grateful for every ugly second of it, because it's making you a much better version of yourself."

JOCELYN WADSWORTH is the author of the middle-grade series *Wisher*, available on Amazon. She is also an autism activist, sharing her story to encourage and uplift other families. She lives with her husband and children in rural Idaho. Follow her journey on **Facebook:** Jocelyn Wadsworth

DONNA KRECH'S STORY

Donna and I have been connected on Facebook for a while now, each of us inspiring the other's journey. When she saw my initial post she messaged me, and I'm so grateful she did because hearing her story inspired me at the perfect time.

"My initial dream was to feed my daughter, whom I had no money to feed," Donna began. "Some people would call that survival, but for me that was my dream.

"I remember walking down a gravel road in the blazing Texas heat, sweating and pushing her in a stroller that I paid twenty-five cents for. I was on my way to the nearest store to buy her milk. I was sobbing, because all the money I had in the world was jiggling in my pocket. I was sobbing as I pushed, knowing I could get her milk today, but I had no idea how I'd get it tomorrow (#EarthquakeMoment).

"I went back to the trailer we lived in, wiped my tears, got up the next morning, and went to work. It was 1982, and I'd been working at a fitness facility for minimum wage. I was miserable back then, overweight, and lonely."

So Donna decided to take her daughter, leave Texas, and move back to Ohio to live with her mom. "That's when my dream changed, and I started wanting more (#DreamIT)." Donna took a job at the health club and loved it because she was helping people; she also worked in a grocery store to make ends meet.

"One day I saw an ad for a salesperson in a weight loss center, and got an interview. I was offered the job on the spot." After a month Donna went to her new boss and asked to be promoted to manager. "He gave me the shot," she told me. "So I went out and started blowing away all the sales records."

Donna bought her first weight loss franchise the next year. "I made 90K that year, and that's when my dream became a lifestyle dream, one where I wanted more for my life (#BigPictureDream).

"One night I was kneeling next to my kids' bed doing our nightly routine, when I had a thought. I wondered if my sales team knew how to do this—build a strong home life along with their financial success. I made a conscious decision to teach my team how to make purpose lead profit, instead of just having purpose at home and focusing on profit at work. I believe strongly that you need both to be successful."

During this time Donna was going through a divorce, and the balance between work and home life with her children had never been more important. After her divorce she started dating an executive at her company, and the two married. Donna made the decision to sell her franchise and start a business venture with her new husband.

Together, they have built a women's fitness empire. "The dream once again grew bigger and success followed (#HBRLife). That success turned into a worldwide speaking career and becoming a published author. But I didn't want to solely focus on selling weight loss; I wanted to teach women how to grow as a person and find success in all areas of their life.

"At a certain point those two goals began to conflict with one another. I built this very successful weight loss brand, but my heart's burning desire was against just selling weight loss. That stress made me extremely physically sick; I felt like I was living a double life and wasn't being true to myself. I finally made the decision to create a product that was focused on helping women change their mindset and find success in all areas of their life.

"My dream has definitely evolved over time, and now it is to affect millions of people to change their lives (#ItsTheJourney).

"It hasn't always been easy. We've faced bankruptcy. [My husband] has fought and beaten cancer five times along the way (#EarthquakeMoment). There are days when you feel so inadequate. But you get out of bed no matter what. You put one foot in front of the next and you just DO IT (#TheHustle). You keep working even on the days you don't believe, and the times when you want to give up (#RelentlessPursuit). But when you keep moving forward despite those feelings, belief rises up again (#BelieveIT)."

DONNA'S ADVICE TO YOU

"You need to have a powerful 'why'; there must be a purpose behind your dream. Aligning your purpose with your core values is key, and finding a balance between working on your passion and focusing on financial success. You need both.

"Statistics prove that the absolute best way you can grow is to teach what you know to someone else. Seek wisdom and knowledge, and share it freely. Never stop learning and growing. Your growth will be permanent."

DONNA KRECH is the CEO of The Donna Krech Companies, a bestselling author, and a motivational speaker who's shared the stage with the greats, including Zig Ziglar and Jim Rohn, to audiences around the globe. She's also hosted two national TV shows. Follow her journey on **Twitter:** @DonnaKrech **Facebook:** Donna Krech **Website:** www.donnakrech.com

MARTELL WEBSTER'S STORY

I met Martell and his wife Courtney at his annual charity camp in Portland, where Kanen was learning how to shoot a basketball for the very first time.

They say you can't choose your family, but I've learned over the past six years that you absolutely can, and the Websters are my family. So over Christmas break 2015, I sat in their kitchen, while Courtney cooked and the kids played, and asked Martell to tell me his story.

He explained:"When I was four years old my mom dropped me off at my grandma's house and never came back. We learned later that she'd been murdered. I didn't know what to expect living with my grandma; I was in a state of shock and stuck in limbo. It was my brother, sister, and me, and it was a very tough environment for us at that young age.

"Growing up, I never felt like I fit in; I always felt like a fish out of water. I knew I needed to do more with my life than just stay home all the time. I was about seven years old the first time I watched Michael Jordan play basketball on TV, and I will never forget that feeling. I took my ball, went to the park, and imagined I was him making those game-winning shots. (#CreateAMovieInYourHead) That's when I fell in love with basketball.

"In elementary school, I met my best friend Huston playing basketball. We played for Hoop It Up together in fifth grade. That was the first time I really felt like I could breathe. His house became my home away from home, and it felt like I was living a dream—playing basketball, building our friendship, and becoming part of his family. It exposed me to a different culture. They showed me the importance of values and what a family could look like. Huston's mother became a real role model for me; it was amazing to have that love and support.

"When I first started playing basketball, I wasn't very good, and I wanted to be great overnight. I thought about quitting, but seeing Huston working hard to become a better player built that competitive nature in me and showed me the value of a strong work ethic (#TheHustle). I took the summer off after seventh grade to just practice and improve as a player. I learned how to shoot and dribble the ball, working my butt off to get better. I came back my eighth grade year and won a championship.

"That was the year I began to focus seriously on my dream to play basketball. I started playing with better athletes in programs like YES and Hoopaholics, which used education to help kids get better at sports. Playing with skilled athletes meant there was a ranking system, and I could see my name moving up the list. That really motivated me to be the best.

"I understood that coaches saw potential in me; they could see something special even when I doubted my ability. Their belief in me helped me to believe in myself," he told me. (#BelieveIT)

"My sophomore year I learned that life can be changed in an instant, and that I'm not invincible. I had an injury that could have been career-ending (#EarthquakeMoment). During that time I met my other two best friends; all three of my friends' families really took me in. Having that support pushed me though those difficult times.

"Having those friends in my life helped me see what was possible. When I was growing up in the central district of Seattle, there was a lot of violence and drugs. I could have easily fallen through the cracks and gotten mixed up with the wrong circles, but my friends helped keep me clear of all that (#ChangeYourCrew)."

At the start of Martell's junior year of high school he'd recovered from his injury and was the number-one-ranked high school player in the country. "By that time I just really wanted to get to the NBA. That dream was everything," he said (#BigPictureDream).

Martell was selected by the Portland Trailblazers as the sixth overall pick in the 2005 NBA Draft, after graduating from high school (#ManifestThat!).

"I was very grateful to be only two hours away from home; that was a true blessing and made the transition much easier. It was a surreal experience to be so young and feel like I needed to be the savior for my family; it was a lot to deal with.

"But I've always had great people around me and good business mentors who've taught me about how money works, and how to invest and plan for my family's future once basketball is over (#HBRLife)."

Martell met his wife Courtney three years after going pro. "Meeting my beautiful wife changed everything, especially now that we have children. It changes your perspective; things you used to think were important don't matter anymore. Now it's about being the best husband and father I can be and leaving a legacy.

"It's important for me to teach my children to use their imagination (#CreateAMovieInYourHead) and to dream big. Your mind is a muscle, and it's so important that you keep it exercised. Education is huge; if I could do it all over again I would have paid more attention to education. And I want my kids to always be exploring what makes them happy. I'm very involved in music, and it's a big passion of mine. I want to show them you can have more than just one dream," Martell said (#DreamIT).

MARTELL'S ADVICE TO YOU

"Nothing is ever how it looks in the movies. There are so many variables that happen on your journey (#ItsTheJourney).

Keep good people in your life (#ChangeYourCrew); having that solid foundation of true friendships helps you react to life's fastballs.

At the end of the day, your family and friends are what matter. Success is not the only thing that matters, because it can also bring a lot of unexpected problems. Money can't be the thing that drives you, because it can destroy people and relationships. Don't be driven by the money; be driven by the desire to change and evolve and get better (#MoneyAintAThing!). It's all about living a happy life, because money alone is empty."

MARTELL WEBSTER is a ten-year NBA veteran. In 2014 he started for the Washington Wizards, leading them to the playoffs. He's overcome multiple injuries including three back surgeries. Martell and his wife Courtney have four girls and live in Portland, Oregon. Follow his journey on **Twitter:** @martellwebster **Instagram:** @suiisme **Website:** www.eyrst.com

MANIFESTING

STEP 8: #LIVEIT

"Go confidently in the direction of your dreams! Live the life you've imagined." —Thoreau

#HBRSoundtrack: "I Made It" —Kevin Rudolf

MANIFESTING

Finally! The chapter you've been waiting for, the one where you learn how to "Receive" (manifest), and live your #BigPictureDream for life!

To be honest I don't love the word "manifesting." I think there's a misconception of what it means to many people. People think "things" just magically appear in your life with little or no effort simply because you "thought" about them. I think that's bullshit. But try as I might, I couldn't come up with, or invent a word that could replace it, so I've decided to give it my own definition (see Definitions at the beginning of the book).

Manifesting is an *opportunity;* it requires you to take action in order to receive the reward. It is brought about by #TheHustle and requires you to step out on faith to make the choice that is not based in fear.

In the same way that it took me taking a leap of faith to book the flights to Baltimore for the Ravens game, and then all the rest of the trip "magically" came together, manifesting shows you an opportunity. You're faced with fear and doubt, you push past them, you take the leap of faith, and BAM! The rest falls into place. No matter what I've manifested the past several years, I can always trace it back to me taking action, and it being connected to #TheHustle I'd put in long before the opportunity even showed up. That is why the #HBRMethod sets you up for success: you will be aware, present, grateful, and prepared.

#MANIFESTTHAT!

You may remember me mentioning that manifesting has two levels. This is Level One, and it often shows up in your life through #MoneyAintAThing! These manifestations begin almost immediately but are often subtle and unexpected, and therefore easy to miss if you're not practicing #GetGrateful. They are what some people would call a "lucky break" or "good fortune"—like getting bumped to first class on a flight, or finding a twenty-dollar bill on the sidewalk, or running out of gas at the gas station instead of on the highway (*wha-a-at??*).

But as we know, there's no such thing as "good luck" or "random" anything for that matter; instead they are the rewards for our work and belief.

This level whets your appetite for success. It gives you the *experience* of living out aspects of your dream as part of your journey to reach your ultimate goal. It fuels your passion and reinvigorates your #RelentlessPursuit.

When you live out one of these moments they feel magical and fill your soul with pure joy! It makes you want to pinch yourself, and gives you an enormous boost of confidence. It's one of those moments in your life when you pause and think, *Holy shit! Is this really my life!?* It's a new milestone, a new marker of success, a new memory, and it makes you realize that all the work and sacrifice are worth it. It's like a drug; you want to feel that alive every day. That joy, exuberance, and gratitude send a powerful message to the Universe, and you'll notice that more #ManifestThat! moments often happen quickly after.

EXAMPLE

The first time I ever went to an NBA basketball game was with Kanen for his eighth birthday. I'd recently started working with Anthony Tolliver and he'd offered to give Kanen tickets for his birthday. I remember walking to the train station on our way home after the game and Kanen's eyes shining, as he recounted every detail of our night.

It was magical, from the "random" suite level pass a friend had given us, to the postgame meet and greet. All of it was a dream come true for an eight-year-old. And I was grateful because it hadn't cost me a single penny (#MoneyAintAThing!).

Four years later I lived my #HBRLife moment when I took Kanen and three of his buddies to an NBA game and was able to purchase all the tickets for my son's twelfth birthday.

This is the perfect example of #ManifestThat! along with the dozens I've already provided. It's the realization of an experience you've wanted to live out, and the creation of memories. When it happens it feels nothing short of magical. It seems to happen "randomly" and shows up in a way you'd never expect.

EXAMPLE #2:

Brandon Morehead (Facebook: Search his name plus "Chino Hills, CA," for location).

"I started manifesting my dreams when I was in sixth grade," Brandon told me. "A lot of people say 'I wish I could meet someone famous' that they admire, but I looked at it from a different angle. I thought *why can't I?* People made fun of me a lot growing up, and I was bullied pretty bad. Part of my motivation to succeed has been to prove those bullies wrong.

"I've been able to manifest meeting so many famous people, including my idol Marc Cuban, and have even manifested an internship with the Dr. Phil show. But this is my best #ManifestThat! moment.

"My favorite band growing up was Korn; I idolized them. I always said I would meet the band someday (#SayIT), and fourteen years later I was on Myspace and I saw they were playing a concert nearby. I just told myself, 'I'm gonna meet these guys no mater what' (#MottoForLife)."

Brandon showed up at the concert location at ten A.M., long before any other fans (#RelentlessPursuit). "I had this feeling, I just knew it would happen (#BelieveIT)." You can still hear the excitement in his voice. "Then I saw a member of the crew setting up the stage, and I asked him if I could help out (#TheHustle). I worked with him the whole day, and when we were finished he asked me if I wanted to meet the band as a thank-you. He gave me backstage passes to the show and introduced me to the band. It was the happiest day of my life (#ManifestThat!)."

#HBRLIFE

Level two is when you've advanced up the ladder of success and are in a position to be able to afford some of the experiences on your #FutureBoard or #BucketList. It's when you've actually grown into the person you created in your #LifePlan (and trust me, you will get there), and now you're actually in a position to fully enjoy the lifestyle you've worked so hard for.

This is the step where money starts to flow easily into your life. I know that might seem impossible from where you sit now, but if you've followed the steps in #MoneyAintAThing! then you've already taught yourself how to change your thinking around your finances from "I'm broke" to "I've got this." This is the next level of success, and the transition from *the struggle* to *thriving*.

I told you in the first chapter that the #HBRMethod will deliver material and financial success as a side effect of you focusing on your heart's desire, and your hustle. And yes, I got the Mercedes! It wasn't new or free, but it was under Blue Book! I promised I'd give you examples, so here are just a few of them. I have many more on my Pinterest under "My Reality Board." Check them out for more proof that regardless of your dream, if you apply this method, you will live it.

EXAMPLE #1

The first time I took my son to that Baltimore Ravens game in 2011, I didn't have the money to buy tickets, so the Universe gave them to me. Being in that stadium gave my son and me the experience of being at a football game (ManifestThat!), and made us want to find a way to have that experience again (#HBRLife).

In 2014 I was able to fly my three kids to Washington, DC, and take all three of them to a Ravens game. Even my twin girls, who were just seven at the time (and let's be honest, not super excited to go) enjoyed it, but for me it was a huge moment. It was the first time I'd bought tickets to a professional sporting event, and could actually afford to do so. And it was the first time I'd ever been able to take my daughters to a game of any kind. There is something amazing about the feeling of manifesting with #HBRLife. It's a sense of pride, a feeling of accomplishment, of *I did this on my own. I made this happen.* It's addicting, and nothing feels quite as gratifying. That feeling is what keeps the cycle of blessings, hustle, and belief thriving in your life.

EXAMPLE #2

I happen to love designer handbags. And even though I never focused my attention on material objects I did put up handbags and shoes on my #FutureBoard as goals I wanted to reach. I told myself that if I ever made a commission check worth $10,000 that I would buy myself a Louis Vuitton bag. I'd had a picture of one on my wall at work for years, and it was a promise I'd always made to myself to help motivate me.

In the spring of 2013 the unthinkable happened—I got my first-ever $10,000 commission check! You bet your ass I walked right into the Louis Vuitton store and bought the first and only item of theirs that I've ever purchased brand-new—a wallet (I couldn't stomach the price tag for the bag!). But the feeling of walking in and knowing that in my checking account was enough to clear that transaction was insane. It felt better than I could have imagined, and it once again fueled my desire to keep working my ass off to advance my life to the next level.

EXAMPLE #3

In 2011 I took a video and posted it to my YouTube channel of me in a beautiful New York hotel room, on one of my trips for work. I was so excited walking around that huge two-bedroom, two-bathroom condo/hotel that I couldn't resist jumping for joy and posting about it. I remember sitting on the couch in the living room on the 38th floor looking up at the unobstructed view of the Chrysler Building outside the window. I was filled with childlike joy, yet there was a deep sadness under it, as there always is whenever I experience something amazing that I'm not able to share with my kids. I just kept wishing they could be there, see that room, and fall in love with Manhattan the way I had.

But of course I didn't have anywhere near the kind of money needed to make that happen then, so I just enjoyed the moment and let it go (#ChillOut!).

In May of 2015 I lived out my #HBRLife moment. I'd acquired enough miles to take my three children and myself to New York (I only had to pay the booking fee of $25 each ticket #MoneyAintAThing!) for a six-day trip to my favorite city. By this time my kids were very used to me traveling to NYC for work and could recognize all the landmarks in every movie. We'd talked and dreamed about going together since my first trip back in 2010.

I always remembered that hotel from 2011, and when I looked it up to book our trip, I was disappointed to learn that they'd turned it into a time-share, with very few rooms available. Still, I booked one of their standard rooms with two double beds, thinking I could at least tell the kids that it was the same hotel, even though none of the big two bedroom/condo-style rooms were available.

When we arrived at our hotel at midnight the front desk looked worried. The clerk went to get her manager and after a few minutes of looking at our reservation and whispering behind the desk, he said "I'm so sorry, but it looks like we've given away your room for tonight. I could however upgrade you just for tonight and tomorrow to our two-bedroom suite at no additional charge." I screamed quietly inside and graciously took the keys (#MoneyAintAThing!).

When we walked into the room, my kids and I all started screaming. It was the same room I'd stayed in four years before! Kanen had his own bedroom with a panoramic view of the Chrysler Building, and his own bathroom. The girls and I shared the master bedroom and bath. It was beyond a dream come true (#ManifestThat!)!

As I write this book I've not achieved anywhere near the kind of financial success I am working towards, so I was grateful that #MoneyAintAThing! was constantly at work on that trip! However, it was still a next-level #HBRLife manifestation, because instead of someone else (work) giving me this moment for free, I used #TheHustle to earn the miles, save the money, and take my family on a vacation of a lifetime.

#HBRLife is all about living successfully for your entire life. It's about applying what you've learned over and over again to reach the next level of achievement. If you've not planned what your life will look and feel like when you've "made it," then as soon as it comes it will disappear.

This step was a challenge for me; it's still something I'm daily growing into. I have been so fortunate this past year in that I've been able to, in a way, be mentored on this step by everyone who's in this book—people who've gone before me and made the transition from struggle to success. It's a tricky thing to do, and it requires preparation.

If the struggle and #TheHustle are all you've ever known (as in my case), it's difficult to realize when you've transitioned past that. It requires you to break old bad habits. Even though I'd learned how to positively think about money, and manifested the best financial situation of my life, I was still living paycheck to paycheck. My habits were those of the struggle. I'd always lived that way, and so I realized that regardless of my income, I found a way to go back to that familiar pattern. I'd never had money just sitting in my bank account before, so I didn't know what that felt like. I did, however, know what it felt like to pay all my bills on payday and struggle for the next thirteen days until I got paid again.

I decided it was time to make a change. I knew that I'd never really find financial freedom with this destructive habit actively sabotaging my efforts. So I signed up for my work's 401k plan and started contributing the max amount. I wanted to get used to seeing statements that showed "I had money" in a way that I couldn't spend it. Once I got used to that, I started putting money in savings each month. Not that it always stayed there, but I needed to train my brain to not panic when I did have money. I needed to address the anxiety of paydays and turn it into *calm*. Instead of scheduling my life around my payday I began to make appointments and plans that came between paychecks, trusting that I'd be able to hold onto my money longer and cover things as they came up.

All of these little changes enabled me to transition from lack and struggle to a place where money wasn't an issue, and then finally to a place of financial comfort. It took me actively making a conscious decision to get my mind in a place that could sustain success.

#HBRLife is the level that naturally follows #FakeIT. When you're starting out you have to pretend to be successful, as we discussed, but over time a natural transition is made through #BelieveIT and wins with #ManifestThat!, which transition you into *actually* becoming a boss. It becomes your new identity; you are perceived by yourself and your peers as someone who is successfully living your dream.

But it doesn't stop there, oh no. Any successful person will tell you that to maintain their success, they refuse to be satisfied. They are hungry for that next challenge, for the next level of achievement, and they always have an evolving #LifePlan for their future. That plan may look very different than the original, but they keep it current. They keep their goals clearly in view and continue to use all the tools that got them success in the first place to help them continue moving up the ladder.

YOUR HUSTLE

- Commit to write your own story in your journal regularly. Write about your progress, your struggles, and your wins. Recognize every manifestation and log it.
- Make a "reality board"—either a physical board or one like mine on Pinterest. This is basically a picture memory board. Take a picture every time you are living out a moment/experience from your #FutureBoard, and put it on your new "reality board." That reality board could be your refrigerator or a beautiful corkboard, but somehow have a place where you can visually see and be reminded

of those wins and memories. I love to do side-by-side photo comparisons of a picture of my #FutureBoard (before) and my living almost exactly the same moment (after). I have a bunch posted on my Pinterest as examples.

- What is your TEN-YEAR plan? (quick bullet points are fine here; you can always refine it using the #HBRMethod later).
- What is the most important thing you've learned from #HBR?
- How can you mentor others and share what you know?
- The best way to keep moving forward is to realize how far you've come. Look back over your journey often, let your journal be proof of your progress, and let that inspire you to never give up!

#HBRSTORIES

KOREY McCRAY

JONATHAN STEWART

DANIEL JACOBS

ANNA CENTRELLA THAYER

KOREY McCRAY'S STORY

I met Korey briefly after a UCLA men's basketball game in 2012. I'd taken my son to watch my client play, and Korey was one of his coaches. I'd seen what a positive force he'd been in my client's life and liked the mindset of his social media posts, so I reached out to him on Instagram to see if he'd be willing to share his story.

"I come from a beautiful family; I am very close with my mom, dad, and sister. From a young age my father, who is my role model and best friend, was also my basketball coach. My dad coached me through high school, and the best part was spending time with him in the car going to and from practice. That was my time to learn from him and talk about everything."

Korey went on to play basketball in college. "Instead of taking offers to play overseas after graduation, I made the decision that it was time to give back, and follow my passion to become a coach (#BigPictureDream). That's what I love most about being a coach; it's a chance to encourage, teach, and uplift these young guys."

During grad school Korey worked as a coaching graduate assistant at Florida State. "After grad school I went back to Atlanta to coach an elite AU team; it was a great opportunity to give back to my community. I was coaching very talented kids and building relationships with other coaches. I took that role very seriously and was happy to be doing something I loved."

Korey started applying for college assistant coaching positions, and the rejection letters followed. "That's the advantage of being an athlete—you learn how to deal with rejection, and how to brush it off. That is also my job as a coach, to equip my players with tools to handle it as well. While I was applying and interviewing for coaching jobs, I was constantly working to become great at my current level (#RelentlessPursuit). It was a great opportunity because I had one of the best teams in the country and I was able to coach them to the national championship (#ManifestThat!)."

During that time Korey began to build a reputation for training elite basketball players who were preparing to go into the NBA. "I trained John Wall, Dwight Howard, and many other elite players during that time. I was constantly doing everything within my power to be great at what I did (#TheHustle)."

"I believe it's so important to always work while you're waiting. What's your hustle in the quiet time? You've gotta always be perfecting your craft so you're ready when the opportunity comes."

Korey was turned down by college after college and then he got his big break, an interview with UCLA. When the chance came he was prepared. While at UCLA Korey coached the team to a Pac-12 victory, and was instrumental in making UCLA the number-one recruiting class in the country, according to ESPN. Korey has coached men's basketball at UCLA, LSU, Mississippi State, Mercer University, and Florida State.

"I believe that sports prepares you for life. It teaches you how to deal with adversity [and] success, how to come back from losing, and how to stay mentally tough.

"My dream is to one day be a head coach at the highest level, and to be successful when I get there. (#BigPictureDream) I have big dreams, and I feel like I still have a long way to go to reach my big goals, but I know I'm on the right path. God has blessed me. He's placed this vision inside me, and I won't stop 'til I get there.

"I think people should talk about success more (#HBRLife). You need to plan and prepare for it. If you hand a kid millions of dollars there's a good chance they will blow it. When you move financial brackets you have to look at what success will do to you. It's my responsibility to make these kids go to class and be successful in life beyond basketball. You need to put your goals on paper (#WriteIT), put your plan together (#LifePlan). Have something written down that anticipates your dream coming true and what you will do when it does.

"A lot of guys plan to make it to the NBA, but they forget to plan for how to sustain success for the rest of their life. When the money comes they want to spend it taking care of their friends and family, but it's just as important to plan on how to sustain it for a lifetime. And once you've planned that, you need to think about how you can give back.

"I am fortunate to have a great father and a great support system. Even though I have a plan for my future, I'm still excited and open with changes that come in life."

KOREY'S ADVICE TO YOU

"You have to visualize yourself winning (#CreateAMovieIn-YourHead). I tell my players to work hard (#TheHustle), be prepared, and believe (#BelieveIT) you will win. You can't be cocky because that's just talk; you need the work ethic to back it up. You will have to sacrifice to be successful; your talent will take you only so far (#RelentlessPursuit).

"You have to have faith. There are times when you do things wrong and your faith is what keeps you going, and times when you do things right and you still get criticized. Faith is what gets you through all of that. Practice faith over fear.

KOREY McCRAY is the assistant men's basketball coach at Mississippi State University. Prior to becoming an assistant coach at UCLA, Korey was a skills development coach for NBA players. He's consistently coached teams throughout his career who've ranked in the top 10 nationally. Follow his journey on **Twitter:** @Coach_KAM and **Instagram:** @Kam_Austin

JONATHAN STEWART'S STORY

In May of 2014 when I decided to write the blog series "Inside the Mind of an Athlete" featuring five Oregon football players in five stages of their dream, I did so with Jonathan Stewart in mind. There was only one problem—he was the only one, out of the five players I profiled, whom I did not personally know.

But I was convinced that it had to be him for the "veteran player" piece I wanted to write. I just knew he'd be perfect. I've known *of* Jonathan for several years, as we have many common friends and have followed him on social media, so I knew his reputation for being an upstanding positive guy and devout Christian was exactly what I wanted this piece to be about.

In true #HBRMethod form I even wrote out the interview questions specifically for him over a month beforehand, yet had *no idea* how I was going to make it happen. I was determined to get the story idea in front of him, but it's difficult. After all, when someone has the fan base he does, it's hard for someone like me to stand out in the crowd. But at last I tagged him in a post on Instagram where I'd posted the story of Kenjon Barner (a personal friend of his), and he'd responded! He said he'd be happy to share his story. I was beyond thrilled!

One day a few weeks later my phone rang as I was running out the door, and boy, was I glad I'd taken the time to write out my questions a month beforehand!

It was then that Jonathan told me his story . . .

"I was always the little kid growing up, out there playing catch with my older brother and his friends, getting teased for being the little guy." He laughs.

Jonathan's parents divorced when he was in fourth grade, and his mom began dating a man named James Parker. "James really fell into that father-figure role in my life. He'd come to our apartment complex and we'd go to the field across the street, and he'd be out there throwing the ball with me for hours. He'd leave work early, or drop whatever he was doing to come teach me the game of football and spend time with me. He introduced me to flag football my fifth grade year, and always encouraged me, never pushed or forced, just encouraged. So football came with a sense of comfort and a connection with someone who really cared about me—it came from a place of love."

In seventh grade Jonathan began playing select league tackle football and started to notice two things: (1) He was always the smallest kid on the team, and (2) he was starting to love it, and he was pretty good, too. In high school Jonathan racked up the most yards of anyone on the varsity team as a nonstarting freshman, and then the "high school hype" started. Jonathan turned to his roots and upbringing to get him through the limelight of being a break-out star athlete.

"My mom raised me in church, and that's always been really important to me. I was blessed to see that at a very young age and always put God first in everything I do. So in high school I just wanted to play football, honor God, and focus on school. I felt like football was my tool to honor God. Everything I did was for that end, and to make sure I was living up to that potential."

In 2008 when Jonathan was drafted, he signed a deal with the Carolina Panthers for $14 million, and re-signed with them in 2012 for a reported $35.5 million on a five-year contract.

Knowing what I do about money and athletes, and seeing firsthand how it destroys perfectly good people, I needed to know how Jonathan's been able to keep his head about him after seven seasons in the league—especially with the distraction that type of money can bring. Many players unravel when they reach this level of success. They lose a grasp on reality and are not able to think past it. The "be careful what you wish for" factor tends to take effect.

"The key to staying grounded is to stay yourself. You remember where you came from and you don't change; you *adapt*. You refuse to change for anyone and surround yourself with the people who have always been there for you. If you are true to yourself that is the kind of people you will attract. Those are the people who are drawn to me. I think it's like if you go to a country music concert you'll see mostly country fans, because that's what's on the stage, that's what people are attracted to. So if your heart is true, that's what is playing on your 'stage,' and those are the types of people you will attract to yourself.

"You also need to have good internal radar to know who's real and who's fake, to steer clear of the mess (#ChangeYourCrew). I don't ever want to be seen as something I'm not. I watch who I interact with because I know you will be judged by the company you keep. You become very aware of that, and the company you keep becomes who you want to be. If you really want to be successful you need to filter what comes at you."

I asked Jonathan where that strength and mental toughness comes from, and he said, "When your mind, body, and spirit are connected, that's when it really begins to have its full effect on your life. When my body is not where I want it to be, I have to make sure my mind and spirit are top notch, so that I'm in line with where I need to be. I turn to the Word of God, and the Bible to maintain a positive spirit, and remind myself that whatever I'm going through, I will be okay. Especially when I'm going through struggles (#EarthquakeMoments), I remind myself that God has been faithful to me through everything. I've made it through difficulties before; I can do it again (#BelieveIT). And having gratitude, no matter what (#GetGrateful). If something is going wrong I focus on what God's given me, and not on my problems. It especially helps when you're faced with an injury, it's easy to get down and upset because you're not out there doing what you need to do. But I don't let myself dwell in self-pity (#ChangeTheVoicesInYourHead). Your mind is such a powerful thing (#ThinkIT); it's critical to keep it full of gratitude, because that energy affects everything, including your physical health and recovery."

I wanted to know what it must feel like for Jonathan to be living his dream, and was shocked by his answer. "To play football was never really my dream. I always thought it would be great if I could, but I never necessarily made that my goal. In high school I wanted to go to college, and football was the way to do that. I always had the mindset that if I do everything within my power (#TheHustle) that God will open the doors and take me where I should go, so I didn't worry about the outcome."

Then I realized that maybe his dream was bigger than football . . .

"I have joy," Jonathan told me.

"Happiness is temporary, but joy is forever. I've always let joy guide me. Making sure I keep and live in that joy is what has always been the most important thing to me. That really is my dream at the end of the day, to always have joy, to not worry about the outcome, and to glorify God (#BigPictureDream).

"My mom was a single mom, raising two boys, and I never saw her worry. I know she must have, but she never showed that to me. She had faith that God would provide (#BelieveIT), and He always did (#ManifestThat!). She never focused on what we didn't have, or tell me we didn't have money even though I know times were tight; she didn't focus on that (#MoneyAintA-Thing!). So I've always been the same, not worrying about what will happen, just working hard (#TheHustle) and living in the joy of the moment, and trusting God with the rest. God gives me peace and provides everything I need when I need it, so I just try to glorify Him.

"I want to uplift people. My goal is to inspire others; it's the backbone of my life, to reach a place where I could motivate people to reach their goals and dreams. I want them to see that they can accomplish something greater than they can even imagine. Football is a platform for me to make an impact on people's lives and I try to use it to create momentum to affect others in a positive way." In 2016, Jonathan went to the Super Bowl with the Carolina Panthers (and scored a touchdown!).

JONATHAN'S ADVICE TO YOU

"Never settle. I have a kids' football camp every year, it's the 'Jonathan Stewart Never Settle football camp.' I tell the kids to be extraordinary. Do extra in everything that you do. Do that consistently, and when you do over time it becomes who you are. Whether it's a goal or a dream, seek out people who can help hold you accountable to that goal [and] find things and ways to push you that extra mile, so it becomes who you are. It's a lifestyle that you create and attract to yourself."

JONATHAN STEWART is a running back in the NFL for the New York Giants. He was the 13th overall draft pick in the 2008 draft from the University of Oregon. Follow his journey on **Twitter:** @jonathanstewar1 and **Instagram:** @jonathanstewar1

DANIEL JACOBS'S STORY

I first met Daniel (Danny) Jacobs in New York. I'd been invited to my very first red-carpet charity event by Kimberley Hatchett, and I'd excitedly called my girl Lisa to join me. Lisa and I were trying to take in the magnitude of what a big deal this was. I mean, a girl's first red-carpet event is kind of major. It was one of those moments when we felt like we were *living our dream*. I had no idea when I arrived what the charity was benefiting, or that it would turn out to be such a pivotal part of my *#Hustle-BelieveReceive* journey.

The event was Kicked It In Heels, hosted by Janna Andrews.

When Janna introduced one of the night's honored guests, she motioned to the side of the stage where a handsome young man in a white sweater waved as she told the crowd who he was. When the announcements were over, I crossed the room to meet Daniel. I knew I had to hear his story, and somehow I needed to convince him to be featured in my book. I'd never met a boxer before, and I was a little nervous. I knew I had to pitch quickly, so I blurted out my idea for featuring him in my book, and before I'd finished he said, "Yes, of course, I'd love to be part of it." We talked for just a minute more, and he gave me a small snippet of his story. There was something so humble and graceful about his presence, and I couldn't help but give him a big hug after we'd set up a time for our interview.

It's November 19, 2014, the day of our scheduled interview. I've been anticipating this day since the night I met Danny in New

York a few weeks prior, and when he called I eagerly asked him to tell me his story.

"It's ironic because I was never the fighter type," he began. "I was a mama's boy, raised around women, lots of aunts and cousins. I was more of a lover, not a fighter.

"But when I was in the eighth grade, there was this bully in school, and every week he'd pick a new victim to beat up. When my day came, I stood up for myself and didn't let him beat me up. I was the only kid who'd defended himself against him, and I realized that I wasn't helpless.

"I learned later that he trained at a local boxing gym, so one day I went down to check it out. That was it; immediately I loved it. It was so strange because the energy of conflict had never sat well with me, so it came as a total surprise. But I loved everything about it. I loved the grit and sweat of it, the dirty ring, and the smell. I stuck with it, and learned the art of boxing, the craft of the sport, and became more passionate about it (#TheHustle)."

He was a natural boxer from the start. A few months after being introduced to the sport and starting his training he began to win matches. He became the most successful amateur boxer to date in the state of New York, and he was even chosen as an Olympic alternate in 2008.

In 2009 Danny decided it was time to cross over into the professional boxing ring. From the beginning he was slated as a star prospect, fighting on TV and in huge key matches. He was featured on fight cards with the greats, including Oscar De La Hoya and Floyd Mayweather, and the fans loved him. They nicknamed him "The Golden Child." "It was fitting," Danny said, "because it was all just so picture-perfect."

In 2011 his grandmother became very ill with cancer, while at the same time he'd been offered the opportunity of his career—a chance to fight for the world championship. "I couldn't keep my mind clear though," he told me. "Four days before the world championship match, my grandmother passed away. My family and I were all there with her when they turned off the machines, and sat with her when she passed. It was a really hard moment for all of us. But the next day I had to get on a flight and have the biggest fight of my life with one of the toughest opponents. Needless to say, I wasn't prepared."

That match was Danny's first loss. "I was 23 years old, and in the same week suffered two of the most difficult losses in my life, back to back (#EarthquakeMoments)."

For the next eight months he trained and started slowly climbing back up the ladder, getting win after win, making his comeback (#RelentlessPursuit). Soon he was back at the top of his game, with a record of 28-1, with 25 of those 28 wins being knockouts (#ManifestThat!).

The money and fame came quick. "It was hard to handle," Danny told me. "It came so fast, and I was just a kid, who'd come from very little. So to have it all so quickly can really mess with your head. But at the core of who I am is a person who wanted to work hard and stay humble. I always wanted to stay the same guy. But it was a struggle. I remember one day I was reading the Bible and I came across the word 'meek.' The passage: 'The meek shall inherit the earth.' And I asked God to show me what that word really meant, and to find a way to make me 'meek.'

"Then I got a call from Oscar De La Hoya, my promoter, and he said he wanted to feature me on a tour in Iraq to support the troops. I was really excited to go, but toward the end of the trip I suddenly became very, very weak. I had the chills, and felt like I had gotten the flu. My legs kept getting weaker and weaker, to the point that I wasn't able to finish the tour. I knew something was wrong. By the time I got back home to Brooklyn my left leg was so weak I was dragging it a little."

Danny went to his local general doctor, who couldn't explain why he'd suddenly gotten so sick, or why he was quickly losing the function in his legs. He told Danny it was likely a pinched nerve, gave him a prescription, and sent him home to rest. "I was just so confused. I was healthy, had a great diet, I trained constantly, and had just been fighting. It didn't make any sense. But I believed him; I mean when your doctor tells you something, you usually just believe them. So I took the pills and it got worse fast."

In just two short weeks from the time Danny's symptoms first showed up in Iraq, he had gone from his leg being weak, to needing to use his grandmother's walker. "I kept thinking; *this must be a really bad pinched nerve*. But at the same time I knew I was getting progressively worse and fast. At first, I was just so embarrassed. How had I gone from a healthy fighter to not being able to use my legs in the span of three weeks?"

One night Danny drove home in what was the scariest drive of his life. He could feel his condition worsening by the minute, and the use of his legs evaporating, making it nearly impossible to drive that night. When he got home, he labored up the stairs to his room, dragging his legs up each step. When he reached his bed he realized he'd left his phone down in the car. "I knew there was no way I could go back down to get it and still make it back up the stairs that night. So I went to bed and thought, *I'll get it in the morning.*"

The next morning he woke to the sound of someone knocking loudly on his front door. He tried to sit up and get out of bed, but his legs didn't move. He was paralyzed from the waist down. "I had to pull myself out of bed, *commando style,* and crawl down the stairs. I had to pull my body across the room to the door, and when I opened it my godmother started crying seeing me on the floor like that. She was my guardian angel that day. We still don't know how she'd picked that particular day to stop by my apartment unannounced. Or how she'd made it past the doorman. Or why she didn't leave when it took me so long to answer the door. But she saved me."

By the time Danny made it to the hospital that Friday afternoon, it was clear this was no pinched nerve. The doctors knew immediately something was very wrong and ordered an MRI. As soon as the test was over the doctor came into his room bearing the most horrific news. He told Danny, "I don't know how to break this to you Mr. Jacobs, but you have a massive cancerous tumor and it's wrapped around your spine. Had you waited 'til Monday to come in, chances are you would have been dead." (#EarthquakeMoment)

"I couldn't understand it," Danny told me. "At first I was just thinking, *okay, well go take it out and let's move on.* It didn't sink in that it could be anything serious. I figured I'd have surgery and be just fine."

The doctors told Danny they weren't equipped to treat his condition and that he'd need to be moved to Cornell Medical Center in New York and undergo a six-hour surgery to remove the tumor. During surgery the doctors had to remove so much tissue from Danny's spine to fully get the tumor out that they were forced to fuse his spine together with titanium rods.

"Once I was out of surgery, I just kept thinking; *I need to get on with my rehab so I could get back to boxing.* That's all I was thinking about, how quickly I could find a way to recover so I could box and continue to provide for my family. I had a two-year-old son, and boxing was not only my passion, and my dream, it was our only livelihood."

But one day, a few weeks into Danny's recovery all his doctors and therapist came into his room. They walked him through his diagnosis, his progress, his treatment plan, and then they told him the most devastating news of all. "They told me I would never box again," Danny told me, the emotion still fresh in his voice (#EarthquakeMoment). The doctors told him that if he ever got hurt in the ring that it would likely be fatal. They warned him that the nerves in his legs might never fully return to full sensation and feeling. They encouraged him to focus on fighting the cancer and getting well, but not to think about ever boxing again.

"Those words were verbal death," Danny said. "Everything I'd ever worked for was gone with those words. The teenage years I missed because I was fighting and training. All the dreams I'd had for my future. My job and my income. All of it was gone. It was like a death. Emotionally it could break you. And there were nights I'd lay awake crying and ask God *Why? Why was he doing this to me?* I was questioning everything and feeling sorry for myself.

"Then I remembered something. About two months before all this happened, I'd asked God to find a way to make me 'meek.' That's when I realized that everything I'd been through was all part of God's plan for me and the bigger plan for my life. Once I accepted that, then I began to see that anything was possible (#BelieveIT).

"I've been fortunate because I was trained in a sport that teaches mental toughness (#ThinkIT). It taught me that with hard work (#TheHustle) I could achieve anything. The same skills I used in the ring to get and keep my positive focus, are the same ones I used to turn my dark thoughts around (#ChangeTheVoicesInYourHead). I started to see the doctor's words as motivation. I treated them, and the cancer, like my opponent, and I was determined to fight and win. I wanted to raise my hands high like a champion (#BigPictureDream)."

When Danny was finally released from the hospital, he was broke. Just as fast as the money had come, it had imploded with the cost of his treatment. He had lost everything—his car, apartment, and all his fancy things. There was nothing left. The cancer had not only threatened his life, but it had taken his dream, his body, everything he owned, and every penny he had. Before he knew it, he was struggling to simply find his next meal, and desperate to find a way to financially take care of his girlfriend and young son.

But he was finally able to walk on his own, though still wearing his back brace, and that was all the hope he needed. "The first chance I got, I disobeyed the doctors' orders and went back to the gym." He laughs. "It had been all I was focusing on (#CreateAMovieInYourHead) when I was in the hospital, and there was no way I wasn't going to reward myself. I could tell I was getting better, slowly, but I was improving. I was even able to run again. I knew it was coming together the way I'd planned (#LifePlan), and I really started working on my craft again and began to believe I would make a comeback (#BelieveIT).

"No one expected me to come back to boxing," Danny explained. "Not my managers, or promoters, or doctors. No one expected that. But I called my manager and told him to look out for me, because I was comin' back! I remember reading when I was in the hospital about the plan to open the new Barclays Center in my hometown of Brooklyn, and that the owners of the arena intended to hold a major boxing match as soon as it opened. I'd put it in my mind that I wanted to be on that fight card (#CreateAMovieInYourHead). So I went to the gym every day and I worked and worked (#TheHustle) and that was a huge motivation for me."

Miraculously Danny got the "all clear" from his doctors and from the boxing commission to fight again. Then one day the call came that he had been added to De La Hoya's fight card to box in the new Barclays Center. "It was just how I'd been envisioning it to happen, that was my dream (#ManifestThat!)."

When the media and press got wind of Danny's amazing story, they swarmed. It was one of the biggest stories the boxing world had ever seen. On the night the Barclays Center opened one of the owners called Danny directly to invite him to sit in the front row for the opening ceremony. At the opening Brett Yormark, CEO of the Brooklyn Nets and the Barclays Center, recognized Danny and his incredibly inspiring story. "It was the hugest thing in the world to me! Beyond amazing," Danny told me, his voice still full of excitement.

In August of 2014 Danny stood in the boxing ring facing the crowd in the middle of the Barclays Center. It was his first fight since being diagnosed with cancer, and it was exactly how he'd envisioned it. Sitting ringside were all of his doctors and physical therapists, including Janna Andrews. They watched Danny deliver a fifth round knockout punch to become the first ever, cancer-surviving Middleweight World Champion (#HBRLife).

He had achieved his dream and was able to raise his hands as not only a World Champion boxer, but a champion over cancer.

He has since been appropriately renamed by his fans: *The Miracle Man*.

DANNY'S ADVICE TO YOU

"You really don't know who you are until you hit rock-bottom. You will never be given more than you can handle. When something devastating happens to you, the only thing you can do is go up from there. You have got to believe that the difficult times are part of the plan for your life and have faith that you will get through them and be better off for it."

DANIEL JACOBS was the WBA middleweight champion from 2014 to 2017. His story has been featured in the HBO boxing documentary *My Story*. In October 2018 he was the last fighter to be televised on HBO for a match at Madison Square Garden. Follow his incredible journey on **Twitter**: @danielJacobsTKO and **Instagram:** @dannyjacobs718

ANNA CENTRELLA THAYER'S STORY

Anna is my aunt. Growing up I didn't have many positive role models in my life. I had lots of examples of what not to do, which in their own way motivated me to choose a different path, but I had very few people I could point to and say, "I wanna be like that." But Anna, her siblings, and her mother (my beloved Nonie) were my light in an otherwise very difficult childhood.

It was Anna who took a chance, back when I was still trying to finish college, and gave me my first job in corporate sales. Her belief and ability to see my potential made me believe that something other than what I'd known my whole life might be possible. She was my first positive mentor/"crew."

I remember her coming to my office one day and asking why all my walls were bare. She then asked when I planned to buy a house. I'll never forget how my mind spun with that last question. I'd never even considered buying a house before, not once. I'd grown up homeless for much of my childhood, and the rest I'd spent bouncing from one rent-free place to the next. The concept that I could ever buy a house was totally foreign to me. Up to that point I'd been patting myself on the back because I was the first person (out of my parents and siblings) to go to college; but buy a house? It seemed impossible.

Still, Anna told me to hang up pictures on my wall of the house I'd like to buy, and things I could work towards and reward myself with once I hit specific sales goals. And that is how the first picture of a Louis Vuitton bag ended up on my office wall. Though I didn't realize it then, that wall was my first

#FutureBoard. Less than a year after hanging up a photo of the house I dreamed of buying, my then-husband and I bought that exact house (#ManifestThat!)! This was in 2004, so two years before I'd seen the infamous Oprah show, yet still I was (without my knowing) already manifesting.

This is not only Anna's story, but it's also her expert advice, which as you will see summarizes all of the #HBRMethod in the most perfect way.

"When I look back at my life and think about when things began to shift, I was a year out of college," Anna began. "I'd taken a job at what was then Airborn Express, and I found myself in an extremely stressful environment. I didn't like it at all, but I refused to quit. I kept thinking, *What am I doing? How can I do this forever?*

"A month later I got offered a promotion to be the company's worldwide trainer, and for seven years they paid me to travel the world training their employees. I remember when I first took the position I thought, *There is no way I can do this!* I was in over my head. But I believe that the Universe rewards action (#TheHustle), so whenever I am faced with fear, I do just one thing to move past it, and I trust that the rest will follow (#CourageOverFear). So I started writing affirmations every day for ten minutes in the morning when I first got to the office (#MottoForLife). I'd write down 'I am confident' [and] 'I am a great teacher and people listen to me.' On the days when I didn't do that it was so obvious, I'd have a bad day. I've continued to do this my entire life. I say them over and over in my mind, especially in the morning when I plan out my day."

When Anna was twenty-seven she got married and moved to the east coast, which led to an opportunity with a start-up company called Intercall. "My exposure in training at my previous position taught me how to recognize success and cultivate it in others. I needed to work for people who were smarter than me because I wanted to be challenged; I immediately saw that quality in the CEO of Intercall. That position gave me a chance to surround myself with people who were extremely smart, and taught me the importance of becoming a lifelong learner. It also showed me that my strength lays in my passion. For the first time I could let it shine and create a successful environment for my team and myself."

Anna's hustle and passion got her noticed, and she was given the opportunity to open twelve offices on the west coast, rising to the rank of vice president of sales. "I started to notice that what I visualized became my future, and I began teaching my team how to visualize their success (#CreateAMovieInYour-Head). I even made them all make #FutureBoards as a team building exercise!" She laughed, knowing I remember sitting in our boardroom surrounded by magazines that became my office wallpaper. "I wanted them to physically see (#SeeIT) what they were working towards so they could be self-motivated, especially since I was overseeing offices in multiple locations. Then I made them all write out (#WriteIT) their personal and professional goals in specific detail, quarterly, annually, and for the next five years (#LifePlan).

"That position revealed my purpose, which wasn't trying to sell the most; it was helping people see that they could achieve their goals and their dreams (#DreamIT). I understood my success depended on theirs and I wanted to build in them the belief that they could do it (#BelieveIT). I stopped looking at the quota number or how I'd achieve it; instead I focused on teaching my team to go after the LIFE they wanted (#BigPictureDream). I had to shift my focus off just money, and turn it to the lifestyle we wanted to create (#MoneyAintAThing!). That shift in thinking and my leadership style resulted in my team being one of the most celebrated sales teams in the country! Every one of my offices hit their number for the first time ever (#ManifestThat!)!

"When I transitioned out of corporate life into building companies, consulting, and being a mom I had to refocus my purpose into these new areas. But the results showed in exactly the same way!"

ANNA'S ADVICE TO YOU

"You have to create your life. Begin with the end in mind and then back it out from there (#BigPictureDream).

"If you ever feel like you are starting to slip, look around and see who you are associating yourself with. Who have you let into your life? Take the time to pull the weeds. Negative people will suck the life out of you and bleed you dry. Get rid of them (#ChangeYourCrew)!

"Give yourself the gift of ten minutes a day to visualize and write affirmations for the life you want. Write what you're grateful for (#GetGrateful). If you make this a daily habit it will change your life."

ANNA THAYER is a keynote speaker, a sought-after corporate trainer, and a start-up business consultant. She is a mother of four who lives with her family in Palo Alto, California. (And most importantly, she is my personal lifelong mentor!) Follow her journey on: **LinkedIn:** Anna Centrella Thayer **Instagram:** @AnnaCentrellaThayer

LASTLY . . .

My wish is that this book, and all the stories you have read, were able to destroy your doubt, obliterate your excuses, and empower you with the tools you need to change your life and live your dream. No matter who you are, where you live, or what your current situation is, this book is PROOF that you can and *deserve to* have the life of your dreams!

If you put in the work and believe with all your heart, the reward will find you. I can't wait to hear YOUR story!

YOUR HUSTLE

I want you to find the most successful person you know and interview them. Ask them the same questions I asked the people in this book.

- When did you first identify your dream? (Who you wanted to be, and what you wanted to accomplish?)
- Tell me your story. How did you get from that idea to where you are today?
- Was there ever a time when you felt like giving up?

- What's the biggest obstacle you ever faced on your journey, and how did you get through it? Why didn't you quit then?
- What was your hustle when you started pursuing your passion? What is it now?
- Did you ever visualize your future success? If so, how do you think that impacted your outcome?
- What is your advice for me, someone who's just starting my journey, to live my dream?

When you are finished, write their story. Then see if you can place the appropriate hashtag steps (#HBRMethod) in their story the way I've done here.

WHAT MORE PROOF DO YOU NEED??! ☺